Expanded Praise for
The Self-Publishing Roadmap

"I may be the original influencer, but these two know how to take you from 'I should write a book' to holding it in your hands—without losing your mind or your vibe. A must-read for anyone ready to finally hit Publish. This is easy. And it works! Jenna is one of the best collaborators I've ever created with!"

— **Perez Hilton, Queen of All Media**

"Essential, comprehensive, actionable, and a delight to read—what every author must know about getting books published today."

— **Michael Levin, *New York Times* bestselling author and "the Michael Jordan of ghostwriting"**

"*The Self-Publishing Roadmap* is the book I wish I'd had when I was still clicking around all alone in the wilderness. Comprehensive, detailed, and concise, it's the perfect resource for anyone who thinks they know where they might want to go in the indie-publishing world but have no idea how to get there."

— **Dave Mason, author of the multi-award-winning historical-fiction novel *EO-N***

THE
SELF-PUBLISHING
ROADMAP

THE SELF-PUBLISHING ROADMAP

Everything You Need to Know About Becoming an Indie Author

FROM THE CREATORS OF
THE BOOK-A-GO-GO PODCAST

**JENNA ROSE ROBBINS
& SARA STRATTON**

Redwood
Publishing

Published by Redwood Publishing, LLC
Orange County, CA
www.redwooddigitalpublishing.com

ISBN: 978-1-966333-25-8 (hardcover)
ISBN: 978-1-956470-95-6 (paperback)
ISBN: 978-1-966333-30-2 (e-book)

Cover by Lluvia Arras, lluviaarras.com
Interior Design by Jose Pepito
Additional Design by Chris Bielinski

For inquiries, please contact:
info@bookagogo.com
www.bookagogo.com

To the writers, dreamers, and creators

CONTENTS

Introduction

The book you're holding is really quite meta: It's a book about making books. The steps and advice provided within these pages were instrumental in the book's creation. Many of the forms, charts, and other resources are the actual ones we used throughout the publishing process.

The Self-Publishing Roadmap started as Book-A-Go-Go, a podcast about self-publishing books. After writing the first eighteen "Reference Episodes," which were designed as a roadmap to guide authors through the process, we realized that we also had the makings of a book. Both the Reference Episodes and this book begin with setting goals and building your author platform, then move on to topics such as finding the right editorial and design teams, and wrap up with the basics of marketing and distribution.

Book-A-Go-Go's co-hosts and this book's authors, Jenna Rose Robbins and Sara Stratton, first met in 2011, when Sara was helping to build the DIY-publishing division of a well-regarded ghostwriting firm. The two worked on several projects together—Jenna writing and editing, and Sara publishing. Afterward, Sara left to start Redwood Publishing, which she describes as a self-publishing concierge. A few years later, she helped Jenna publish her book *Faithful and Devoted: Confessions of a Music Addict.*

After many phone calls where we shared our knowledge and experiences on our respective roles in the book process, we realized that we should share the most commonly sought information with a wider audience, rather than just one client at a time. The result was Book-A-Go-Go, the podcast that will take you from writer to published author.

While our professional backgrounds are similar, we—Jenna and Sara—have two distinct areas of knowledge: writing and publishing. Although there is some overlap between the two, we have mainly worked as a tag team: Once Jenna finishes a manuscript with a self-publishing client, she hands it off to Sara's team at Redwood to usher it through the publication process. Between the two of us, we've written, edited, and/or published more than fifty books.

In the course of researching this book, we came across numerous others that offer similar advice on self-publishing. Despite that—or perhaps because of it—we still saw a place in the market for ours because the vast majority of these books were written for authors who are simply looking to produce a book quickly, regardless of the quality, or to turn a quick buck. Such information is fine for people trying to create passive income but not for someone who aspires to become a name author by creating quality content they can be proud of. One author we reviewed went so far as to state he uses pseudonyms for most of his books, which he says was because it's not feasible for someone to specialize in multiple niches (yet he himself does so). More likely the reason he doesn't use his own name is because he doesn't want to be associated with those books. That's understandable, because some of the strategies he suggests could actually get you in trouble with some publishing services.[1] If a book promises you'll be making money quickly through self-publishing, beware: It's more than likely just another get-rich-quick scheme.

In some cases, the books we read contained content more suitable for a website, in that the information will most likely be dated in just a few months, such as screenshots of setting up a Goodreads Author profile. If you purchase such a book more than six months after its release date, you'll probably find that a good portion of the content is now irrelevant. Other self-publishing guides were written by authors who, while successful at what they'd accomplished so far, seemed inexperienced or unfamiliar with the professional aspects of book publishing, in that they'd never written for a traditional publishing house and most likely learned the ropes through trial and error. As commendable as that is—and we don't ever want to discourage someone from pulling themself up by their own bootstraps—their books reflect that inexperience, with grammatical errors and run-on sentences, poor formatting, and even inaccurate information.

Of the reputable books we found, few had been updated in the last couple of years. With the rapid evolution of technology and the publishing world, much of their content is also now outdated. We took note of that and believe our book has found a way to solve that issue: through our online resources, which we will update regularly. Late in the writing process, we discovered the one book we felt might give us the most competition. (We didn't come across it during our earlier research, probably because the title wasn't keyword friendly.) But upon review of the book, we found that it had quite a few formatting issues and broken links and could have benefited from a professional proofread (despite the author's insistence that readers hire a professional themselves).

We wrote *The Self-Publishing Roadmap* for authors who are looking to produce a professional, high-quality book on par with those of traditional publishing houses. We don't cut corners, but we do offer DIY and more economical options, in addition to the professional route.

This book is comprehensive in that it covers each step of the publishing journey. However, each individual step is an overview, with resources for further exploration. After reading this book or listening to the full library of Reference Episodes (which can be found at bookagogo.com/reference-episodes), you'll understand what you need to accomplish to get your finished manuscript into published form. You'll then have the option to explore each topic in more depth, either through the sources we provide at the end of each chapter (Further Resources) or on your own.

We also wanted to acknowledge how increasingly common AI (artificial intelligence) has become as a writing and editing tool. Some writers now rely on this disruptive tool to write entire books. However, due to the fact that the legal landscape surrounding AI is still in flux (more on this is chapter 8), we did not fully explore this topic but plan to do so on upcoming episodes.

Many of the topics in each chapter of this book are so broad that whole books and podcasts have been dedicated to them, the authors of which are far more experienced than we are in those niches. Where relevant, we point you to these reputable experts. If you want to know more about a chapter's subject, you can explore the endnotes, appendices, and Further Resources sections at the end of each chapter. A complete list of the endnotes, Further Resources, and their respective hyperlinks can be found at bookagogo.com/books/endnotes and bookagogo.com/books/further-resources, which we plan to keep maintained with the most up-to-date information for as long as readers such as you let us know you have a need. Appendices with graphics can be viewed in a larger, color format at bookagogo.com/infographics, while worksheets mentioned in appendices can be downloaded at bookagogo.com/worksheets so that you can fill them out as you move forward on your book journey.

Further Resources

Companies, Individuals & Resources Mentioned in This Chapter
- Redwood Publishing: redwooddigitalpublishing.com
- Jenna's website: jennarobbins.com
- Jenna's book, *Faithful and Devoted*: amazon.com/Faithful-Devoted-Confessions-Music-Addict/dp/1952106826

From Book-A-Go-Go
- Further resources: bookagogo.com/books/further-resources
- Endnotes: bookagogo.com/books/endnotes
- Infographics: bookagogo.com/infographics
- Worksheets: bookagogo.com/worksheets
- Podcast: bookagogo.com/podcast
- Reference episodes: bookagogo.com/reference-episodes

Setting Goals & Expectations When Writing Your Book

W henever a new client comes to one of us for editorial or publishing help, they always have a ton of questions: *What's the process like? How long will it take? How much will this cost?* We hope to answer those questions and many more in the course of this book.

But the first question a writer should ask themselves is *Why am I writing this book?* When asked that question, our clients often say they can't wait to see their name on the bestseller list, or they tell us their plans to buy a new home with the book's profits. While those are commendable goals, we want to manage expectations by explaining the realities of the publishing world.

When you're deciding why you want to write a book, your goals should be realistic. Of course, everyone wants to have a *New York Times* bestseller or sell thousands of copies of their book, but there are other practical reasons you should also consider. If you choose the proper main goal for your book, financial and personal success is far more likely to follow.

It's important to establish a reasonable goal at the very beginning so you can track your progress each step of the way, which is why the end of nearly each chapter in this book includes a reminder for you to check in on your goal. It's also fine if, in the course of learning about the publishing process, you decide to change goals at any point. Just make sure that your goal—which we refer to as your BAGG (Book and Author Gameplan and Goal)—is always front of mind when you're making decisions.

What's your BAGG? It might be one or two of the following goals. In some cases, it might even be three, but we recommend sticking to fewer so you can be more focused. Throughout this book, we will mention other subgoals, all of which should work toward supporting your BAGG.

9 Common Goals in Publishing a Book

There are numerous reasons why you might want to write a book, but here are the nine most common and practical ones we've heard:

1. **Income: Either as a side hustle or full-time career.**
    While not every author can make a living solely by selling books, it's not impossible. Of the 3.2 million titles tracked in 2021, fewer than 1% sold more than 5,000 copies.[2] Even if you don't reach the lofty goal of writing books full time, you could still create a steady stream of passive income, particularly if your book's topic is timeless and can be marketed for more than just a few years. Although this is by far the most common goal we hear from clients, it also requires the most work.

2. **Promotion: To use the book as a calling card or marketing tool.**
    One of Jenna's clients was also able to impress a slew of his own clients with the fact that he was the man who'd written a book on the very topic they needed help with. The idea took root when he realized he

was always relaying the same information to his clients. He started out disseminating that info in bite-sized chunks on his blog, which earned him the notice of new clients looking for those very answers. Later he compiled the dozens of blog posts he and Jenna had written together over two years and made them into a book, which he gifted to new clients. Both the blog and the book helped firmly establish him in his industry, even though he was a relative newcomer. "Our ghostwriting clients have found self-published nonfiction books are most valuable as lead generation tools, not as revenue streams in their own right," says Andy Earle, CEO of Write It Great, a service that caters to business professionals seeking to share their ideas in book form.

3. **Reputation: To establish yourself as a professional writer or as an expert in your field.**

Many of our clients have written books to be recognized as thought leaders in their specific niche or to demonstrate their writing prowess. One of Jenna's clients wrote a book about narcissism in relationships because, although she was already an established psychologist, she wanted to be recognized for her authority in this area. Other clients of hers published with the sole intent of booking speaking engagements—any book proceeds were icing on the cake. One client had the single-minded goal of landing her own television show and used her book to get airtime on numerous news and talk shows.

4. **Education: To share info about a new idea or experience.**

This is a common goal for academics, instructors, experts, and even some memoirists, particularly those who've experienced a unique struggle. A client of ours wrote one of the first memoirs about being dually diagnosed with bipolar disorder and addiction. Conor Bezane saw a hole in the market and decided to write about his experiences as a way to help others who are dually diagnosed and their loved ones. The result: the book entitled *The Bipolar Addict: Drinks, Drugs, Delirium & Why Sober Is the New Cool.*

5. **Persuasion: To convince others regarding an opinion you hold.**
Much like an essay, a book may be written with the purpose of swaying others to your point of view. Although political books such as Rush Limbaugh's *The Way Things Ought to Be* and Hillary Clinton's *It Takes a Village: And Other Lessons Children Teach Us* are most likely the first examples to come to mind, others include Rachel Carson's seminal environmental book *Silent Spring* or even fiction works such as Harriet Beecher Stowe's *Uncle Tom's Cabin* or T. C. Boyle's *The Tortilla Curtain.*

6. **Documentation: To preserve information for posterity.**
This could be anything from leaving a legacy by writing your family's history to compiling a collection of notes from a research project. You can ensure your family's story or important research lives on for future generations.

7. **Catharsis: As a form of self-therapy.**
For authors who have undergone a traumatic experience, such as a tragic accident or surviving an illness, writing can be a therapeutic outlet and a way to potentially help others who are in similar situations, even if it's just to remind others that they aren't alone.

8. **Self-Expression: The joy of creation.**
Writing is an art and, as with many artists, a writer's desire and need to express themselves often can't be suppressed—they *have* to get it out of their system. The process itself is reason enough to write.

9. **Satisfaction/Gratification: To have a finished piece of work you can take pride in.**

    As Jenna can attest, the day you finally hold the completed book in your hands is one you will remember for a long time. It's a symbol of your many hours of hard work made tangible—and something you can take as much pride in as any trophy or medal.

Once you've identified your BAGG, attach a quantifiable measure of success to it—a certain number of book sales (Income), new clients (Promotion), or new speaking engagements (Reputation)—so that you can measure your success over time. You can then determine your ROI (return on investment), a measure of profitability, such as the cost of publishing versus book sales. Some goals, such as Documentation or Satisfaction, have a simple binary ROI: Are you or are you not satisfied with the results? However you decide to measure ROI, note it now. We will return to this topic in chapter 16.

Setting Expectations: Timing

Once you've identified your BAGG, focus next on your expectations, such as what the process—from putting the first letter on the page to getting the book on the store shelf—looks like. Unless you've already published a book, you might not be aware of how time-consuming it can be. The process consists of far more than just writing the manuscript. In that respect, we find that a lot of clients think that writing and publishing a book is as simple as redecorating a room, when it's really more comparable to renovating an entire five-bedroom, three-bathroom house. It's that big of a project. You'll need to interview editors, book designers, self-publishing experts, and everyone else involved in the production line—all of whom we'll cover in this book—just as you would home contractors, to ensure that the professionals you'll be working with for the next several months are the right ones for the tasks at hand.

As with home renovation, timelines get pushed around and unforeseen problems arise. You might forget to have a release form signed and now your centerpiece interview for the book can't be used. Or maybe you discover that another young-adult book with the same plotline hit the shelves six months ago. Or perhaps you're writing a cookbook of spinach recipes when suddenly there's a spinach recall due to *E. coli* (as happened in 2006).

When the 2020 pandemic first hit, Sara had a number of authors rush to publish through her company, Redwood Publishing. She and her team were able to help several clients with quick turnarounds, but once they were ready to release the book for online sales, Amazon barred some of those authors from publishing based on new rules it had just implemented that prohibited books containing certain pandemic-related phrases.[3] The authors and Redwood had to revise titles, rewrite content, and, in one case, redesign the entire cover. So despite speeding through the first half of the process faster than usual, they had no way of anticipating the roadblocks they would hit.

Part of the purpose of this book is to provide first-time authors with an overview of the process so they can manage their expectations, especially in terms of timing. Jenna once had a prospective client call in September saying he wanted his book on shelves by December. Aside from the actual writing itself, the publishing process alone generally takes far longer than that. Could his goal have been accomplished? Sure. But at great financial cost and probably with some degree of sacrifice in quality.

On the flip side, at the start of the pandemic lockdown, several authors Jenna knew were tapped by a publishing house to produce manuscripts within six weeks. Their books ended up being far shorter than traditional books, but they still made their deadlines—albeit with the resources of an entire publishing house behind them. Had they self-published, the time and money it would have taken to get their books out by such a short deadline would have been many times the usual cost.

Timing can also be affected by minor setbacks, such as your changing a design element of the book. Sara once worked with an author who, after approving the final design and then reviewing the proof copy (the term for a sample printed book), decided he wanted to move the start of his chapter up by about an inch on the page. He felt strongly about the change, even though he knew it meant pushed deadlines and added costs, and asked Redwood to make the adjustment. This seemingly small change affected every single page of text, thereby adding an additional week and a half and an extra $500 to the project timeline.

The above examples demonstrate how numerous factors can influence the length of the publishing process. The writing portion itself might include research, interviewing sources, or other tasks aside from just putting words on a page. When given all the necessary materials from the client (interview transcripts, research, etc.), Jenna has written a full book in less than a month—and once even ghostwrote four books in four months. However, the majority of her clients come with merely an idea, in which case the average time from first discussion to book launch is two years.

Once the manuscript is completed, there's still a lot to be done, from the interior and cover design to deciding on distribution to marketing and PR. At Redwood, it usually takes about six to eight weeks to get a completed manuscript on Amazon. After that comes marketing and PR, hiring a distributor, fulfilling orders, and much, much more.

For a rough estimate as to how long each of the steps of the publishing process takes, see the sample self-publishing timeline in Appendix A.

Setting Expectations: Costs

The cost of publishing your book depends on how much help—and what kind—you need. The first professionals usually hired to work on a manuscript are writers and editors, of which there are a few varieties. Proofreaders are generally the least expensive, while ghostwriters can command some serious cash. In one of Jenna's ghostwriting forums, the general opinion is that no one should accept a ghostwriting project for less than $75,000. Other ghostwriters, Jenna included, don't usually offer flat rates for ghostwriting and instead feel that hourly rates are fairer—both for the ghost and the client. We discuss writing collaborators and editorial teams in chapters 5 and 6.

After your manuscript has been professionally edited, you may decide to pay for beta readers, a lawyer (if your manuscript requires it), and possibly a web designer, social media consultant, marketing and/or PR expert, and any of a number of other professionals.

Then there are publishing costs, which include such items as cover design, interior design/layout, e-book conversion, copyright filings, barcode purchases, distribution costs, printing, etc. Appendix B contains a chart of the different costs you might incur throughout the book-writing process.

You can either handle each of these tasks yourself, hire separate individuals for each of them, or hire a one-stop shop to take care of it all. Such companies are called hybrid publishers or self-publishing houses. (The differences between these two and traditional publishers are discussed more in chapter 9.) In our experience, it's pretty obvious which authors handle everything themselves or cut corners to save a few cents, as the end result generally looks unprofessional. Hiring different people for each task generally results in the highest-quality product, but this strategy also tends to be more costly.

This book presents many situations where you can decide between DIY and hiring a professional. It's a good idea to begin thinking about this now so that you're not faced with the dilemma of deciding whom—if anyone—to hire at every one of the many milestones in the publishing process. While outsourcing from an online freelance marketplace, such as Fiverr (fiverr.com) or Upwork (upwork.com), can be an affordable and viable option, you could be making more work for yourself by having to find someone each step of the way. You also risk the chance that, if they weren't directly recommended, the quality of their work won't be up to snuff, or that they might leave the marketplace, making it impossible to contact them down the road when you need an update to the materials.

Using a contractor from an online marketplace may also require a lot more work on your part, as there could be time zone differences or language barriers to navigate, or the freelancer may be designing as a side gig and is not available to respond as quickly as you'd like. Another consideration is that book-formatting standards differ in other countries, so the designer you hire must have experience in the requirements for your market, e.g., American— not British—books.

It's almost always more beneficial for both you and the freelancer to work together directly, both to avoid the fees invariably associated with a third-party site and to be able to communicate as you wish, rather than being trapped within a messaging system, for example. In one indie-author forum that Jenna belongs to, editors stated that they do more and better work for clients when they work with them directly, as they're getting paid more due to the lack of fees. One forum member mentioned a site that charges $18 per 1,000 words for a line edit but pays the freelancer only a third of that. At that rate, the member posited, "How in-depth of an edit do you think you will get?" You could instead pay that full amount to a more professional editor, ensuring that *all* of your payment goes to the editor's work, not fees and taxes.

But don't dismiss online marketplaces altogether. Such sites can fill a need, especially if you're on a tight budget and if you're savvy about working with them. After using Fiverr for many years, Sara has learned to navigate its pitfalls. Although she has a stable of professional creatives she calls upon for most of her work, she sometimes taps the hive mind of an online marketplace for out-of-the-box ideas or brainstorming. Over the years, she's developed relationships with creatives on the site, whom she and Jenna turned to for smaller projects related to this book, such as creating downloadable forms and website icons. So don't completely count out the benefits of online marketplaces.

Even though it's entirely possible to handle all the book-publishing tasks yourself and not spend a dime, DIY is not always the more economical option.

As the saying goes, time is money—especially your own time. While a task might take only an hour for a professional, there's likely to be a learning curve for someone new to the process. DIY could also end up costing you if you make an egregious mistake, such as uploading an incorrect file type that results in the delay of your book's release, miscalculating the spine width, or aligning the text in the wrong direction.

As when hiring any professional, ask to see samples of their work, particularly as it relates to your topic. References from past clients can also provide insight into the quality of their work and working style, such as whether they are organized or how quickly they can turn projects around.

In our chart of publishing-related expenses in Appendix B, we've included a column for you to fill in the cost associated with different tasks. Call some publishers and find out their one-stop pricing, then add up the fees of all the professionals you'd need to hire individually. Be sure to also estimate the time it would take you to find and interview each of them. We're willing to bet that, in the majority of cases, the cost to work with a hybrid or self-publishing company will be the more affordable—and efficient—option.

Next Steps

- Write down the BAGG(s) you've identified. You'll be referring to this often throughout your publishing journey.
- Review Appendix A and make notes as to where your timeline might deviate.
- Fill out the expenses chart in Appendix B. Update this chart as you finish each chapter and revisit your budget periodically.
- Determine how you will calculate your ROI and write it down for later reference.

Further Resources

For the complete collection of all links in this book, visit bookagogo.com/books/further-resources.

Companies, Individuals & Resources Mentioned in This Chapter
- Andy Earle, CEO of Write It Great: writeitgreat.com
- Conor Bezane's book, *The Bipolar Addict: Drinks, Drugs, Delirium & Why Sober Is the New Cool*: amazon.com/Bipolar-Addict-Drinks-Drugs-Delirium/dp/1947341340
- Fiverr: fiverr.com
- Upwork: upwork.com

What to Expect When Writing and Publishing a Book
- "Getting Published Takes Time: A Guide to Self-Publishing Your Book": forbes.com/sites/forbesbusinesscouncil/2021/11/17/getting-published-takes-time-a-guide-to-self-publishing-your-book
- Interview with Conor Bezane about his experience getting published: jennarobbins.com/2019/05/what-expect-book-writing-process

Author Platform: What It Is & Why You Need One

One of the steps in the publishing process that many writers overlook is building an author platform. This is such a crucial step—whether you're self-publishing or going the traditional route—that you should begin working on it as soon as possible, and that could mean even before you start writing your book.

Out of all the authors we've worked with, the ones who have been the most successful are those who embraced the idea of building their author platform. Keep in my mind that success isn't always defined by sales figures. Sara once had a fiction author who committed to her platform so intensely—even going so far as to create an entire social media profile for her fictional character—that she gained enough of a following to catch the attention of an agent and eventually have her book optioned for a Lifetime movie. Another author got his foot in the door with Netflix based solely on his author platform.

Definition of an Author Platform

Depending on whom you ask, the exact components of an author platform can vary. Publishing-industry expert Jane Friedman defines the author platform as the ability to sell books because of who you are or whom you can reach—an ability that comes in many forms.[4] *Writer's Digest* defines it as your *visibility as an author.*[5] The publication goes on to break down the author platform into three components:

1. **Who you are.** If you're already known in your field, this adds to your credibility. If you've already written a book, is it in the same genre as the one you are writing now? That's to say, will your next book be for an existing audience, or will you have to attract new followers? If writing nonfiction, are you known as an expert in your field?
2. **Your connections, both personal and professional.** Do you have a lot of media connections? Can you ask them to review your book, interview you, or perhaps provide a blurb for your book? (We'll discuss blurbs more in chapter 10.)
3. **The platforms you can use to eventually sell your book.** This can be anything from the obvious, such as social media, your website, traditional media, and mailing lists, to less obvious examples, such as at events of organizations you belong to.

Anyone who's ever had a blog or tried to gain followers on social media knows that it takes time, which is why you should begin working on your platform as early as possible—even before you write a single word of your actual book. If you're self-publishing, starting early gives you time to build a foundation for marketing later on. If you end up going with traditional publishing, you will want to include your numbers—Facebook fans, website views, newsletter subscribers, etc.—in your book proposal, as well as media connections that you can tap (an address book full of journalists; podcast, radio, and television outlets; etc.) and your offline following (classes, speaking engagements, and local influence, such as a position as a public official, a leader of a prominent organization or business, etc.).

In 2020, a prospective client asked Jenna to co-author a book with her. The client wasn't even a writer—she's a visual artist—but she'd been approached by a big-name publishing house simply because of her platform: some 100,000 Instagram followers at the time. She'd also received numerous write-ups for her art shows in publications such as the *New York Times*. The publishing house saw she had a platform and offered her a book deal on that basis alone because they saw there was already a healthy crop of potential buyers of her book.

Self-published writers can leverage their author platforms the same way, in addition to reaching out for help before publication. For example, you could ask your followers to weigh in when you're deciding on a title, choosing a book cover, or naming a character.

As you grow and engage your followers, they will become increasingly interested in what you have to say and how your book is progressing. They become your tribe, to use marketing expert Seth Godin's term. Although much of the goal in developing this tribe is to help you on your book journey, you must always remember that you, too, are a tribe member and so must give as much as you receive. If you do so, and do so altruistically, you'll be better positioned to call on them to help down the line, such as when you begin marketing your book. Once your tribe decides they like your product, they will like and share your posts and even talk about your book to *their* followers in an effort to share the new author they've found. They will, in effect, be marketing for you.

Building Your Tribe

Godin's idea of tribal belonging is very closely tied to the concept of social proof, which is when individuals behave a certain way because they see that behavior in others. This concept plays out in our daily lives, such as when a friend raves about a product or service, thereby influencing us via their recommendation.

Once you've built out your tribe and they begin to connect with your content, they may begin to market you to their friends and followers, bringing you more members to add to your tribe. This makes selling subsequent books or related items, such as memberships or tickets to a seminar you're hosting, much easier.

At this stage in the publishing process, many authors are hesitant about talking about their books for fear of seeming too self-promotional. It's something we hear often from our clients, many of whom are reluctant to replace their author hats with sales hats. That's perfectly understandable—most authors don't start writing a book with the intention of getting a job in sales, and many feel uncomfortable in that role.

If self-promotion is uncomfortable for you, take a look at products and individuals you hold in high esteem. Watch how they promote themselves and think of how you could translate that to your author platform. At this point, if all you're comfortable with is posting photos on Instagram that relate to your book, do that. Start in your comfort zone and slowly work your way up to higher levels of visibility.

In addition to potentially boosting your sales, talking about your book can help it seem real to you—and help hold you accountable—much in the same way someone tells their friends they're on a diet so that they don't order a double-fudge brownie sundae when they're out to dinner. Talking about your book while it's in its beginning stages is a ramp-up to telling people that you're working on becoming a published author.

If you already have a Facebook account, post a short description of your book. Just take the first step—make it a baby step—and then take another one in a week, and another one the next week. After a while, it will start to feel much more natural to talk about your book project and yourself as an author.

When you first start out building your author platform, you won't be talking *that* much about your book. The steps we are recommending you take right now will just lay the groundwork to promote your book once the publishing date approaches much later on. If you're writing a book about event planning, you can start by posting pictures of events or articles written by other professionals in the field, or you may just use your account to share helpful tips and tricks for throwing an event. If you're writing a novel centered around astrology, you might share horoscopes, talk about the history of astrology, or even post trivia questions to your followers. You're simply sharing relevant content at this stage, not promoting yourself or your book.

Author and naturalist Melanie Choukas-Bradley gives talks and leads outdoor excursions for prominent organizations in the Washington, DC, area. "To promote my events," she says, "these organizations often include the titles of relevant books in their marketing and registration copy, sometimes with sales links to area bookstores. I've never done much with social media myself, but I benefit from the social media activity of the organizations that engage me for events."

First Steps

Let's jump right into the groundwork of building your author platform. We completely understand if reading all these steps seems daunting, but you don't have to do them all in one sitting—or even in one month. Set aside an hour or two a week at first to tackle a few items, then slowly add more time as allows.

Claim your social handles.

This is crucial. Even if you never plan to use TikTok or Instagram, you should claim your name so that someone else doesn't squat on it. Try to use the same handle everywhere, if possible, so that you're easy to find. For example, Jenna tries to claim @StJenna whenever a new service crops up, before someone else gets to it. Make sure you claim your author name first; your book title is secondary, because when your second book comes out, you won't have to rebuild a whole new author platform from scratch.

Decide where to focus your efforts.

It's easy to get overwhelmed, so concentrate on one or two services at first, and then expand if you have the time and wherewithal. To decide where to start, research the following questions:

- Where does your demographic spend most of its time? Which strategy makes the most sense for your topic? See where other authors in your genre spend most of their time on social media. There's probably a reason they chose Pinterest over Instagram, for example. Remember to think offline as well, such as booking speaking engagements with relevant organizations.
- What services are you most comfortable using? For example, because Instagram is visual by its very nature, you need to be able to create images or be willing to buy them. Or maybe you're already familiar with Facebook; if so, start there.

As of the writing of this book, TikTok has become extremely influential in the book industry due to the #BookTok community and hashtag. Because of the ever-changing nature of social media, and the BookTok trend specifically, we recommend researching the most up-to-date information on the topic.

Begin building your newsletter subscriber list.

Start with your personal contacts, then collect new subscribers through your website and any events you may host or participate in, such as speaking engagements. You can pass around an old-school signup form on a clipboard, or you can have attendees enter their name and email on a tablet.

Claim your Amazon and Goodreads author pages.

Because these services require you to already have a book listed, make a note to claim your author pages as soon as the book link is up. Both of these services are discussed in more detail in chapter 17.

Build a content calendar.

This can help keep you on track—and also help you avoid writer's block. You can start with holiday-related content—even the offbeat ones, like International Talk Like a Pirate Day—if they're relevant to your book. Then keep a running list of ideas so that you're not starting from scratch each time you sit down to post.

Blog about your topic.

In marketing, there's something called the 80/20 Rule: Only 20% of your content should be self-promotional, while the other 80% should be informative or entertaining content related to your topic. Blogging is covered further in chapter 4. (Note that this is not to be confused with the 80–20 rule, otherwise known as the Pareto Principle, which posits that 80% of outcomes are the result of 20% of all causes.)

Warm up those old contacts.

You don't want to be reaching out to a colleague from ten years ago just when you need a favor, so begin rekindling those relationships now, particularly ones with individuals whom you may want to review your book, interview you, or in some way help with marketing. Since it can take a while to write your book, one way to go about this is to make sure to contact colleagues on their birthdays, and to do so in as personal a manner as possible. If you stick to it, you'll have communicated with everyone in your contact list by the time the year is out.

Write for other outlets.

Offer to write a guest blog on a site that caters to your audience, or write articles for outlets targeted to your demographic.

Join relevant associations—and be active in them.

These organizations can be online or in person. For example, if you're writing a book about wine, join some wine lovers' groups, online and off. Be active in their online forums and attend any in-person events you can. Start doing all of this now. As with reaching out to old contacts, you don't want your first activity with the association to be a request to promote your book.

Start guest-speaking.

Although it's best to do this closer to the date of your book's release, you can start guest-speaking on related topics now. Guest-speaking is more common for nonfiction authors than for fiction authors, but if you're a fiction author who can think of a related topic to speak on, go for it.

Hire a PR firm or social media agency.

Public relations firms and their online counterparts can cost a pretty penny, so engaging one is by no means a must, but you might want to consider it if your budget allows. PR agencies can book you on TV and radio shows or get you interviewed in the press. A social media agency can help manage your author platform, drive traffic, buy online ads, or even get your blog posts syndicated. We've had clients use both PR agencies and social media firms, with widely varying results, so make sure you interview other authors to find a reputable firm that specializes in promoting books, especially those on your particular topic. Public relations is discussed further in chapter 16.

While this isn't a comprehensive list of everything you can do to build your author platform, these steps are the most common and most important. Remember, you don't have to do them all now, but start to get comfortable with each step and slowly wade in once you're ready.

Keep in mind that author platform numbers do not translate directly to book sales. Just because you have 10,000 newsletter subscribers doesn't mean that 10,000 copies of your book will sell. A small percentage of your followers will buy from you right away, and another percentage will buy somewhere down the road, but the vast majority may never buy your book at all. However, if they're engaged, they may promote you to their own networks by sharing your posts, forwarding your newsletter, or via old-fashioned word-of-mouth. Think of it this way: Just because Coca-Cola has 108 million followers on Facebook doesn't mean that every time they post content, they sell 108 million bottles of Coke. But it does keep the brand front of mind and builds goodwill with their customer base.

While your author platform doesn't guarantee book sales, it is your starting point. When your book is eventually available on Amazon, Barnes & Noble, Bookshop.org (a partner of IndieBound), or your website, you can post these links to the various components of your platform—over and over again (keeping in mind the 80/20 Rule we mentioned earlier). Closer to the date of launch, you may want to engage social media marketing teams, publicists, and other PR teams.

Look at it this way: If you were to start building an author platform two years before writing a book, think about how many friends, subscribers, followers, etc., you could collect in the meantime. This gives any professionals you hire a head start, as they don't have to spend the first months of their contracts trying to amass enough followers to see your posts.

If this is all new to you, ask for help, get recommendations, hire a coach until you get the hang of it, or just hire a company to do it for you. You want to make sure you do it right, like creating a Facebook business page as an author rather than a profile, which is what private individuals (not public figures) use.

Hiring a Professional

Before you sign a contract with a social media manager, should you decide to go this route, there are two very important points you should research to ensure they are clearly spelled out:

1. **Methodology.** If you're hiring a company to build your following, ask how they do so. Jenna has seen clients pay a flat fee to get thousands of followers on X (back when it was called Twitter), only to have their numbers plummet after a few weeks, with the remaining followers consisting mainly of fake accounts. Trust us, publishers and agents can tell when your numbers are artificially inflated. Make sure you ask *how* the company plans to grow your numbers—and get it in writing that it won't be with fake accounts.

2. **Reporting.** Make it clear that you want to receive regular reports on progress—how many pageviews you received after a campaign, for example—and that the company is willing to explain them if you're unsure about the jargon. Ask to see examples of such reports that the company has done for similar clients.

There are many other questions to ask, but these are the biggies. See Further Resources for additional questions.

Many first-time authors don't realize that an author platform plays such a crucial role in the self-publishing process, and they feel overwhelmed. For now, if there's just one action you take after reading this chapter, make it claiming your domain name and social handles *everywhere*.

Next Steps

- Make sure your author strategy aligns with your BAGG (Book and Author Gameplan and Goals).
- Follow the First Steps mentioned earlier in this chapter. Refer to this list on a regular basis.
- Claim your domain name and social handles *everywhere*.
- Store any account passwords in a secure location.

Further Resources

Visit bookagogo.com/books/further-resources for the complete collection of all links in this book.

Companies, Individuals & Resources Mentioned in This Chapter
- **BookTok:** en.wikipedia.org/wiki/BookTok
- **Melanie Choukas-Bradley:** melaniechoukas-bradley.com
- **Seth Godin,** *Tribes*: amazon.com/Tribes-We-Need-You-Lead/dp/1491514736

Building Your Author Platform
- **"The Author Platform: What It Is and Why You Need One":** laeditorsandwritersgroup.com/what-is-author-platform-why-you-need-one
- **Author platform coaching:** jennarobbins.com/author-platform
- **Facebook profiles vs. Pages:** laeditorsandwritersgroup.com/facebook-tips-for-writers-profiles-vs-pages
- **Choosing a newsletter tool:** monsterinsights.com/best-email-newsletter-tools-compared-pros-and-cons

Claiming Your Author Pages
- **Amazon:** author.amazon.com
- **Goodreads:** goodreads.com/author/program

Social Media

- **Social proof:** entrepreneur.com/article/342883
- **Working with social media managers:** linkedin.com/pulse/16-questions-ask-your-social-media-marketing-agency-matin-wallister
- **Questions to ask social media agencies:** forbes.com/sites/forbesagencycouncil/2021/10/29/6-questions-to-ask-a-social-media-agency-before-hiring
- **Social media guide for authors:** kindlepreneur.com/social-media-for-writers

Author Website: Why You Need One & What It Should Include

One of the most essential parts of your author platform is a website. Despite that, many authors often question why they even need one. But trust us when we tell you: You need a website—even if it's just a few simple pages. The blog for IngramSpark, a self-publishing and distribution competitor to Amazon, even ventures to state that "a professional-looking website ... is, by far, the most important element of a book marketing strategy."[6]

Writer's Digest calls a website an author's "primary piece of real estate on the internet," as it's the first place you'll be able to build credibility and connect with your audience.[7] If it takes two years to write your book, you could be using that time to begin forming the tribe of readers we mentioned in the previous chapter. Even if you do only the bare minimum with your website, it becomes a way to increase your visibility when readers search the web for you or your book.

Choosing a Domain Name

One of the most common questions authors ask is what domain name they should use: their own name or the book title? We always recommend using your author name. That's because you're going to spend a lot of time—and possibly money—getting traffic to your website. If you decide to publish a second book down the road, you don't want to start from scratch—you want to build upon the foundation you've already invested in, which you can do if you use your author name. Starting a new website for each new book would be like starting a new social media account for each one: You'd start off with zero followers and lose all the momentum you've built.

That doesn't mean you shouldn't buy the domain name for your book as well, because you can then redirect it to your author site. For example, before her memoir *Faithful and Devoted: Confessions of a Music Addict* was released, Jenna bought faithfulanddevoted.com. Because she's had jennarobbins.com since 2001, she set up a redirect that sent visitors of faithfulanddevoted.com to her book page on jennarobbins.com. Although it's not necessary to buy your book title as a domain name, it can help keep it safe from cybersquatters or hackers posing as you, or just help avoid confusion if someone else has the same book title.

If this is your first book, you may want to think about how to make your author name and related domain name unique, particularly if many people share your name or have a similar one. Jenna began using her middle name, Rose, after finding several other individuals with the name Jenna Robbins. So far, she's the only other Jenna Rose Robbins she's found. Another way to make your name unique is to add any relevant titles or degrees—for example, Dr. or MBA. Be sure that the name you choose is something you then consistently use in your branding, such as on Facebook, X, LinkedIn, and in marketing materials. Once you've decided on your author name, set up a Google Alert so that you are notified whenever you are mentioned online.

If you're an author who writes in several distinct genres with different audiences, you may want to consider different names and websites for each.

For example, if you write both nonfiction business books and children's books, you should probably have a website for each and possibly even use a different author name. This allows you to brand each for the proper audience and prevent confusion.

Once you've decided what name you want to use for your website domain, you can purchase and manage it through a kind of company known as a domain host, while the actual website is managed on a web host. In many cases, the web host and domain host are the same company, but not always. See Further Resources for more information.

Website Builders

Although hiring a website developer (a person who builds the website) isn't a requirement, we highly recommend you do so if you're not tech savvy. We also recommend the site be built in WordPress (wordpress.org), the most popular website builder by far, and to avoid website builders such as Wix (wix.com) or Squarespace (squarespace.com) due to the limitations in functionality, although both services have improved greatly over the last few years.[8] If using one of those options is the only way you're going to get your website off the ground, it's definitely better than no website at all. You want to look professional, so your website needs to reflect that.

Since most authors don't have much experience in HTML (the coding language used to build websites), if you decide to go with WordPress, you will most likely need a developer at some point. Some web hosting companies will now install WordPress for you. The next step is to choose a theme, which is sort of like a template, complete with fonts, layout, and sometimes even special functionality. For example, themes that are built specifically for recipes often have built-in capabilities for displaying ingredients, instructions, and nutritional information. Most themes come with documentation that guides you through the set-up process, while others come with technical support. If you get stuck or want functionality outside of what comes with WordPress or your theme, you can have a developer help you over the hump. Just make sure that any functionality the developer creates isn't proprietary, so that if you need to change developers, a new one can easily take over the former's work.

One of Jenna's clients came to her with a website that was built in WordPress but had custom functionality added and a high-end plugin installed. In order for Jenna to take over management of the website, she needed to rebuild that portion of the website the plugin controlled so that any developer could take over at any point and the client didn't have to pay the plugin's annual fee. While this meant additional up-front costs, the client opted to do so for the peace of mind and the longer-term cost savings.

If you hire a developer to do the whole kit and caboodle, make sure that you have all the passwords and that you own your domain name. This isn't only because there are some unscrupulous individuals out there who hold sites hostage for more money. If you somehow lose contact with a developer, you may have trouble reaching them when you need to make updates. Jenna has had several new clients ask her to make updates to their sites, only to then tell her they had no idea how to log into them. Then, when they try to contact their developers, they're unable to get a hold of them. See Further Resources for more about making sure you have complete control over your digital assets.

Remember to keep your passwords in a safe place. Better yet, *memorize* them. Jenna has developed a way to create secure, memorable passwords; see the link in Further Resources.

Design & Content

When it comes to brainstorming design ideas, look at websites of other authors in your genre, particularly those who've recently published books so that you can see if there are any new trends in book marketing. In the early 2010s, book trailers (the publishing equivalent of movie trailers) were pretty much de rigueur, but as of the writing of this book, they've fallen out of fashion. (More about book trailers and other marketing tools in chapter 16.) Reviewing the websites of authors in your genre can help you determine whether there are specific pages you might need for your demographic.

Make a list of your website's goals, such as collecting emails for your newsletter and building a social media following for your author platform. Make sure that every single one of your pages has at least one goal on it with a CTA (call to action). Some of the most common goals for author websites are:

- Signing up for a newsletter
- Contacting you or your business
- Buying your book
- Booking speaking engagements
- Downloading media kits

See Further Resources for an article that lists more website goals.

Your website doesn't have to be a behemoth. Although it could be as small as a single page, there are four pages we recommend every author include. Think of these pages as the heart of your website and the focus of your website menu.

1. **About.** This page is all about you (or your company, if you chose Promotion or Reputation as your BAGG; see chapter 1), so it should include a photo and bio of you.

2. **Books.** If your title is not yet available for purchase, this page should reference when it will be released, even if that is just a general time frame, like "fall 2025." After that should go your book's synopsis and any blurbs, awards, or reviews, which you can add as you receive them. Include a prominent "Buy" button to purchase your book,

either directly from your site or from a third party such as Amazon, as well as a signup form so subscribers receive alerts when there are updates about your book. You can also offer a sneak peek, such as a free chapter to download, or additional content freebies, such as outtakes or background information.

3. **Contact.** Include a contact form along with your phone number, email address, and social handles, as well as those of anyone working for you, such as a publicist or agent. It's also a good idea to include a link to this contact page on every page of the site, preferably in the footer. Links to your social media profiles should also go in a universal location, usually the header or footer, and the accounts themselves should all point back to your website.

4. **Newsletter.** Make it easy to share a link to your signup form by putting it on its own page. Just ask for an email address—that's it. Don't include any distractions on this page, just the signup form. Once you start collecting emails, you can begin marketing to your subscribers immediately, or you can build out a list and market to them when the time feels right. Be sure to include a signup form on every page of your website, such as in the footer.

Authors with other products or services to offer may want to consider building a fifth page, which would be your store.

Once your book launches or is about to do so, you can build out additional pages such as:

- **Press.** This is optional, but once you get interviewed, this is where to add press hits, such as magazine articles that feature you or your book, press and video interviews, any guest-blogging you've done, etc.

- **Testimonials.** Any recommendations from clients about your work or services would go here. For example, on Jenna's website, she includes reviews for her memoir on the book's page, but recommendations from clients about her ghostwriting and editing services on a separate page.

- **Events.** When you start to book author appearances and book signings, or other activities such as seminars, webinars, or conferences, post them to this page.

Website Functionality

Your site should have some basic functionality. If you decide to enable purchasing a book directly from your site, your profit margins will be larger than if you point them to Amazon or your distributor's site. However, you then have to determine who will fulfill those orders. We discuss distribution more in chapter 15, but as it relates to your website, just know that it should be flexible enough to allow for these decisions later on.

You also want to ensure you can track website traffic in detail. While some builders such as Wix have that feature built in, we highly recommend going with the industry standard, Google Analytics (analytics.google.com), which is free to use. Not only does it provide much more data—more than most users will ever need—but it also works in conjunction with Google Ads, which you or your marketing professional might eventually decide to use. Google Analytics begins tracking data from the moment it's installed, but since it can't track data retroactively, it's important to have it installed as soon as possible.

As someone who has project managed the launch of numerous websites, including those for companies such as Disney and FIJI Water, Jenna has compiled a multipage document of requirements she gives to a developer before they begin work. Some of these more common requirements are included in Appendix C.

All of this functionality does not have to be available when you first launch your site. But this is one of the reasons you want to choose a website builder that is scalable: You can add functionality as you and your marketing strategy evolve and grow. Of the builders we've discussed, WordPress is by far the most scalable, but if you don't foresee ever needing a store or some major bells and whistles, then you might be fine with Wix or Squarespace. Just make sure that you choose a website builder that allows anyone with the login information to make updates. If your developer used proprietary code to build your site, you might be beholden to them to make all updates—not to mention the fact that such a site probably won't rank as highly in search engines as one developed on a builder such as Wix or WordPress, which are designed to increase your content's ranking in search results (a process known as search engine optimization, or SEO). Choosing the right website builder is important because you don't want to launch on one, only to discover six months from now that you have to move to another, costing you both time and money. That's another reason to work with a reputable developer or web consultant: They can help guide you in this decision.

Keep in mind that since technology and design trends are constantly changing, you will most likely need to update your site occasionally. The basic rule of thumb is that sites should get a full revamp every five years so that they don't look dated and they possess the most up-to-date functionality, including security features. Even if you originally build in WordPress, there is the possibility that your theme will, at some point, no longer be supported or a plugin with key functionality will be abandoned. So make sure you budget for such inevitabilities.

Once you have the website's basic framework in place, you can keep adding to it little by little. Set aside just an hour a week, for example. Even if you work on it just once a month, you'll eventually get it to where you want it. Of course, this only works when you've given yourself enough time to build out your site before the launch of your book, which is why we're covering this topic so early in our overall timeline. Possibly the most efficient way to add to your site incrementally is by blogging, which also happens to be one of the best ways to increase your visibility in search engines. (More about blogging in the next chapter.)

Don't let your website overwhelm you. Start by buying the domain and building a simple landing page with the basics: who you are, what your book is about, how to get in touch with you, and a newsletter signup form. If you have even this little bit, it's not just a good first step—it's also a way to start building your email list and getting your site recognized and indexed by search engines. So start small, but map out a strategy for incremental improvements from now until your book launches.

Next Steps

- Make sure your website reflects your BAGG as much as possible.
- Decide which domain name(s) to buy, ensuring that the main one is your author name.
- Identify the pages of your website and which CTA/goal will appear on each.
- Make sure you, in addition to your developer, have all the passwords for your website and that you own the domain name and any accounts associated with your website.
- Store your passwords in a secure location.
- Ensure Google Analytics is installed on your site.
- Update the Appendix B worksheet to reflect any changes based on this chapter.

Further Resources

Visit bookagogo.com/books/further-resources for the complete collection of all links in this book.

Companies, Individuals & Resources Mentioned in This Chapter

- **Google Alerts:** google.com/alerts
- **Google Analytics:** analytics.google.com

Advice About Author Websites

- **Jane Friedman:** janefriedman.com/author-websites
- **Website goals:** intechnic.com/blog/best-examples-of-website-goals-and-objectives

Book Trailers

- **Determining if you need a book trailer:** rachellegardner.com/should-you-have-a-book-trailer

Digital Security

- **Retaining control over your digital assets:** siteseeingmedia.com/the-one-thing/ensure-your-digital-assets-are-yours
- **Creating secure passwords:** siteseeingmedia.com/the-one-thing/create-a-secure-password-system

How-Tos

- **Domain hosts vs. web hosts:** wpbeginner.com/beginners-guide/whats-the-difference-between-domain-name-and-web-hosting-explained
- **Choosing a domain name:** jinand.co/articles/5-recommendations-choosing-right-domain-name-author-illustrator-websites
- **Setting up Google Alerts:** authorimprints.com/google-alerts-authors-book-marketing

Website Builders

- **Squarespace:** squarespace.com
- **Wix:** wix.com
- **WordPress:** wordpress.org

Why Blogging Is Important for Authors

You probably already know that blogs can play a big role in your marketing strategy by boosting your web presence. But there are many other benefits to blogging. We meet so many clients who are reluctant or even completely averse to blogging that we want to start out with the unsung reasons why you should make it a core part of your author platform.

8 Reasons Writers Should Blog

Although we've included eight reasons, many others have been written about extensively, so see Further Resources for where to find more info.

1. **Different audience.** Blogging offers you a different medium for your message, which means you have another outlet for promotion. Social media is important for your author platform, but that's more appropriate for short-form content. Blogging, on the other hand, gives

you the opportunity to go more in-depth on your topic (although likely not as in-depth as you do in your book), further demonstrating your experience and knowledge, which in turn allows you to build trust and instill confidence. Just make sure that you remember the 80/20 Rule discussed on page 19.

2. **Long-lasting content.** Blogs allow you to create content with legs. Social media is often ephemeral—a Facebook post, for example, doesn't often get many eyeballs a few weeks beyond when it was first created. Solid, credible web content, on the other hand, can have a much longer shelf life, provided it is well written. That's because this content can still turn up in search engines—and because others may link to it from their own sites and even share it on their social accounts.

    If you find that a post is still getting traffic years after you first wrote it, you can always update it, providing you with an opportunity to have your content rediscovered all over again. As an example, a post on the website for Jenna's writers' group has been so popular that it accounts for more than a quarter of the site traffic—even more than the homepage (which is highly unusual, as that is almost always a site's most visited page). "Memoir: Do I Use Their Real Names?" has proven so popular more than seven years after it was originally posted that the group decided to update it—and that further increased their site's traffic.

3. **Multipurpose content.** For nonfiction authors, blogging can be a way to share information with clients and prospects. When a question comes up in meetings or on phone calls, you can follow up by sending a blog post that addresses the issue. This not only increases your SEO (more about this in reason 7) by providing highly sought-after content, but also allows you to be more efficient and thorough with your answers.

    In fact, the idea of using blogs as a way to share helpful information was the genesis of our podcast and this book. We both found ourselves answering a lot of the same questions for our authors, and this prompted the idea of answering these questions in the form of a podcast, which we would then transcribe and turn into a blog post. Those blog posts, in turn, became the book you're holding in your hand.

Digital content can have many outlets, so ensure that your work gets repurposed wherever relevant. Once you've published a blog post, don't just wait for people to find it: Serve it up to them by posting on social networks, sending out a newsletter, and sharing the link in relative forums and websites such as Reddit and Quora. This way, you're using this content in numerous components of your author platform.

4. **Personability.** Blogging connects readers directly to your brand (or, in this case, your book) on a more personal level. As you blog and update your website with new content, the awareness of your brand can continue to grow. You can engage with readers by sharing behind-the-scenes details, such as why you decided to write a book, or who (if anybody) inspired you to write. If you're a nonfiction author, blogging is also a great way for you to build clout with your readers and position yourself as an industry expert.

5. **True ownership.** Blogging allows you to create content you will always own. Even though it's unlikely Facebook or YouTube will go away anytime soon, they could eventually pull a Google+ and do just that—and take your content with them. No matter what new legalese the social media networks roll out, you can rest assured that your content remains yours when it's on your blog. To that end, ensure that content backups/downloads are a functionality of whichever website builder you choose (which is another reason to go with WordPress, discussed in the previous chapter).

6. **Accountability to write regularly.** Beyond just marketing, blogging could lead to ideas for a future book. After you've been blogging for

a while, you may find that you can compile your posts into a book manuscript, or you might find that the posts are the seeds of a future book—ideas waiting to be expanded upon.

7. **SEO (search engine optimization).** The content you create and the way you code and structure your website determines how easily users can find your site—that's SEO in a nutshell. Blogging helps increase SEO by letting search engines know that your site is being updated regularly, and the more regularly you update your site, the more likely it will rank higher in search engines, meaning an increase in organic (unpaid) traffic. More organic traffic means paying less for ads down the road.

Another SEO benefit of blogging is the increased opportunities to use keywords, which are words or phrases that relate to a specific topic. If you're writing a book about event planning, you might want to attract readers to your website who want to learn about flower arrangements and centerpieces, so your keyword/phrase might be "flowers in event planning." For your site to rank highly for this keyword, you have to use it often on your site, so you could blog about centerpieces, corsages, bridesmaids' bouquets, etc. If you stick to only the four core pages discussed in the previous chapter, you won't have many opportunities to rank for different keywords. Blogging greatly expands those opportunities.

Some bloggers have garnered enough of a following to land publishing contracts. The story of *The Martian*, which became a 2015 blockbuster film starring Matt Damon, began as blog posts on Andy Weir's personal website, releasing a new short story every six to eight weeks. In interviews, he has said that his blog visitors were the ones who critiqued his writing and scientific data, which allowed him to improve with every post.[9] He eventually amassed enough of a following to be noticed by an editor at Crown Publishing, a division of Random House. The rest is history.

8. **Practice, practice, practice.** The most obvious reason to blog: It helps you polish your writing chops. Whether you're writing fiction or nonfiction, blogging is one of the best ways to find your voice and style. Just as athletes and musicians need to practice to hone their skills, so do writers.

   There's a common misconception that blogging is only relevant for nonfiction writers, but that's far from the truth. For fiction authors, a blog could be a great way to test out new ideas (plot concepts, characters, etc.) for future books or just serve as a creative release—a place where you can write whatever you want to write, not material specifically geared toward your book. For nonfiction authors, a blog can be used as an educational tool—a place where you can write about the topics you discuss in further detail in your book. In doing so, you demonstrate value to your readers, and in turn, value in your book.

The print-on-demand publisher IngramSpark highly recommends that authors blog and mentions many of the reasons above, as well as some others.

Getting Over Getting Started

Many of our clients never get rolling with blogging because they never even start. And the reason most don't start is that they're afraid of putting their writing out there, which many admit is rather contradictory, since the reason they *should* start blogging is because they want to promote their writing.

If fear is the reason keeping you from blogging, consider this: Once your book is printed, it's completed—you can't make changes. (Yes, there are some exceptions, such as reprints and new editions, but that doesn't apply to 99% of books, so for the sake of argument, let's just say your book won't ever be changed once it's printed.) On the other hand, blogs live on the web, which means they can always be changed, updated, edited—and all within a few seconds and with little to no cost. You can even delete a post, if necessary.

Another reason often cited for not getting started is lack of time, which is a valid concern. If that's what's holding you back, rather than thinking of this task as "blogging," think of it as "marketing." You will eventually need to market your book if you have goals of selling copies. But you may not have realized that the earlier you get started with marketing, the easier—and possibly more affordable—it will be.

Thousands of books are published on any given day. According to *Publishers Weekly*, 1.68 million books were self-published in 2018, up a whopping 40% from the year before.[10] By 2023, that number had surpassed two million.[11] With that kind of competition, you have to find a way to cut through the clutter.

A blog can help you do just that, if you give it the proper time and attention. As you build a following, you'll garner more awareness before your book is even published. If you put in the time to blog, you will see results, possibly without having to pay a marketing professional. Although you might still need one down the line, if you make significant progress with your blog, you'll likely need fewer of their services. So blogging is indeed an investment worth making.

In a Q&A with the Authors Guild, Jane Friedman gave the following advice: "If you're a serious blogger, usually you need [to] be posting at least 2x week. I'd avoid keeping a blog if you can't post something at least a couple times per month. Otherwise, things look dusty."[12]

Another common barrier to starting a blog is good ol' writer's block. But there are numerous ways to come up with blog topics. For fiction, since so much of the success of your book depends on your unique voice, showcase it. Talk about the topics that interest you. In a Medium article Shaunta Grimes wrote about the benefits of blogging for fiction writers, she discusses how she didn't blog before the release of her first book, which didn't sell very well.[13] When she sold another book a few years later, she put in the time and effort to blog and build her email list. The result: That next book had about 1,000 presales, which, as Grimes notes, is a big deal.

Guest-blogging can also be an effective marketing strategy. You can either guest-blog for someone else's site or invite someone to blog on yours. It's really a win-win for you both: The guest-blogger gets exposure to a whole new audience, while the host blogger gets a short break from writing the blog.

If this chapter hasn't succeeded in convincing you to blog, that's fine. Blogging is by no means a requirement. We just wanted to make sure you have time to get as much of a head start as possible before you reach chapter 16, which covers marketing and public relations.

⌖ Next Steps

- Make sure your blogging strategy reflects your BAGG (see chapter 1).
- Create an editorial calendar for the next month.
- Write your first blog post.
- Set up a schedule for regular content creation and analysis of website traffic.

⌖ Further Resources

Visit bookagogo.com/books/further-resources for the complete collection of all links in this book.

Companies, Individuals & Resources Mentioned in This Chapter

- **About *The Martian* by Andy Weir:** wsj.com/articles/SB10001424052 7023045588045793751614611671196
- **IngramSparks's blogging advice:** ingramspark.com/blog/blogging-for-authors-increase-reader-engagement-and-sell-more-books
- **LAEWG's most popular webpage:** "Memoir: Do I Use Their Real Names?": laeditorsandwritersgroup.com/memoir-do-i-use-their-real-names

Blogging Advice

- **From Jane Friedman:** janefriedman.com/blogging-for-writers
- **Blogging tips:** bookmarketingtools.com/blog/7-blogging-tips-for-fiction-writers
- **For fiction writers:** yourwriterplatform.com/blogging-fiction-writers
- **For nonfiction writers:** ignitedinkwriting.com/ignite-your-ink-blog-for-writers/how-to-effectively-blog-your-nonfiction-book/2020

Blogging to Land a Book Deal

- **From** *The Writer* **magazine:** writermag.com/get-published/the-publishing-industry/blog-to-book-deal

5

Writing Collaborators: Ghostwriters vs. Co-Authors vs. Writing Coaches vs. Flying Solo

Some authors complete their manuscript without ever needing help from a ghostwriter, co-author, or writing coach. Other authors—whether it's due to time constraints or their writing skills—benefit greatly from working with one or more of these professionals. This chapter will help you decide if that applies to you.

Keep in mind this is *not* about the editorial help you need once your first draft is finished, such as developmental editors, line editors, copyeditors, and proofreaders, which we'll cover in the next chapter. To differentiate these roles from the editors you may need once your manuscript is complete, we'll refer to someone who acts as a ghostwriter, co-author, or writing coach as a writing collaborator, and the editors as your editing team. Both teams fall under the category of editorial, but while a writing collaborator creates the actual content, the editing team organizes, refines, and polishes that content. An author usually has only one writing collaborator, but there is often more than one member of the editing team.

All of these writing-collaborator roles—ghostwriters, co-authors, writing coaches—may be fluid and change throughout the process: A writing coach might transition into being your ghostwriter, or vice versa.

Ghostwriters

A ghostwriter is someone hired to anonymously write a book. In most cases, the client's name goes on the cover, while the ghost gets absolutely no credit and is often contractually obligated *not* to mention their involvement in the project.

Some people are shocked to learn that, as a ghostwriter, Jenna cannot talk about any of the more than two dozen books she's written for clients. Some even see it as deceptive on the part of the client or mistake it as a form of plagiarism. For that reason, clients often don't want to admit they've used a ghostwriter even though it's a very common and acceptable practice. However, that tide is turning. In recent years, several notable authors have been very up front about using a ghost, including Prince Harry, who enlisted Pulitzer Prize-winning journalist J. R. Moehringer to help him pen his blockbuster bestselling autobiography, *Spare*.

Almost all nonfiction books written by nonwriter celebrities—politicians, athletes, actors, musicians, etc.—have used a ghostwriter. Often, the client hiring the ghostwriter isn't a writer themself or simply might not have the time to write, so they turn to a professional to help them produce the manuscript. In the end, the ideas and thoughts communicated in the book *usually* come from the author whose name is on the front, but they've used the professional services of a ghostwriter to get the information on the page in a clear, organized manner.

Although ghostwriting is a more common practice in nonfiction than it is in fiction, some very well-known fiction books have been ghostwritten.

James Patterson, for example, is very open about the fact that he has a stable of ghostwriters who churn out the many books that bear his name.[14] When a series becomes a brand unto itself, such as the Baby-Sitters Club or the Jason Bourne series, the best way to turn a quick buck is to keep churning out material, and so ghosts are often brought on board to further the saga. Even classic series such as Nancy Drew and the Hardy Boys were ghostwritten by multiple authors, although each book bore the name "Carolyn Keene" or "Franklin W. Dixon" on the cover.

Of the two dozen books Jenna has ghostwritten, two became *New York Times* bestsellers. The process for each book was quite different due to the fact that each client's needs were different. For some, Jenna did all the legwork, from finding sources to interview to burying her nose in microfiche in Los Angeles's downtown library. For others, she was given transcripts of recordings of the client discussing the topic at hand, which she would then edit into chapters.

But even though Jenna was doing all of the legwork, the client still needed to take time to review what she had written—both for content and to ensure she had captured their unique voice. So just because you hire a ghostwriter doesn't always mean you can step back from the process and wait for the published manuscript to land in your hands. You might be able to do so if you've previously worked with the ghost and trust that they will get your voice and tone. But just like beginning any new relationship, you need to earn each other's trust and get to know each other's work and communication styles so that the process can flow smoothly.

Ghostwriting rates can be quite steep, but it really depends on the ghostwriter. As mentioned earlier, many never take a gig ghostwriting a book for less than $75,000, while others command upwards of six figures.

Sara's first job out of college was at a ghostwriting firm. When she started, the company was charging $35,000 to $60,000 for each book project. Over the next several years, the firm continued to expand its team of award-winning writers, got more *New York Times* bestsellers under its belt, and had more manuscripts optioned for film and television. Such success allowed the firm to raise its rates to more than $100,000 dollars per book. It's not uncommon to see price tags like that when dealing with ghosts who have such stellar credentials.

Jenna, on the other hand, rarely offers a flat rate for a ghostwriting project and instead charges hourly, which she feels is fairer for both parties because it's a true reflection of the amount of time she puts into the project. She also offers a hybrid ghostwriting/writing coach service, where she writes the more challenging portions of the manuscript while mentoring the client on the remainder. Many clients prefer this option because it's much more affordable.

In a LinkedIn post, Jane Friedman reported that the attendees of the January 2024 Gathering of the Ghosts conference in New York City came to the consensus that "a writer who charges less than $50,000 for a book of 50,000 words or more is going to starve."[15] Ghostwriter Michael Levin (for whom both Jenna and Sara have worked in different capacities) suggested to the audience that ghostwriters should "take whatever they're charging now, double it, and add 20 percent."[16] That gives you a good idea of how competitive industry rates can be.

By law, when someone creates a work, they own the rights to it. But when you hire a ghostwriter, you are more often than not contracting for the ghost to create what is known as a work for hire, which is a legal term meaning that you, the client, wholly own the work that the ghost creates for you. That means that you keep 100% of the profits and all of the rights in perpetuity, as long as the contract states that the piece is a work for hire.

That's another reason ghostwriters charge such steep rates: They know they're not entitled to a piece of the back end if the work is a smashing success. Imagine if J. K. Rowling had used a ghost for the Harry Potter series: The ghost likely would have received a flat fee up front and none of the billions of dollars that the series spawned in merchandising, film rights, and all the other revenue streams that made Rowling one of the wealthiest people in the world.

Also, since the ghost is contractually obligated to be anonymous, they are constrained in how they can market themselves. If Rowling had used a ghost, that person—who would have been just as, if not more, responsible than Rowling for the success of the book—wouldn't even be able to claim a shred of credit. For that reason, the ghost is compensated financially up front, no matter how successful the resulting work is. (Just a quick disclaimer that we are in no way saying that Rowling used a ghostwriter. We've just used her as a high-profile what-if.)

Of course, you can make different arrangements with your ghost, such as offering back end in lieu of up-front cash. Every client–ghost relationship is different and every ghost is different. Some ghosts are open to working out a partial-pay–partial-royalty share, and others are not.

Co-Authors

Although the term *co-author* is sometimes used interchangeably with *ghostwriter,* there is one significant difference: The hired co-author gets credit for the work. That's significant because they can speak openly about the project and use it as part of their personal marketing package.

For example, if you visit Jenna's Amazon Author Page, you will see three books: this one, her memoir, and a book about grief that she co-authored. Although she's written more than two dozen books for clients, the only one she can talk about in detail is the book on grief. For the books she ghostwrote, she can only speak generally about the subject matter and the book-writing process for each one, but she can't say anything that might give away the identity of the book or the client. Being able to speak openly about a project has value to a writer, so many offer reduced rates when hired as a co-author rather than as a ghostwriter. Rates can also vary depending on how prominent the co-author's credit is, such as whether their name appears on the cover or just on the inside.

That's not to say every ghostwriter offers each client the option of co-authoring. Because an author is a brand, a ghostwriter might not choose to co-author a project that doesn't reflect their brand, such as a project outside the genre they are known for. Some might pass on having their name associated with a controversial subject but might not have a problem working on the project as a ghost. For example, if an author is known for children's books, they might not choose to co-author a steamy romance novel, no matter how much potential it might have.

Many times, a co-authoring arrangement is actually just that: a fair sharing of duties and profits between the two parties, with no money changing hands up front. You might split up the chapters of the book so that each of you writes an equal amount, or you can divvy up the workload as you see fit—one writer researching and interviewing, while the other does the actual writing. The book you are reading was co-authored, with each of us writing on the topics of our expertise and sharing additional responsibilities according to our strengths.

Writing Coaches

Hiring a ghostwriter or co-author may not be necessary if you know what you want to write about and how to write. In that case, you might just need a writing coach, whose main job is to assist you, whether that be helping when you get stuck, keeping you on track, or providing feedback. For example, you can set up an accountability schedule, where you turn in a chapter every two weeks for the coach to edit and critique.

A writing coach, also referred to as an author coach, should be somebody who isn't personally close to you, so they can give you honest and candid feedback on your work. They can also advise how to shape the content you've already written and how to develop future chapters. Individuals who work best with writing coaches are often those who do well in a classroom setting, as the coach acts as a hybrid teacher/mentor.

Just keep in mind that if you hire a writing coach, *all* of the writing responsibility falls on you, so you need to be certain you can dedicate the time to write, interview, research, and perform any other tasks related to your book. A writing coach generally does *not* act as a ghostwriter or co-author.

Writing coaches can charge set fees or by the hour, billing each month for the time they spend with you on phone calls, reading content, and, if they do it, editing. For example, Sara works with a coach who charges $4,500 for ninety days of coaching, which includes reviewing and providing feedback on all content the client sends him. He does set limits on hours and material, but it's very reasonable.

When Jenna works as a writing coach, she bills by the hour but also offers retainers at reduced rates for clients who purchase a minimum number of hours per month. Other writing coaches have different ways of billing, so check around to see whose fees fit your budget.

Flying Solo

You don't have to use any of the three above-mentioned writing collaborators. Not everyone needs one. However, if you decide to fly solo, you'll still need a schedule that works for you, including setting goals to finish the book.

If all you require is motivational support, consider joining a writing group or meetup. Doing so also offers you the opportunity to get feedback on your work, bounce questions off your peers, and even receive encouragement to stay on schedule.

You will still eventually need an editing team—whether that be a copyeditor, proofreader, or both—once your manuscript is completed. That's because the first rule of editorial is: "Two sets of eyes on everything." You just can't edit your own work, unless you let it sit for an extensive amount of time. And even then, it can be hard to notice your own idiosyncrasies. Even though Jenna is an editor, she always has someone copyedit her work. In fact, she had three different editors read her memoir before it went to print. If the writing doesn't need to be quite so polished, such as for her blog, she lets it "marinate": She writes the piece, sets it aside for a few days, and then returns to it with a fresh set of eyes.

When choosing your writing collaborator, remember that just because someone is a good writer doesn't mean they're the right one for *you*. Don't get starstruck because a writer happened to work on a book with a celebrity or a well-known executive in your industry. You and your writing collaborator need to have chemistry, as the two of you will be working together for months, maybe even years. So pick wisely. Not only do you want to ensure the two of you get along on a personal level, but you also want someone who can communicate your ideas clearly and in your voice, not theirs.

Because Jenna believes so strongly in the chemistry between a writing collaborator and a client, she requires all prospective clients to take a five-hour test drive with her. During those five hours, they get to see the quality of her work and whether or not she gets their style and voice, while the two feel each other out and see if they mesh. If those five hours go smoothly for both parties, they then sign a contract for the remainder of the project or a portion of it. This gives the client a peek into the process and the quality of her work, while allowing Jenna to see if she wants to work on the project long-term.

Sometimes it's preferable to have a writing collaborator who isn't very familiar with your subject matter. For example, if you're working on a technical nonfiction topic intended for laypeople, a co-author who is in your target audience can help point out jargon that needs to be defined or concepts that need better explanation for your audience. When it comes to fiction, you may need someone familiar with your genre so they can point out overused plot points and tropes.

You may also need to work with someone who is extremely organized and detail-oriented. For example, Jenna once worked on a book based on true-crime cases. To protect the identities of the victims, she and the client relocated the story to Los Angeles. This required numerous documents to keep track of all the changed names and locations, as well as maps to make sure that the new locations made logistical sense. She and the author also kept extensive timelines and character sheets to ensure consistency.

Tools of the Trade

Several brands of software are commonly used when writing a book. Jenna loves Scrivener for its organizational features, which allow her to jot down ideas and compile research. Jenna and Sara used Google Docs to write the majority of this book, as it allowed them to collaborate in real time on a single master document. (We also tried using the collaborative feature in Microsoft Word but found it too cumbersome. However, we both plan to give it another chance soon.) Note that screenplays are most often written in Final Draft.

Jenna uses Google Docs for some clients, usually those with smaller projects, such as blog posts. For longer manuscripts, however, its collaborative feature is precisely the reason she does *not* use it: There's too great of a chance that the client will make edits without tracking the changes, thereby making it impossible to identify newly added material or record previous versions. There's just too much room for error.

For book manuscripts, the industry standard is Microsoft Word, so even if you start out using Scrivener or Google Docs, you'll more than likely transition to it at some point. Features such as customizable styles (e.g., for headers, chapter titles, etc.), automatic generation of tables of contents, indexing, and macros—along with many, many more—make getting your manuscript ready for your interior designer simpler and more efficient. (Despite this seemingly glowing review, the software does have its problems, which accounts for Jenna's love-hate relationship with Word.) Plus, since it's the industry standard, there's less possibility for problems with file compatibility—since all industry professionals use it, you don't have to worry about, say, your ghostwriter being unable to open your document. So while you can work on your manuscript solo in Apple's Pages software, any writing collaborators or editors you work with probably won't own that. The best route is to invest in the most recent version of Word until your book is on the shelf.

When working with a writing collaborator or one of the members of your editorial team mentioned in the next chapter, the two features of Word you need to become proficient in are Comments and Track Changes. The first is just as it sounds: You (or your collaborator or editor) can add a note anywhere in the manuscript, and the other can reply. As the comments are addressed, they can be closed, allowing them to act as a checklist of sorts. For example, we created comments in several locations of this book to indicate information that needed to be verified before the book file went to the designer.

When turned on, Track Changes keeps a record of any and all edits to the manuscript, from adding a comma to changing the size of a heading. You can then choose to view the document with these changes shown or hidden, or even view the original text without having to open an archived file or reverting the changes. Depending on your settings and your version of Word, changes are shown either inline or in balloons to the side of the document.

Using these two features, the process between you and your writing collaborator and/or editor usually looks something like this: You send the collaborator the most recent version of your manuscript in Word. They then do a pass, commenting and making edits where needed, and return the file to you. During your review, you can reply to comments or close them out, accept or reject edits, and add comments or edits of your own, after which you return it to your collaborator. Some edits or comments may be extensive enough to require spoken discussion, such as on a phone call. The back-and-forth process continues until the manuscript is free of all edits and comments.

Timing & Costs

As you will hear often in this book, every project differs. Ghostwriting and co-authoring projects can last for years, depending on the complexity of the material and how much time each party commits. But it's also not uncommon for a project to be completed in as little as ninety days.

As mentioned in the introduction, Jenna and Sara began this book as a podcast, then took the transcripts of the first eighteen episodes and turned them into this book. We met virtually once a week for two years before we were happy with the episodes, then began the book-writing process. By this point, we were meeting twice a week. Towards the end, we powered through with extra hours each week, bringing it to a total estimate of more than 1,000 hours of work. Keep in mind that also involved recording the podcasts and other tasks, such as building the website, hiring a musician to produce our theme song, and working with graphic designers on logos, infographics, and charts. We deliberately took our time, as we didn't want our project to get in the way of our work with clients or our personal lives. That took a lot of pressure off us, although we still gave ourselves deadlines.

So, before you embark on your book journey, think about how quickly (or slowly) you want to move through the process. Perhaps you travel a lot for work, or you have a nine-to-five job that leaves time to write or meet with a writing collaborator only after hours or on the weekends. If that's the case, you may not want—or even be able—to turn around a full manuscript in a matter of weeks. On the flip side, maybe you've already spent a lot of time thinking about your book and have even gone so far as to develop a detailed outline, conduct your own research and pull together resource materials, and written very rough drafts of potential chapters. If that's the case, you might be in a good position to hit the ground running and have your first draft of the manuscript completed on an expedited timeline. Refer back to your BAGG, and remember that there can—and most likely will—be setbacks.

The quality of work you are looking for may also dictate just how long you spend on the writing process. Quality writing takes time and should not be rushed.

Writing collaborators don't come cheap. If you find someone who is charging what seems like a steal, there's probably a reason for it. The ghostwriting firm where Sara worked knew they were on the higher end of the price range for ghostwriters, but they also knew that their ghostwriters and co-authors were worth it. Many had books under their belts that had already been published by traditional publishers, or they'd worked for one of the "Big Five" publishing companies: Penguin Random House, Simon & Schuster, Hachette Book Group, Macmillan, and HarperCollins. One ghostwriter in their stable even had manuscripts optioned for film and TV.

Potential clients often experienced sticker shock when the firm quoted prices, and many countered by quoting much lower rates they'd received elsewhere. Oftentimes, this ghostwriter the client mentioned had not written any other books or was new to the industry, such as an editor transitioning into the world of ghostwriting. In any industry, newcomers generally have lower rates, which they raise as they gain experience and credibility. But if your expectation for working with a writing collaborator is that you won't have to do much heavy lifting, then you should look for someone with a proven track record. A less seasoned or less expensive writing collaborator could very well produce a professional manuscript, but there will likely be more bumps in the journey as they learn to navigate the road.

Being a ghostwriter requires more than a knack for writing. The ghost also needs to be able to channel their client's voice, extract information that the client doesn't realize they aren't expressing, and possess a number of other skills that other types of writers might not be familiar with. Established ghostwriters command the rates they do because of their experience and professionalism.

Hiring an inexperienced ghostwriter could end up being more than just a poor financial decision. If a ghost fails to accurately portray your voice or produces low-quality work, you could lose faith in your project and not want to continue. The book-writing journey is very emotional, so make sure to choose a writing collaborator who will make the process as smooth as possible.

Next Steps

- Decide if you will work with a ghostwriter, co-author, or writing coach, or if you will fly solo.
- Communicate your BAGG to each writing collaborator you interview so that they understand what you hope to accomplish.
- Review Appendix A again to see if your timeline has shifted after reading the last few chapters.

Further Resources

Visit bookagogo.com/books/further-resources for the complete collection of all links in this book.

Companies, Individuals & Resources Mentioned in This Chapter
- **Jenna's Amazon Author Page:** amazon.com/Jenna-Rose-Robbins/ e/B00ZP44VKG
- **Sara's Amazon Author Page:** amazon.com/Sara-Stratton/e/ B0G6RCHB96
- **Scrivener:** literatureandlatte.com/scrivener/overview

Advice on Hiring a Ghostwriter
- **From Jenna:** clearvoice.com/blog/hiring-a-ghostwriter-secrets-from-a-ghostwriting-professional

How-Tos

- **Using Comments in Microsoft Word:** support.microsoft.com/en-us/office/using-modern-comments-in-word-edc6ae71-0a2d-49fe-8faa-986f1e48136a

- **Using Track Changes in Microsoft Word:** support.microsoft.com/en-us/office/video-track-changes-and-show-markup-3faf8a07-26ed-4b76-b6a0-43cca013e6d3

Choosing the Members of
Your Editorial Team

As we mentioned earlier, the first rule of editorial is "Two sets of eyes on everything." That's because it's very, very difficult to edit your own work, so, more likely than not, you'll need professional editorial help to polish your manuscript before it's published.

There are several types of editors, all of whom work on manuscripts at different stages. The four most common are developmental editors, line editors, copyeditors, and proofreaders.

Unfortunately, there is no formal consensus within the editing community about where the responsibilities of one type of editor end and another begin. Some editors believe that copyediting and proofreading are one and the same, for example.

"Copyediting and proofreading are fairly easy to define, with line editing being a bit of an outlier," says Mark Allen, a board member of ACES: The Society for Editing. "All of them mean different things to different people. I consider what I do copyediting. Depending on the client's needs, I might do some big rewriting and rearranging. Usually if I see an opportunity for improvement, I write a margin note."

For the purposes of this book, we will refer to the services each type of editor offers based on our collective experience, which is how we both market our respective services.

Although this chapter provides examples of each type of editorial process and their associated fees, every editor defines their services differently and has a different work style, so always ask how your editor operates before you sign a contract. Fees and time frames also depend on the state of your copy and the complexity of your manuscript, which may require more than one pass, or read-through. Expect to pay extra if your book requires specialty knowledge, such as for technical, medical, or legal texts. For more about costs associated with working with various editors, see Appendix B.

You most likely will not need every single one of these editors, so make sure you're comfortable with the editor you hire and confirm which services they offer.

Developmental Editors

The first kind of editor you might need for your manuscript is a developmental editor, whose job is to create an overall organization for your manuscript, giving it structure. A developmental editor usually works on a manuscript at the very early stages, before the first word is even written. In a sense, they provide an outline for the book. If that is all you're asking of a developmental editor, you then take their proposed structure and craft your manuscript to their guidelines. A developmental editor can also be brought in on the first draft of a manuscript so you can receive feedback early on as to whether or not the manuscript is properly structured. When this type of editor is brought on before any work has begun, the role may also be referred to as a book planner. Although that term is less frequently used, some professionals prefer it so as to clarify the sort of work they do: only planning and outlining, not organizing existing content.

"A book plan is so much more than just an outline," says Bree Barton, who worked as a ghostwriter, editor, and coach before shifting her focus exclusively to book planning. "It answers the fundamental why of a book, clarifies the what, and offers guidance on the how. All writing performs a kind of alchemy, smelting words from ideas. I set the stage for that alchemy by putting those ideas in the right order. I also love riffing on titles, so my plans always include engaging titles and subtitles to grab the reader. Then I'll make suggestions on how best to divide the content into larger sections and individual chapters."

Note that, rather than having a developmental edit, you may prefer to have a manuscript critique, which is usually less detailed and doesn't go line by line, as a developmental edit often does. Another difference is that the editor providing the critique is not hands-on, whereas a developmental editor can be, if you so desire.

Developmental editors can charge hourly, by the word, by set rate, or a combination of the three. For example, a colleague of ours charges $2,500 to $4,500, depending on the manuscript's length and complexity, for an extensive manuscript critique and then offers his services as a developmental editor for an additional fee. Once hired for this critique, he reviews the manuscript and provides extensive notes (sometimes thirty to forty pages in length) to the author, detailing his suggestions for rewrites, restructuring content, inconsistencies in the storyline, and even ideas for further development. The author can then decide if they'd like to engage him on an hourly basis to make the changes or if they'd like to make the changes themselves. If the author decides to make the changes on their own, the developmental editor offers one further full read (a "pass") of the newly revised manuscript as part of his initial fee.

When hiring a developmental editor, you have to be open to significant changes being made to your book. However, most editors discuss these changes with clients beforehand so you can decide together which changes you agree on and which you do not want implemented.

Jenna once had a client with a 300,000-plus-word manuscript about protecting yourself from sexual assault, based on real-life cases. Keep in mind that a good word count to shoot for is 50,000 to 100,000 words, so the client's manuscript probably would have turned off its intended audience of college-bound females, not to mention any potential publishers or agents.[17] After reading the manuscript, Jenna found that many of the cases were not pertinent to the intended audience, and so she provided the author with criteria for which ones to keep. That alone reduced the word count by about a third. She then instructed the author to delete cases that were too similar, which further reduced the manuscript to about half its original length. She and the author then worked on the order that the remaining cases should go in so that they made sense for the reader. Once that was in place, the line editing process began (discussed below).

Tasks & Responsibilities

Developmental editors:

- **Do** provide structure for the overall manuscript by looking at the big picture: concept, thesis, structure, narrative arc, character development, style, voice, language, point of view, and organization.
- **Do not** fact-check or review mechanics such as grammar, punctuation, or typos, which are handled by the other editors discussed in this chapter. They do not get granular in their edits but rather review the material from a high level.

Timing & Costs

Expect a developmental editor to be the most expensive of the editors on your editing team. Rates may be charged hourly (with $200 being average), per word ($.09), or per page ($15), with totals usually landing between $3,000 to $6,000. Your engagement with a developmental editor will also probably be the longest of that of any member of your editorial team. Depending on the level of work your manuscript needs and how much time you need to execute these changes, this is usually a one- to three-month process.

Depending on scope and genre, Barton charges $3,000 to $5,000 per book plan, a document that provides big-picture thoughts on the why, what, and how by laying out a suggested structure, organizing principles, and providing an annotated chapter-by-chapter outline, title, and subtitle options.

Line Editors

Moving one step down from a high-level perspective, a line editor takes a deeper dive into the material than a developmental editor does, but does not fine-tune the nuts and bolts, as a copyeditor or proofreader does. As mentioned earlier, there's some discrepancy, even among editors, as to the difference between a line editor and a copyeditor, so make sure you clarify which services you will be receiving.

"I've seen two definitions of line editing: a big-picture review done prior to copyediting and one a deeper level of copyediting," says Allen. "Line editing to some means looking for higher-level changes but not the nitty-gritty of usage and style. To others, it's a type of copyediting that includes a deeper level of rewriting, including moving or deleting paragraphs to help clarity, flow, and structure. Some people just call that copyediting (I do), but some people limit copyediting to more basic spelling, usage, grammar, and style."

Despite the discrepancy within the industry, one point universally agreed upon is that a line editor's job is to focus on your use of language, ensuring your writing is clear and applicable to your intended audience and that the copy flows and makes for an enjoyable read. A line editor points out repetitious exposition, sections that are confusing or that would benefit from being rewritten for clarity and pacing, and word choice. They might even fix these issues rather than merely query them, after which you can determine if further adjustment is necessary.

"Modest rewrites are often the most efficient way to achieve the goal of a satisfying reader experience," says seasoned line editor Kate Zentall, "especially once trust and confidence between client and editor have been established." She says this underscores why a good client–editor fit is so important: This way, your editor will understand your voice and can help "speak" for you.

Tasks & Responsibilities

Line editors:

- **Do** focus on a more granular level than developmental editors do. The focus of their work is overall clarity, language, and flow.
- **Do not** maintain responsibility for reviewing overall story structure, high-level plot development, fact-checking, or checking for typos, grammar, and punctuation (although if they spot an egregious error, they may call it out for you to review).

Timing & Costs

Average rates for line editors are $75 to $150 per hour, $12.50 per page, $.06 to $.09 per word, with the average project costing about $3,500. Some line editors may charge a flat fee once they've estimated how much time they believe the line edit will require. Turnaround time is typically two to six weeks.

Copyeditors

We are often asked if a copyeditor and a proofreader have the same responsibilities. Although some believe these two roles are interchangeable, they actually serve two distinct—and crucial—functions in the final stages of refining a manuscript. Copyeditors do perform some proofreading while copyediting (they don't just ignore obvious typos they come across), but that is not the focus of their job. To catch the mechanical errors, it's vital that the manuscript undergo proofreading.

A copyeditor looks for issues of sentence structure, grammar, and consistency in punctuation and, sometimes, formatting. At Redwood Publishing, copyeditors are more like hybrid copyeditors/line editors, as they also fact-check, call out issues with the language and flow, and ensure any referenced works are properly cited. Redwood offers all these services in this editing phase because Sara sees the copyedit as the last real chance an author has to make more in-depth changes before moving forward, when major changes could affect timeline and budget. Verify with your copyeditor which of these services they include.

For some authors, particularly those in nonfiction, fact-checking is a crucial step in the publishing process, especially because most publishers do not fact-check. Instead, they require their authors to sign agreements acknowledging that all information in their books is factually accurate, taking the burden off themselves and placing it firmly on the authors. (Fact-checking is discussed further in chapter 8, which also covers legal review and compliance.)

Make sure your copyeditor is proficient in editing per *The Chicago Manual of Style* (CMOS), the standard for spelling, usage, and punctuation for books—and thus used by all traditional publishers. You can tell quite easily if a book has not been professionally edited if it doesn't adhere to Chicago style or, in the case of medical and scientific texts, the *AMA Manual of Style*. When interviewing copyeditors, confirm they will be editing per Chicago, not Associated Press (AP) style (the standard for newspapers, magazines, and professional journals).

Since copyeditors are the first editors to review a manuscript at the level of the individual words, many compile a style sheet specific to each manuscript. This document includes any proper names, industry jargon or other special vocabulary, and topics either not covered in the *CMOS* or that deviate from it. For example, many music aficionados (such as Jenna) choose to format band names differently than what CMOS dictates: Chicago says to lowercase *the* if it begins a band's name (the Beatles), while music fans generally prefer to capitalize it (The Beatles) since it's an official part of the name. This deviation would be noted in the style sheet so that future editors working on the book know the capitalization is not an error. Depending on your book's topic, there may be other styles that deviate from Chicago. For example, if you prefer *okay* to Chicago's style of *OK*, that's okay. Just make sure that's included in your style sheet, which can also be consulted for marketing materials, the website, and other related work. (If there are any copyeditors reading this book, you may notice several such deviations, as Jenna is a strong proponent of em dashes over semicolons and several other punctuation choices that she feels makes writing more legible and reader friendly.)

The term *style guide* can refer to one of the three main style guides—*The Chicago Manual of Style*, the *AMA Manual of Style*, and *The Associated Press Stylebook*—or a brand style guide, which is a document that contains style sheets in addition to design information, such as brand colors and fonts. Make sure your copyeditor provides a style sheet so that you can pass it on to any subsequent editors and, down the road, your designers, who can update the document with information on the cover and interior design details to create a more detailed style guide.

The fiftieth-anniversary edition of J. R. R. Tolkien's *The Fellowship of the Ring* goes into great detail about the efforts made to produce a volume more closely mirroring that of the author's intent, as previous editions had contained inconsistencies, typos, and even deliberate word changes by typesetters. Tolkien's son Christopher spent years poring through his father's notes, marginal scribblings, and first drafts to ensure the term *Dark Power* was capitalized when referring to Sauron and that *Breehill* was written as one word, not two. The younger Tolkien's job would have been far more expedient had his father compiled a proper style sheet (which no doubt would have been as long as *The Silmarillion*).[18]

If you haven't already done so yourself, your copyeditor could also compile a list of potential glossary words. While not all books could benefit from having a glossary, yours might if it is instructional, as this book is, so you should weigh whether the additional cost is worth it.

Both of us agree that your copyeditor (which is two words according to AP style, but one per *CMOS*) should be someone who has not worked on the manuscript up to this point, as you want somebody who will see your material with fresh eyes, which makes them the first official reader of a final manuscript.

For her book *Faithful and Devoted: Confessions of a Music Addict*, Jenna had three editors review it before it even went to Redwood to start the publishing process. On the very last pass of the book, three separate people read the manuscript, and each found different issues—about fifty in all. That just goes to show that different sets of eyes notice different things.

Also note that very few books make it to publication without a few errors. When Jenna read the final Harry Potter book, she noticed three errors within the first fifty pages. Such a blockbuster book surely had dozens of eyes on it before it went to press, yet the final product was not perfect. Having more than a handful of errors in an entire book, however, looks unprofessional, so it's worth hiring a professional to clean up as many errors as possible.

The copyediting stage is also the time to consider having a beta reader or sensitivity reader review your book, as you can often find one person who can do both at the same time. A beta reader is simply a reader who gives you feedback, pointing out plot holes, character inconsistencies, confusing points, and the like.[19] Although this is similar to a manuscript critique, beta readers are usually not professionals and so often provide this service for free simply because they love reading, although some do charge. Some beta readers specialize in specific genres, while others are simply avid readers who take on most any literary project. Sensitivity readers, on the other hand, are editorial professionals who review how characters of certain backgrounds are represented.[20] Using a beta or sensitivity reader is by no means necessary, and few writers use them, but those who do appreciate the additional feedback. More info about beta readers and sensitivity readers is available in Further Resources, and a sample letter that you can use to send to beta readers is included in Appendix D.

Tasks & Responsibilities

Copyeditors:

- **Do** focus on word choice and sentence structure to ensure consistency in style and tone. They often serve as one of the first readers of the final manuscript.
- **Do** fact-check.
- **Do** compile a style sheet and/or glossary as they review the work. Ensure this is included as part of their service.
- **Do not** focus on high-level issues such as character development and plot.

Timing & Costs

Copyeditors charge either by the hour ($65–$100), the page ($6–$9), or the word ($.04–$.06). Plan on the process taking between two to six weeks.

Proofreaders

A proofreader is an editorial professional you should *always* hire, even if you don't bring on board any of the other editors mentioned in this chapter. The proofreader's job is to catch and correct issues such as missing words, typos, and punctuation mistakes in the proof copy, or the version of the manuscript created as a sample just before the book is officially published. Compared to the work of a developmental editor, line editor, or copyeditor, the proofreader's work is much less subjective and is simply a matter of determining whether something is correct or incorrect. *Is a comma needed? Is formatting consistent? Are there any extraneous spaces or carriage returns?*

A manuscript that is clean of obvious errors projects a professional image. Browse through the Amazon reviews of any book—particularly self-published ones—and you're bound to see comments about the presence or lack of typos. Many books lose stars in their ratings solely based on typos, which should be sufficient enough of an argument for you to hire a proofreader. Is the cost of hiring a proofreader worth an extra star in your review? We wholeheartedly think so.

"Generally, proofreading is the final stage of editing, usually on page proofs, with a check for typos and formatting issues," says Allen. "Of course, if there are basic issues that might fall under copyediting, the proofreader should mark that too."

Proofreaders are typically the least expensive member of your editorial team, as the work is relatively straightforward and less intensive: They focus on the words and punctuation and do not call out issues related to storyline, consistency, character development, etc. By the time a proofreader receives your manuscript, it should be relatively clean, having already been reviewed by at least a handful of other editors, professional or otherwise.

A design proofreader possesses a special skill set, with an eye for design elements such as identifying bad breaks, the accuracy of page numbers in the table of contents and on each page, consistency between chapter titles in the table of contents and the body of the book, and consistency in the formatting of headers, to name just a few of these skills. Most professional proofreaders are able to perform both a text proofread and a design proofread.

If your budget allows, consider hiring a proofreader *before* your manuscript goes to the interior designer, then again once the manuscript is in the final layout. But if you can afford only one proofreading pass, it should be performed after layout is complete. Authors on the single-pass route should try to find someone who can perform both a proofread and a design proofread. Ideally, you want your interior designer to make as few changes as possible because each change runs the risk of disrupting the formatting your designer has so carefully worked to create. So although it might seem faster and more economical to do only one proofreading pass, what you saved on the second pass might instead end up going to the designer.

When you opt to have the manuscript proofread before and after formatting, the design proofread should include only changes related to design, such as an unintended double indent. If you save a complete proofreading until after the book is laid out, your designer may have to make subsequent changes, which could increase your design fees. Even something as small as removing a comma or italicizing a word can force the subsequent pages to reformat, which might require the designer to spend unscheduled time fixing the flow of your book. To see for yourself how even relatively small changes can affect design, watch the video mentioned in Further Resources.

Tasks & Responsibilities

Proofreaders:

- **Do** focus on missing words, typos, and punctuation; in the design proofread, they also check the design and layout for accuracy and consistency.

- **Do** look for issues in visual layout, such as consistency in formatting and multiple stacked hyphenated words.
- **Do not** typically edit line by line or fact-check and **do not** make editorial suggestions that pertain to word choice, sentence structure, storyline, etc.

Timing & Costs

Proofreaders and design proofreaders typically charge an hourly rate starting around $40. A proofreader usually turns around a manuscript in two or three weeks, while a design proofreader can take an additional week.

If your budget won't allow for both proofreading passes, you can perform the design proofread yourself. We've included a checklist in Appendix E.

Remember that even when you hire any professional editor, you still need to be involved in the process, accepting or rejecting suggested edits and asking questions about changes you don't understand. Anytime an editor takes a pass and incorporates edits, you should review the manuscript. At the end of the day, it's you signing off on your book, not your editors. So if your book goes to print with a typo on the first page, that's on you—not them.

It is, however, a good idea to give yourself boundaries with your manuscript. Once you've sent it off to a copyeditor, don't look at it again until the proofreader has finished their pass. Giving yourself a break both keeps you from getting burned out and allows you to approach changes to the manuscript with a fresh perspective.

Next Steps

- Decide which type(s) of editors you need, ensuring that you at the very least hire a proofreader.
- As with hiring writing collaborators, make sure your editorial team is aware of your BAGG, as this can influence editorial decisions.

- Ensure your copyeditor provides you with a style sheet that you can provide to other editors and designers.
- Update the Appendix B worksheet to reflect any changes based on the information in this chapter.

Further Resources

Visit bookagogo.com/books/further-resources for the complete collection of all links in this book.

Indicates a source recommended by The Chicago Manual of Style.

Companies, Individuals & Resources Mentioned in This Chapter
- ACES: The Society for Editing: aceseditors.org
- *The Chicago Manual of Style*: chicagomanualofstyle.org
- Kate Zentall: laeditorsandwritersgroup.com/member/kate-zentall
- Video showing small edit affecting interior design: Watch at bookagogo.com/books/further-resources

Additional Books on the Subject
- *The Subversive Copyeditor: Advice from Chicago (or, How to Negotiate Good Relationships With Your Writers, Your Colleagues, and Yourself)* by Carol Fisher Saller: amazon.com/Subversive-Copy-Editor-Second-Relationships-ebook/dp/B01DGPSNWW

Types of Editors
- Jenna's article: clearvoice.com/blog/types-of-editors
- Jane Friedman's article: janefriedman.com/the-differences-between-line-editing-copy-editing-and-proofreading

CHAPTER 7

Choosing a Title for Your Book

Even if you have a completed manuscript, you might not yet have a title. That's quite common. A title is important because it's typically your first opportunity to connect with your reader on an emotional level. The book title—and subtitle, if you decide to include one—does more than just give your reader a sense of the subject matter: It also evokes a feeling and the essence of your book. The title (combined with an eye-catching cover, discussed in chapter 12) is how you will (or will not) capture your audience.

Publishing agent Jillian Manus sums it up nicely: "The title must be a 'heart' message designed to elicit a powerful emotional response from the reader. The subtitle is a 'head' message that informs the reader as to the primary benefit they will receive from buying and reading the book."[21]

Even though, as a rule, titles consist of only a few words, they can be the most important—and difficult—words of the entire book-writing process. Because it's such a personal process, you don't want to postpone the task of naming your book until the very end. The title has to resonate with you, so take time for reflection to make sure it's just right.

There are different strategies for choosing titles for a nonfiction book versus a novel, but regardless of the genre, the title needs to be catchy and memorable.

Titles for Nonfiction Works

Compared to that of a work of fiction, a nonfiction title has a lot more room to work with, as it's currently more common than not to have both a title and a subtitle. Your title (your heart) can be short and creative to get that initial emotional response, while the subtitle (your head) can appeal to the straightforward side of your reader, letting them know what to expect from your book.

Your title and subtitle must be able to capture everything about the book—its features, benefits, and so on—and that has to be conveyed to potential readers in a matter of seconds.

Cheryl Mendelson gave her 1999 book the alluringly cozy title of *Home Comforts*. Its subtitle, *The Art and Science of Keeping House*, zeroes in on its target demographic. Malcolm Gladwell's book *Talking to Strangers* bears the subtitle *What We Should Know About the People We Don't Know,* which makes it clear from the start that the book is about how we interact with strangers and how to improve upon those interactions.

This title-naming strategy can also apply to memoirs, even though, as narratives, biographies are more literary. One of our clients gave his memoir the following straightforward title: *The Bipolar Addict*. Right off the bat, you know the general subject matter. But it was his subtitle that told readers the flavor of the story inside: *Drinks, Drugs, Delirium & Why Sober Is the New Cool*. Sure, it alludes to how it ends—he overcame his addiction—but it also offers a beat-by-beat outline of what readers can expect from the story, as well as the mystique of *how* he got over the addiction and continues to cope with his bipolar disorder diagnosis.

Some other good examples of nonfiction titles and subtitles include:

- *The Night of the Gun: A Reporter Investigates the Darkest Story of His Life. His Own* (by David Carr)
- *The Lost City of Z: A Tale of Deadly Obsession in the Amazon* (by David Grann)
- *The New Jim Crow: Mass Incarceration in the Age of Colorblindness* (by Michelle Alexander)
- *Going Clear: Scientology, Hollywood, & the Prison of Belief* (by Lawrence Wright)
- *How to Win Friends & Influence People: The Only Book You Need to Lead You to Success* (by Dale Carnegie)

In choosing the title of her memoir about her obsession with the band Depeche Mode, Jenna knew that she had to go with something that would appeal to fans. She considered using the title of their song "Just Can't Get Enough," since those words so perfectly echo the sentiment of a fan. However, since that's quite possibly her least favorite song in their vast catalog, she could never fully embrace it. When she finally realized that *Faithful and Devoted*—a play on the title of their album *Songs of Faith and Devotion*—conveyed the same sentiment, she knew she'd found her title. To make sure the book also appealed to non-Depeche Mode fans, she added a subtitle, *Confessions of a Music Addict,* which further conveyed the plot and opened up her audience to all music lovers, which had been her intention while writing the book.

But a subtitle isn't required. Once in a while, a title all by itself lures the reader in with tacit promises and an aura of mystique. Perhaps the best title—ever—is Dave Eggers's *A Heartbreaking Work of Staggering Genius.* Try forgetting that one! *Eating Animals,* by Jonathan Safran Foer, is both telling and provocative—in just two words.

Titles for Fiction Works

Fiction titles require a little more finesse because you really have to know your audience and genre. When choosing words that will resonate with readers, you have a few options. For example, you could choose a line from the book that represents the overall theme, or just put the theme right in the title, such as *Pride and Prejudice.* On that same note, if you saw the book *Pride and Prejudice and Zombies* in a bookstore, you could pretty much guess what the genre is—and assume that it doesn't take itself too seriously.

Try to keep the title short so it's easy to remember, but not so short that it's generic. However, if a longer title truly connotes what your book is about, go for it. Neither of us can ever remember the full title of *The Curious Incident of the Dog in the Night-Time,* but we don't need to in order to find it online. Even if you just drop a few words from the title in conversation, anyone familiar with it will most likely know which book you're talking about.

A short title could also cause confusion in search engines—unless it's unique. Before J. R. R. Tolkien wrote *The Hobbit,* the word was not in use in the English language, so even though he published his fantasy masterpiece well before the invention of the internet, his choice of title was still relatively easy to remember and pronounce. But if Jane Austen had written *Emma* today, her publisher might have asked her to change it to something more along the lines of *Pride and Prejudice.* Michelle Obama can get away with naming her book *Becoming* because many readers probably found the book by searching for "Michelle Obama book," not the actual title.

Let's play a little game. You probably know most of the following fiction titles, but if you don't, see if you can guess the genre and basic plot from the title alone. (Answers on page 81 at the end of the chapter.)

1. *Miss Peregrine's Home for Peculiar Children*
2. *Nick & Norah's Infinite Playlist*

3. *Ready Player One*
4. *The Hitchhiker's Guide to the Galaxy*
5. *The Devil Wears Prada*

Brainstorming a Book Title

If you're struggling to come up with the best title and/or subtitle, begin by jotting down the easy ideas, the ones that simply explain the book, e.g., *How to [Insert Book Info Here]* or *The Biography of Jane Smith*. When Sara worked with an author who was writing a book about the afterlife, their list started with *How to Achieve a Higher Purpose*, which evolved into *How to Understand the Spiritual World and Prepare for the Next Life*. Eventually, they arrived at the final title and subtitle: *Journey from Life to Life: Achieving a Higher Purpose*. Between these iterations were thirty or so variations of what became the published title.

Another good exercise is to craft an elevator pitch. If you met Oprah in an elevator and she asked you to explain your book, what would you say? The pitch needs to be specific and enticing yet concise enough that you can say it all before Oprah gets to her floor. Working on this pitch can help you identify words or phrases that you can use as a book title and/or subtitle.

Although being listed on Amazon isn't a requirement for having a bestselling book, not having your title listed there makes that goal much more difficult to achieve. Since so much browsing and shopping are done on the internet, take that into consideration when choosing your title. Think about how your reader would search for a book like yours and try to include those search terms in the title, or at least allude to them, such as in *The Devil Wears Prada*.

Once you've found what you believe is your perfect title, do your due diligence and see if that title is already being used—as a blog, podcast, or even the title of another book. Even if you do find it is already in use, as long as none of those other works are in the same nonfiction genre or on the same topic as yours, go for it. In this sense, choosing a book title is very similar to choosing a name for your business: Avoid confusion by making sure the title is not in use by someone in the same space.

Your subtitle can differentiate your book from others with the same or a similar name. We advise against reusing a fiction title already in use, particularly if it's well known, and even if it's a different genre, as you risk having readers buy your book by accident and leave you a bad review without even reading it. As much as we want to say that you shouldn't worry about reviews, they do affect sales, so it's best not to put yourself at a disadvantage right from the start.

Note that you cannot copyright a title—of a book, a song, a film, or any other creative work—so there may be other titles out there that match yours.[22] You can, however, *trademark* a title if you plan to use it as part of a brand you are building or a new concept you want to market. This is another instance when a subtitle is critical. If your title is a trademarked term that you're debuting, your readers most likely will not be familiar with it. Your subtitle can clarify what they can expect. See Further Resources for more information about copyrights and trademarks for titles.

Since we aren't lawyers, this information is just a starting point to help guide you. If there's any doubt your title might be infringing on someone else's work, we highly advise you to consult with a legal professional. Such legal points are covered more in the next chapter.

Here's a recap of some of the criteria you can use to decide whether a title is the perfect fit for your book.

Dos

1. Ensure your book delivers on the promise of its title. If you read the negative reviews for a book, particularly a nonfiction one, many of the critiques are about this very point: The book fails to deliver.

2. Leave a question unanswered—lure the reader in. In other words, don't give away the whole story in your title.

3. Make the title memorable and easy to pronounce. If your audience can't remember it to type it into a search engine or ask a store clerk for it, you're going to miss out on sales.

Don'ts

1. Don't have a title that is just one word. For a first-time author, this could make it harder to find you—you will get lost in a sea of other books that use that one word in their own titles. However, you can get away with just one word if it's unique or your subtitle does the rest of the work for you.

2. Don't pick a trendy title unless your book is specifically about that topic. You never know when a trend will suddenly lose steam and become irrelevant (or even worse, become something that could offend potential readers).

3. Make sure the title doesn't have an unintended connotation. At first glance, *Penetrating Wagner's Ring* might sound more like a work of erotica than an in-depth look at the German composer's musical opus. For some other books with unintentional innuendos for titles, see Further Resources.

Once you've come up with a few potential titles, do some crowdsourcing. "Once you have a list, test them by getting feedback from beta readers or running surveys to see which titles generate the most interest," says Emanuel Rose, CEO of Strategic eMarketing and author of *Authenticity: Marketing to Generation Z*. "Consider factors like clarity, relevance, and memorability when choosing a final title. Remember, a great title can catch a reader's attention and increase the chances of your book being discovered."

Start by running the list past people well versed in your topic or genre, as they may have specialized insight. If they give one particular title a green light, go ask a gaggle of friends. Don't ask just one or two individuals—make sure you get a critical mass, at least twenty or so opinions. Ask in writers' groups, online or off. You can even poll strangers in person or on social media. X (formerly known as Twitter) is a great place for this, as that social network attracts some rather vocal and opinionated users.

Say your title aloud as often as possible—to friends, family, yourself. Make sure you don't get sick of saying it or explaining what your book is about. You need to be sure you are happy with your title—and not just for emotional reasons. While some sales outlets may allow you to change your title, it's not common or easily done, and many disallow changing it once the book is published. If you want to change it on Amazon, for example, you first have to unpublish the original book and then republish it as a new listing, and you are required to add a disclaimer to the updated book's description, such as "Previously published as [*Book Title*] by [author name]." If you unpublish your book, your customer reviews and Amazon ranking that you've worked so hard to build won't transfer from one listing to the other.

Once you've finalized your title, make sure to buy the domain name. You most likely will not use the book title for your main website, but you also don't want someone squatting on it. As we said in chapter 2, claim everything. Even if you never end up using it, at least you'll own it so there's no risk of somebody pretending to be you. You can then redirect the book domain to your author domain so that you can use either one in your marketing strategy.

With a finalized title, you can also begin designing your book cover. But you have to be absolutely sure that it's final as, more often than not, the title plays directly into the design, from dictating imagery and typography to how the words fit on the cover. The seemingly simple cover for Simon Sinek's *Start With Why* relies entirely on the short title and positioning of the letters. If he had changed his title to *Start With Your Why*, it may have changed the entire look of the cover.

If you plan to hire a marketing and/or PR team, run your title selections by them. They are in the business of selling you and your ideas, so they should be able to offer professional insight as to whether or not a title has merit. If they don't get it, it's likely that the folks they pitch to also won't get it. And that means less interest in you and, in turn, less buzz about the book.

Quiz Answers

1. *Miss Peregrine's Home for Peculiar Children:* a young-adult fantasy about some children with supernatural gifts
2. *Nick & Norah's Infinite Playlist:* a young-adult romance about two music lovers
3. *Ready Player One:* an '80s-obsessed sci-fi action-adventure based primarily in cyberspace
4. *The Hitchhiker's Guide to the Galaxy:* a tongue-in-cheek science-fiction space odyssey
5. *The Devil Wears Prada:* a semi-autobiographical novel about the author's misadventures in the fashion magazine industry

Next Steps

- Your BAGG probably won't play a role when you're choosing your book title—unless you chose Promotion or Reputation, in which case the title should resonate with the audience you are marketing to or hoping to gain visibility in.
- Jot down your ideas for a title, and then get feedback from trusted sources and general audiences, as well as your PR/marketing team.
- While brainstorming a title, start by creating an elevator pitch.
- Buy the book's domain name and redirect it to the domain for your author name.

Further Resources

Visit bookagogo.com/books/further-resources for the complete collection of all links in this book.

Companies, Individuals & Resources Mentioned in This Chapter

- *Start With Why* by Simon Sinek: amazon.com/Start-Why-Leaders-Inspire-Everyone/dp/1591846447

Book Titles: The Good and the Bad

- **The good:** earlybirdbooks.com/best-book-titles
- **The bad:** forreadingaddicts.co.uk/language/20-unintentional-innuendo-book-titles

Tips for Picking Your Book Title

- **Two-week process:** iuniverse.com/en/resources/writing-and-editing/how-to-choose-your-book-title-in-2-weeks
- **Nonfiction books:** bookbuzzr.com/blog/the-10-commandments-of-nonfiction-book-title-success
- **Choosing a business name:** inc.com/serhat-pala/choosing-a-business-name-is-hard-here-is-how-to-make-it-easier.html
- **Copyrights vs. trademarks:** writersdigest.com/copyrights/can-you-copyright-a-title

Legal Review, Fact-Checking & Compliance of Your Book

O nce your title is finalized, determine if your manuscript needs legal review, whether you're going the traditional route or self-publishing. Because neither of us is a lawyer, the information in this chapter is very general and does not constitute legal advice. We just want to make you aware of the most common legal issues involved in book publishing so you can make an informed decision as to whether or not to hire an attorney to review your manuscript.

Nonfiction books are more likely to need a legal review than fiction ones, particularly if you're mentioning individuals or entities who are likely to sue. So although a review is not required, you can put your mind at ease by having a lawyer review your nonfiction book before you send it off for publication.

Although legal reviews are most commonly performed when you have a completed manuscript, you may want to bring in a lawyer early on for guidance. In a book Jenna co-wrote with a former police officer, the two used real-life cases that had been fictionalized for the purpose of providing lessons about protecting yourself against sexual assault. Because they knew there would be legal implications, they consulted an attorney specializing in intellectual property and publishing law who was able to provide guidelines on how to change the characters and settings enough that they would protect the real-life individuals' identities. This saved Jenna and her co-author countless hours of work and revisions, which they would've been faced with if they had gone in the direction they'd originally intended. Due to the sensitive nature of the book, they enlisted the same attorney to do a final review just before it went to the publisher.

Plagiarism & Copyright

Two of the most important legal areas to focus on are plagiarism and copyright. With regard to plagiarism, it's not just verbatim copy you need to worry about: If your entire story idea is too close to that of another book, you might be accused of infringing on that book's copyright. So, if your story is about kids forced to fight to the death against one another, there needs to be enough difference from *The Hunger Games* to ensure that you won't get sued. Note that plagiarism of ideas is far more common in fiction than nonfiction. For examples of famous copyright lawsuits, see Further Resources.

When you've completed your manuscript, run your book through a plagiarism checker to ensure you didn't copy–paste something into your manuscript that you forgot to cite. Some professional editors perform a plagiarism check on every manuscript before agreeing to work on it. Keep in mind that an editor is *not* responsible for catching plagiarism, so just because something gets by yours doesn't mean you're in the clear.

The most popular websites for performing plagiarism checks are Grammarly and Chegg, which charge nominal fees and require a few hours of your time. Doing so may also make you feel more confident that your materials won't cause a legal team to fire off a nasty letter to you at some point (at least not for plagiarizing and republishing content).

Many authors use materials with trademarks or copyrights when they shouldn't because they believe it falls under the umbrella of what is known as fair use. However, fair use allows for the use of such materials only under highly specific conditions. More importantly, fair use is a defense—it does not prevent you from being sued. You would still need to prove in court that you are abiding by the rules of fair use, and that can be costly. For that reason, many authors opt to purchase errors and omissions insurance, which may protect you in such cases. Note that before they will cover you, some insurance companies require a fair use opinion letter from a lawyer, which is a document stating that the attorney has reviewed your manuscript and deemed the content to be within the scope of fair use.

Fair use does not mean that anyone can use any work in whatever manner they please, especially not if that manner is commercial. So do yourself a favor and keep track of any and all works that are not your own but that you plan to include in your book. Then, when you have written approval to use them, make sure you credit them appropriately, including the blurbs for the back of your book. We've created a worksheet for you to keep track of some of the more common third-party items that might need legal review and/or permission. This worksheet is available for download on our Book-A-Go-Go worksheets webpage (bookagogo.com/worksheets). Keep in mind that this worksheet is not comprehensive, but it is a good place to start.

Works such as lyrics, photos, artwork, charts, graphs, other books, and brand names all have legal rights associated with them. To be safe, you should use only those works that you have purchased outright, have paid to use, or for which you have received some form of clearance from the owner. For example, if you pay someone to create an illustration so that you own it outright and you include the proper wording in your agreement, this is considered a work for hire. If you hire a photographer using a work-for-hire contract, the photos they take will be yours—no licensing fee required (although the work might still need to be credited properly). You can then use them in any way you please—on your book cover, on your website, in marketing materials, etc. Note that if your agreement does not specifically state that the work is a work for hire, you are merely purchasing a license in perpetuity, which means the work's creator remains the owner and can potentially license it to others.

Sites such as Flickr (flickr.com) and Wikimedia Commons (commons. wikimedia.org) offer photos, videos, audio files, and other media for free within certain licensing constraints known as Creative Commons licenses. The rights granted range from allowing unlimited use (much like that of a work in the public domain) to rights that require that the author receive credit or that the work not be used for commercial purposes (which includes a book). Works released under the appropriate Creative Commons license can be very helpful for those on a budget.

Here's a quick list of the most commonly used works that require some form of clearance/permission:

- **Lyrics.** Do not use lyrics unless you have clearance; music publishers are some of the most protective owners of copyrights, and if they find out you're using lyrics of theirs, even if just a few words, they can (and usually will) take action.
- **Photos or artwork.** You can use stock photos from sites such as iStock (istockphoto.com) or Dreamstime (dreamstime.com) as long as they are royalty-free and cleared for book use. Some images are cleared only for editorial purposes—newspapers, for example, can use them, but books cannot. If you have artwork that has been given to you or that you commissioned, make sure your contract states in what form and medium you can use it. One of Jenna's authors commissioned an artist to create illustrations for his website. When he later wanted to use them in a book, he had to pay an additional licensing fee, as he had not originally purchased them as a work-for-hire and had

only licensed them for his website. For this reason, it's critical that you review the scope (such as whether commercial use is allowed), medium (e.g., print, web), credit terms (how the work should be credited), and terms of the license (it should be in perpetuity) before you sign an agreement.

Some people live by the rule that it's better to act now and ask for forgiveness later in such matters, but this is one situation where doing so could cost you. If Jenna's client had already printed his books with the illustrations, the artist would have known the author's hands were tied and she could have asked for a lot more, as reprinting the books without the illustrations would have been rather costly. So it's best to just get the proper permissions as early as you can.

If you don't have the budget to use a particular work, consider using an alternative. Jenna and Sara couldn't afford to license the Austin Powers theme song for our podcast, so we instead hired the incredibly talented Bob Malone to come up with a tune in the same genre. In the end, we're even happier with our theme song than if we'd shelled out the money for the original. Plus, it's 100% ours.

- **Other books or publications.** This is where things get a little murky, as it's often more difficult to determine what is and what isn't fair use. For that reason, you should seriously consider getting permission for excerpts of any publications you use or hiring a copyright lawyer to review the manuscript. Even a one-line quote should undergo clearance.

- **Brand names.** You probably won't run into trouble if you use brand names in a way that isn't disparaging, but it's better to err on the side of caution and, where possible, use something else, such as a generic term. For example, you could use "tissues" instead of "Kleenex." However, sometimes brand names can add a particular flavor to a book, such as in the case of Douglas Coupland's *Generation X.* The book is so peppered with brand names that it would have been a completely different work had he not included them. If you do decide your work would benefit from using the brand names, it's best to get clearance.

- **Real individuals/businesses.** Any recognizable individual, even if not mentioned by their real name, should sign a release—or at the very least provide written permission. The same goes for businesses.
- **Likenesses of others.** If you plan to use photos of people who are recognizable, you need them to sign a legal document known as a model release.

If you need to include any of the above in your book, make sure you start reaching out for the rights early on, as obtaining clearance can take time. If your manuscript contains numerous items that require clearance, consider hiring a permissions editor, a professional who specializes in tracking down rights holders, negotiating, and obtaining the proper legal documentation. Although you can hire a lawyer for clearance work, it can be quite expensive, and many law firms simply refer clients to a clearance house, which uses non-lawyers to conduct the work, as a law degree is not required.

When Redwood published a memoir for a music producer who wanted to use a dozen song lyrics, it took nearly two years to secure all the rights. About a month before publication, the author still had not heard back from several of the music publishers, despite his having followed up numerous times. In the end, the author removed all of the lyrics for which he did not receive clearance so that he could finally go to print.

Note that titles, such as those of songs, films, television shows, etc., are not copyrightable, which explains why so many songs have the same name and why the chain Ruby Tuesday was able to use a Rolling Stones song title for its restaurants' name. However, titles can be trademarked, so it's prudent to take care how it is used. For example, if a title is now associated with a brand—say, *Star Wars*—you could be violating a trademark depending on how you use it.

Real-world locations may also be subject to a legal review. Even if you paint a location in a glowing light, the owners might not want the related exposure, or the venue's name itself might have legal protection such as a copyright or trademark. For the book about sexual assault that Jenna worked on, she and the author relocated the entire story to a new city, both to protect the real-life individuals' identities and themselves from being open to lawsuits. Even the college where some of the cases took place was fictionalized, as a lawyer had advised them that a real-life university probably would not want to be associated with numerous sexual assault cases.

Fact-Checking

Fact-checking is entirely separate from a legal review. You don't need to be an attorney or hold any particular credentials to be a fact-checker. While a legal review may call out potential claims on intellectual property, not all legal reviews involve fact-checking. Instead, many legal teams, including those of traditional publishers, assume that all contents submitted by the author have already been fact-checked and are not plagiarized.

In fact, it is the author's legal responsibility to ensure this is the case.[23] Publishers rarely, if ever, fact-check, and contracts will make this clear, with wording such as "The author warrants all statements in the work are factually true." Larger publishers sometimes spring for a legal review, just to make sure they are protected from lawsuits, but if, for example, you have an incorrect date, neither their legal review nor their editorial team is responsible for catching that.

A mistake such as an incorrect date doesn't mean you'll have legal trouble, but readers who catch multiple errors in your book might leave bad reviews, blast you online for being a liar, or even go so far as to question your credibility as an author.

A now-infamous example of how little a publisher or editor fact-checks a book before it goes to print is James Frey's memoir *A Million Little Pieces*, which shot to the top of the charts after being chosen for Oprah's Book Club. When the truth came out that Frey had fabricated key moments in his life, Oprah revoked his Book Club status and grilled him on her show about why he had misled readers.

More recently, Prince Harry came under fire for several claims he makes in his memoir, *Spare*, which outlets around the world were quick to call into question—from memories such as what Meghan Markle was wearing when they first met to easily researched facts, such as the world's largest diamond. The sheer number of fact-checks called out by the media, along with the public distaste for Harry's criticism of his family, was enough for the former royal's popularity to drop precipitously.[24] If Reputation was Harry's BAGG, the book could be considered an epic fail. But if it was Income, he most definitely succeeded, as the book smashed sales records and went on to break the Guinness World Record for the fastest-selling nonfiction book of all time.[25]

Citing sources can be a good way to provide validation of facts. For heavily researched books, we highly recommend keeping a bibliography and/or using footnotes, even if these don't make it into the final published work. For a book she ghostwrote for a well-known publisher of business books, Jenna included more than eighty citations in a single chapter. Even though she knew the publisher wouldn't include them all in the finished book, she and her client wanted to ensure they had done their due diligence, both in the depth of their research and the quality of their sources. The final published book contains only a fraction of those cited sources, but she, the client, and the publisher have them documented should any issues arise.

Emma Copley Eisenberg, who published the true-crime book *The Third Rainbow Girl* with Hachette Books in 2020, wrote an article on the importance of fact-checking, especially in nonfiction books.[26] In it, she makes a case for just how important fact-checking is and insists it should be part of the publisher's standard package—just as standard as receiving a cover design from them. Unfortunately, unless there is a major uprising among published authors, fact-checking will remain your responsibility, even if you're with one of the biggest traditional houses. For this reason, we recommend that you consider budgeting for a fact-checker, whether you plan to independently publish or sign a deal with a traditional publisher.

Traditional book publishers sometimes hire copyeditors to do a two-person job, blending the tasks of copyediting and fact-checking. And although copyeditors typically check for accuracy—names of people and places spelled correctly, dates accurate—a copyeditor still may not feel it is their responsibility to dive into the minutia of fact-checking, as the process may require calling sources, reviewing your notes, listening to recorded interviews, and other time-consuming tasks. If you feel you need a fact-check, ask your copyeditor if they are experienced in both services, as some are.

Legal Reviews

Let's say you've arrived at the point where you've done any necessary fact-checking and the rest of the manuscript is either your own opinion or some form of advice. If you are publishing in certain genres, now is the time to consider paying for a legal review of your book.[27] The manuscripts most frequently in need of legal review are those in the medical, finance, health, or legal genres. Writers in these fields are often required by their companies or respective professional organizations to send their manuscript through compliance before they can go to press. Compliance departments often nitpick on issues such as word choice and even delete or rewrite entire paragraphs of text. If you need a legal compliance review, build that into your timeline, as this step can take weeks or months.

Although those are the most common types of books needing legal review, in reality, *any* book that makes a claim or endorsement, whether for a product or a service, or that offers certain kinds of advice should undergo legal review. Biography and semi-biographical fiction should also undergo legal review, as these genres contain characters based on real people, who are protected by what is known as life rights. These are the permissions required to use someone's personal details and characteristics so as to protect their reputation and privacy. The laws surrounding life rights are somewhat nebulous and depend greatly upon whether the individual is considered a public figure—and, therefore, has less expectation of privacy. However, public figures do have a strong right of publicity, meaning you can't imply their endorsement without their consent. You may or may not need clearance to portray someone in a specific manner, so it's always best to get their approval in writing to avoid lawsuits.

Sara worked with an author who wrote a book about his longtime friendship with a well-known musician, who granted permission to write a book about their adventures. The author approached the book with a playful attitude—more of a trip down memory lane than a sordid tell-all—and the stories themselves were lighthearted. Even though he had the green light from his musician friend to write the book and none of the stories were in any way mean-spirited, he still had the manuscript reviewed by a lawyer, a publicist, and the friend himself. It's always best to err on the side of caution and get written permission from everybody you can before publishing a book. This can protect you down the road, whether or not you pay for a professional legal review.

When Jenna wrote her memoir about her obsession with Depeche Mode, she knew that writing about other individuals could pose legal challenges—and that there would have been no way for her to fight any lawsuits against a band with so many financial resources. Even though she was pretty sure she wasn't committing libel, she was hesitant to publish before she had legal assurance that she wouldn't be taken to court. Paying for a legal review gave her that peace of mind.

Where you source the material for your book and how much of that information is publicly available could also play a role in the legal security of your work. In 2008, J. K. Rowling sued a publisher who planned to print an encyclopedia of Harry Potter lexicon, which the author argued was simply a repackaging of her intellectual property. The content for the encyclopedia already existed on a free fan website, but Rowling drew the line at the content being used for financial profit.[28] Likewise, Olivia de Havilland lost a lawsuit over the way she was portrayed in the television movie *Feud: Bette and Joan*.[29] The court found that the famed actress did not "have the legal right to control, dictate, approve, disapprove, or veto the creator's portrayal of actual people." Furthermore, the movie was based on multiple sources, not merely de Havilland's celebrity, which also made her a public figure. Such nuances can be explained to you after a lawyer reviews your manuscript.

Another benefit of working with a lawyer is that they can help you craft legal copy, such as disclaimers. Every book, both fiction and nonfiction, should contain some sort of legal disclaimer in the front of the book, the wording of which varies depending on the book's content. Pull some different types of books down from your bookshelf, turn to the copyright pages, and compare the different disclaimers you see. See Appendix F for a few sample disclaimers for your review.

Protecting Your Work

Not only do you need to ensure you don't infringe on the rights of another work's owner, you also need to protect your own work. For $65, you can copyright your manuscript on copyright.gov.

You may have heard of a tactic called the poor man's copyright, which entails printing your manuscript, putting it in an envelope addressed to yourself, and leaving it unopened after it arrives.[30] The date stamped on your envelope is supposed to serve as the date you obtained the copyright, but since that tactic does not include registration with the United States Copyright Office, it won't be on record anywhere. The poor man's copyright is not a tested method for defending your work—there isn't even a provision in U.S. copyright law that allows for such protection. Even if there were, you can't sue for copyright infringement until you file a copyright, nor can you issue legal notice to a copyright infringer without an approved copyright application. For these and many other reasons, we highly recommend spending the $65 to properly protect your work.

It's important to register your work as soon as possible. If you do have to file an infringement claim, you can receive statutory damages (financial compensation for harm or loss) only from the date of registration.[31]

"Ensuring proper clearance and protection of your work goes a long way in securing the long-term viability of your book, especially when it comes to derivative works," says Andrew Barcello, an entertainment attorney and a founding partner of the Los Angeles law firm Feig Finkel LLP. "I've seen writers and producers have their option deals fall apart before getting a series or feature green-lit simply because the clearances, copyright, or chain of title weren't handled correctly at the outset. It's a frustrating scenario for everyone involved, but especially for the author who put so much time and effort into their work. My producer clients are far more likely to pursue a project that is fully cleared and properly copyrighted."

One important caveat: You cannot copyright materials created by artificial intelligence (AI), as copyright law protects only "the fruits of intellectual labor" that "are founded in the creative powers of the [human] mind."[32] Although this is an evolving area of law that could change in the future, Barcello says it doesn't seem likely.

Part of the copyright application requires that you swear, under penalty of perjury, that your statements are true, including that you are the author of the work submitted for copyright. If it is later discovered that you submitted AI-created work as your own, you could face serious legal consequences.

Timing & Costs

Hiring a fact-checker can cost anywhere from $1,000 to $4,500, depending on how long the book is, what needs to be checked, and the subject matter.

A 500-plus-page history book about the Civil War, for example, would likely need a lot more fact-checking than would a business book.

Timing and costs for securing the rights to song lyrics, photos, and other third-party works can vary greatly, especially if you are unsure of the copyright holder and need to hunt them down. Start the process as soon as you are certain you want to include the material in your book, but make sure you have a Plan B in case you can't locate the owner or the cost is outside your budget.

Registering your book with the U.S. Copyright Office costs $65 and covers your work immediately (if the application is eventually approved). Although it can take six to eight months to receive the documents in the mail, you don't need to wait for them to move forward to your next publishing milestone.

Legal reviews vary by lawyer. Many attorneys charge by the hour, so it's worth looking for someone who offers a flat fee (often around $4,000) that includes a tailored disclaimer. Plan about one month for the review process and add some buffer time to make any necessary changes based on the feedback. In many regions, particularly major cities, organizations exist to help artists with legal matters either for free or a greatly reduced cost. Search the web or check with your local bar association to see if there's one near you.

Next Steps

- Make sure you've covered yourself in all the areas listed in this chapter, especially if your BAGG is Promotion or Reputation.
- Run your manuscript through a plagiarism checker.
- Use the worksheet in Further Resources to track issues that might require legal advice or clearance.
- Decide whether your book needs a legal review and/or fact-checking, and budget accordingly.
- Decide on the wording for the book's disclaimer.

- Since not every book will require a legal review, consult Appendix A to see if you can remove this segment from your timeline, thereby moving up your publication date.

Further Resources

Visit bookagogo.com/books/further-resources for the complete collection of all links in this book.

*Indicates a source recommended by *The Chicago Manual of Style*.

Companies, Individuals & Resources Mentioned in This Chapter

- **Bob Malone:** bobmalone.com
- **Chegg:** chegg.com/writing
- **Creative Commons FAQ:** creativecommons.org/faq
- **Feig Finkel LLP:** feigfinkel.com
- **Flickr:** flickr.com
- **Grammarly:** grammarly.com
- **Legal clearance worksheet:** bookagogo.com/worksheets
- **U.S. Copyright Office:** copyright.gov
- **Wikimedia Commons:** commons.wikimedia.org

Additional Books on the Subject

- *Book Law for Authors* by Mary Hutchings Reed and David Creasey: amazon.com/Book-Authors-Mary-Hutchings-Reed/dp/1490981020
- *The Chicago Guide to Fact-Checking* by Brooke Borel: amazon.com/Chicago-Fact-Checking-Writing-Editing-Publishing/dp/022681789X
- *The Copyright Handbook: What Every Writer Needs to Know* by Stephen Fishman, JD: amazon.com/Copyright-Handbook-Every-Writer-Needs/dp/1413327834

- **Permissions, A Survival Guide: Blunt Talk About Art as Intellectual Property* by Susan M. Bielstein: amazon.com/Permissions-Survival-Guide-Intellectual-Propery/dp/0226046389

Further Reading

- "The Realities of Using ChatGPT to Write for You": michellegarrett.com/2023/03/11/the-realities-of-using-chatgpt-to-write-for-you-what-to-consider-when-it-comes-to-legalities-reputation-search-and-originality
- Famous copyright lawsuits & their outcomes: mondaq.com/unitedstates/copyright/538096/10-copyright-cases-every-fan-fiction-writer-should-know-about

Legal Resources for Artists

- California Lawyers for the Arts: calawyersforthearts.org
- Lawyers for the Creative Arts: law-arts.org
- Volunteer Lawyers for the Arts: vlany.org

Traditional Publishing vs. Self-Publishing vs. Hybrid Publishing

The publishing world has evolved quite a bit over the last few years, with more routes to publication than ever. These days, there are three main options: traditional publishing with a publishing house, self-publishing (once known as vanity publishing or subsidy publishing), and the relatively recent hybrid publishing.

Because the focus of this book is self-publishing, it doesn't cover the topics of literary agents and book proposals, as those generally relate only to traditional publishing. However, for the purposes of comparison, we will touch briefly on both subjects. While it's not necessary to have an agent to be signed with a publishing house, there are definitely benefits to having one.

A literary agent provides valuable feedback on your book and gives an honest opinion on whether they think they can find a home for it. Agents spend much of their careers developing relationships with individual publishing-house editors, so they are knowledgeable about what each might be looking for and if any would be interested in your project. If an agent decides to represent you, they shop your book around, broker a deal, negotiate contracts, and guide you on decisions. Although an agent is entitled to a percentage of your royalties, that cost is often offset by how much they are able to negotiate on your behalf. Few if any bidding wars have occurred over books that did not have an agent.

Book proposals are documents used to pitch your book to an agent or publisher. More commonly used for nonfiction than fiction, book proposals can be as short as ten pages and as long as fifty, although most land around the thirty-page range. Some publishers require very rigid formats, while others just want the necessary elements, such as marketing plan, sample chapters, and author platform. For this reason, some authors choose to hire a professional to write their book proposal, although this often costs far more per page than even a full ghostwritten manuscript.

Traditional Publishing

Most everyone is familiar with the basics of traditional publishing: You write a book, submit the manuscript to dozens of publishing houses, sign a deal, and begin collecting those royalty checks. Although that's the basic gist, traditional publishing is actually a lot more complicated and time-consuming.

Fiction authors seeking traditional publication typically need a completed manuscript before pitching to publishers. Although it doesn't have to be the final proofread manuscript, it should be pretty close so you can present the most polished version.

Once you begin submitting your book, be prepared to wait. Days. Weeks. Months. Often, you won't even get a rejection from a publisher—you simply won't get a response. Some publishers are courteous enough to list a statement like this on their website: "If you don't hear back from us within twelve weeks, we have respectfully declined your manuscript."

Create a spreadsheet that lists the name of each publishing house, its website, and the date you submitted your manuscript to the publisher. Research the various imprints of each publishing house, as these specialized divisions might be a better fit for your particular audience. A single publishing company may have multiple imprints. For example, Simon & Schuster alone has sixteen imprints for adult books and another eleven for children's books. So while your book may not be a good fit for Simon & Schuster, it might find a home at one of its imprints, each of which has its own review department, editorial staff, press, and marketing team, meaning each imprint should be considered a separate publisher.

Pros of Traditional Publishing

1. **Distribution.** Traditional publishers still have a stronghold on the book distribution network. You can get a self-published title distributed, but traditional publishers have long-established reputations and relationships with bookstores, particularly the big chains.

2. **Prestige.** Being able to say that a big-time publisher accepted their book is a goal of almost every author. You can use that as a calling card when you get ready to publish your next book, and it's certainly an accomplishment.

3. **Money.** You will likely receive an advance for the work on your book, although advances are not as large as they once were. Once the book earns out, or recoups the amount of your advance, you then begin to receive royalties.

Cons of Traditional Publishing

1. **Time.** Traditional publishers are incredibly slow, at least compared with hybrid and self-publishing. They typically schedule their releases about a year out, so you may not see your book published until a year

or more after the date of completion. Traditional publishers are also notorious for bumping a book's release date in favor of a timelier release or one attached to a bigger name.

In 2016, one of Sara's authors signed a deal with a publishing house for a 2017 release. The publication date got bumped twice until, in 2020, three years after the contract was signed, the publisher was finally ready to move forward. The manuscript had been written by the author but was still in need of developmental editing, copyediting, proofreading, and design. If he had waited for the publisher, it would have been another year or two just to get it done. Not wanting any more delays, the author decided to scrap his contract with the publisher and instead self-publish. He was able to release his book toward the end of 2020 on his own.

2. **DIY.** Be prepared to do some of the work yourself. While publishers do have professional teams of editors, proofreaders, and designers to assist with your book, there may be tasks you want performed that publishers may not handle, such as a legal review or fact-checking. Publishers also typically don't do a lot in the way of marketing—only their most established and bestselling authors get that privilege—so that onus will likely also fall on you.

3. **Loss of creative control.** Your publisher makes all of the decisions for you. If they want to go with a certain title, subtitle, or cover design, you won't have much of a choice in the matter. When one of Sara's authors published with a traditional house, she was brought to tears when she saw the title and cover, which focused on the saddest (and shortest) part of her book. The publisher explained it had made that choice because that was what would sell. Although the author finally acquiesced to the publisher's creative demand, it took a long time for her to come to terms with their decision.

Although these are the most common advantages and disadvantages of traditional publishing, there are quite a few others, so we've included some of these in Further Resources at the end of this chapter. Traditional publishing is the right option for some authors, but not all.

If you've always dreamed of publishing with one of the Big Five publishing houses (mentioned in chapter 5) but also want to see your book in print no matter what, you can set a time limit on your traditional publishing journey and then take a detour if that doesn't work out. If you don't reach a certain milestone by a given date—such as signing with an agent within a year—you can switch gears to self-publishing. (Note that the term *indie publishing* is sometimes used as a synonym for *self-publishing*, although it can also be used to mean smaller publishing houses. If you hear that someone is an indie publisher, make sure to clarify what that means.)

Self-Publishing

While traditional publishing can involve a modicum of DIY, self-publishing requires far more of your personal involvement, although you always have the option of hiring professionals to help you over the bumps you can't manage yourself. At the bare minimum, you should assemble a professional team that includes a proofreader, designers (for both the cover and interior of your book), and someone intimately familiar with the process involved with launching your book. The last may be referred to as a self-publishing expert, a book sherpa, or even a self-publishing concierge, as Redwood describes itself. Since this role falls under the more general umbrella of "publishing expert" or "publishing concierge," these professionals often possess different skill sets, such as writing book proposals or assisting with literary agents. You can either hire a person or company to handle it all or hire each professional individually and assemble your own team. Whichever strategy you choose, ask to see portfolios, talk to clients who have worked with the company or individual, and see if they have worked on projects similar to yours. For the sake of simplicity, whenever we refer to Amazon in this chapter, we are referring to any self-publishing outlet, such as Barnes & Noble.

In addition to helping with the Amazon portion of the process, a self-publishing expert can also handle all of the smaller yet still important details, such as purchasing the copyright and ISBN numbers (explained further on page 125), registering for a Library of Congress Control Number, and reviewing designed files and printed proofs. The person or company you hire should be somebody who not only has a lot of experience but has published recently, as the options for self-publishing change on an almost monthly basis. Redwood Publishing offers all of the above and more, as do other similar companies.

Here are some questions to ask prospective self-publishing companies:

- What is the time frame for releasing the book? Will you provide a schedule of milestones?
- Can you provide sample copies of books you have published?
- Do you register my manuscript for copyright, or do I need to do that? Are ISBNs registered to you or to me? Do you take care of Library of Congress registration and submitting the book to the Library once it's published?
- What is your royalty structure? How am I paid?
- How often do you provide sales reports?
- How will those reports be provided?
- Do I pay for printed proofs? Galleys? Final copies of the book?
- In what formats will you publish my book—paperback, hardcover, e-book, audio?
- Do you offer marketing services as part of your publishing package?
- Do you hand over all of my final production files once we have completed our work together?

Pros of Self-Publishing

1. **Total control.** With self-publishing, you are in complete control of how your book gets released to the world. Not only can you make your own design decisions, but you also own all of the files—meaning you can make changes to the text or cover design and release new versions of your book anytime you like.

2. **Faster launch.** With self-publishing, you can typically bring your work to market much faster, releasing it when you're ready rather than adhering to a publisher's schedule. Typically, self-publishing ensures your title is on Amazon within a few days of file submission.

3. **Higher percentage of royalties.** When you work with a traditional publisher, your royalties are shared between you, your publisher, your agent (if you use one), and Amazon. When you self-publish, your royalty is often just between you and Amazon. (Of course, this matters only when comparing apples to apples. Traditionally published books tend to have more sales, but that doesn't mean you can't achieve that on your own.)

Cons of Self-Publishing

1. **Difficulty.** It can be stressful and overwhelming to navigate the self-publishing world. Self-publishing a book involves myriad details that can be easy to miss if you aren't familiar with the process.

2. **Distribution.** The outlets in which your book gets sold can be limited. A typical self-published author releases a title via print on demand, meaning books are printed to order. Often, those POD services distribute to only a certain number of online retailers, meaning many brick-and-mortar stores won't have access to your title or, if they do, they may not be interested in carrying it simply because it is self-published. Even if you use an independent distributor, they likely

won't have the reach of a traditional publisher, so your book won't be available in as many outlets.

3. **Cost.** Self-publishing requires the author to lay out all costs up front and, as with any business venture, there's no guarantee you'll recoup your investment.

Self-publishing has come a long way since it first became an available option to publish a book. Unfortunately, when self-publishing first burst onto the scene, many saw a hole that needed to be filled. As a result, new self-publishing businesses were created left and right, some by people who just didn't understand books or the publishing and distribution world. There are many companies out there—sometimes called POD self-publishers or subsidy/vanity publishers—that simply take advantage of authors. Some of these POD self-publishers offer very cheap publishing packages that, in return, produce poor-quality books. Subsidy publishers typically act as if they are a publishing house, pretending to seek out manuscripts to publish and acting as if they are signing a deal with an author, when in reality, they accept almost every title that they come across. They typically charge more than POD self-publishers and can create nicer quality books, if they have the right team or if they know the book world. Subsidy publishers can also be thought of as hybrid publishers, which we will get into in the next section.

Hybrid Publishing

If you're still not sure which publishing route you'd like to take, you may be a candidate for hybrid publishing, which, as the name implies, is a mix of traditional publishing and self-publishing. Hybrid publishers often treat book publishing as traditional publishers do: They accept a manuscript for review and then decide whether to publish that title. If they accept a title, they work out a deal wherein the author and publisher typically share both the costs and the royalties, but the book is released for sale much as it would be during the self-publishing process.

Pros of Hybrid Publishing

1. **Use of publishing company name.** Hybrid publishers allow for authors to be published under an imprint rather than the author's own name, which can look less prestigious.
2. **Control.** You usually retain all the rights to and creative control over your book. However, some hybrids differ, so make sure to read the fine print before you sign the contract.
3. **Royalty rate.** Your percentage is generally higher than with a traditional publishing house.

Cons of Hybrid Publishing

1. **Distribution.** Many hybrid publishers use the same print-on-demand channels that self-publishing authors use, meaning they are subject to the same distribution difficulties. However, while distribution is often still limited, some hybrids may work with their own distributors, who can help get your book into brick-and-mortar stores.
2. **DIY.** You may still have to be very hands-on, as your hybrid may not offer marketing or other services, which means you have to pay for those out of pocket.
3. **Bad experience.** Because of the surge in popularity of hybrid publishing, new companies are popping up all the time and not all are legitimate, so make sure you do your research before you sign a contract.

These are just three of the most common ways to approach book publishing, but in fact there are many others. Redwood Publishing is something of a hybrid-hybrid publisher. While Sara's authors can use the Redwood Publishing imprint, the company does not handle major distribution to brick-and-mortar bookstores. Redwood also sets up authors with their own accounts so that they are paid directly for book sales—it does not take a cut of royalties or any other sales resulting from the book.

Remember: You can pivot anytime. Even if you publish your first book with a traditional publisher, you don't have to do so the next time around. Or if you start the process of self-publishing but decide you need help, you can find a hybrid. See Appendix G for a flowchart to help you decide which publishing option is best for you.

Whichever you choose, be sure to consult an accountant to make sure you are set up as the proper legal entity. Some traditionally published authors find that an S corporation provides the best financial protection, while successful self-published authors often benefit from having a limited liability company (LLC). Since the process of setting up a business entity can take some time, start early, as you want to make sure it's in place before your first sales.

Timing & Costs

If you decide to go the traditional publishing route, ideally you'll receive an advance of some kind, which you can use to pay yourself or to offset other costs, such as hiring a fact-checker. You will, however, be on the traditional publisher's timetable, which we mention on page 102. This can mean waiting months, or even years, before seeing your book in print.

If you're self-publishing, you must fund the entire writing and publishing process yourself. Revisit Appendix B for a reminder of how much each step might cost. Hiring a self-publishing expert comes with additional fees. For example, Redwood Publishing charges $125 per hour for such tasks as reviewing files and uploading documents, while handling the entire job—from editing through design to publication—is a set fee based on the length of the book and type of design it requires. You can usually control how long it takes to publish your book if you do it all yourself, as you can probably find people, such as editors and designers, who are available to start working right away.

If you instead opt for hybrid publishing, fees can vary greatly, anywhere from $500 to $30,000, depending on the company and publishing package you select. Some hybrid publishers may require the author to pay for all production costs, while others share the costs with the author rather than paying an advance. Still others may provide a small advance but expect the author to pay for certain costs, such as printing. Authors may also be subject to longer lead times with certain hybrid publishers, as some maintain publishing calendars like traditional publishers do, while others might be available to expedite the release of an author's book.

Next Steps

- The BAGG you chose could have a huge impact on which type of publishing you opt for, so make sure the two are in alignment.
- If publishing traditionally or with a hybrid publisher, create a spreadsheet that tracks your submissions to agents and publishers.
- Thoroughly research the publisher and review the contract.
- Decide if you need to establish a legal entity, such as an LLC.

Further Resources

Visit bookagogo.com/books/further-resources for the complete collection of all links in this book.

Additional Books on the Subject

- *How to Write a Book Proposal: The Insider's Step-by-Step Guide to Proposals That Get You Published* by Jody Rein with Michael Larsen: amazon.com/Write-Book-Proposal-Step-Step/dp/1440348170

Choosing a Publishing Route

- **Reedsy:** blog.reedsy.com/self-publishing-vs-traditional-publishing
- **Joanna Penn:** thecreativepenn.com/self-publishing-vs-traditional

Writing a Book Proposal

- **Jane Friedman's advice:** janefriedman.com/start-here-how-to-write-a-book-proposal

Business Entities for Writers

- *Writer's Digest*: writersdigest.com/publishing-insights/when-should-writers-incorporate-or-create-an-llc
- **Author Media:** authormedia.com/the-authors-guide-to-llcs

How to Get Testimonials for Your Book

I n the book-publishing industry, testimonials refer to endorsements of you or your book, usually from someone with a reputation or affiliation that your readers will recognize as relevant to your topic. These testimonials are often solicited by an author, agent, or publisher and are in addition to traditional media coverage, such as interviews and reviews.

More often than not, only a small excerpt of a written testimonial or review is used, a snippet referred to as a blurb. Look at the cover of most any mass-market book and you'll find quotes under the heading "Praise for [*Book Title*]" or simply a list of quotes, usually on the back but sometimes on the front cover or on the book flaps. These are blurbs. In some cases, the word *blurb* is used to describe the short description on the back of a book, but the most common meaning—and the one used in this book—is as a select portion of a third-party testimonial.

There are several ways blurbs can help sell more books. BookBub reports that in a comparison of online ads, those with blurbs had a 22.6% higher click-through rate (CTR) than those without blurbs.[33] That's because blurbs are likely to contain keywords (words or phrases potential readers might use to search for your book), which could help your book rank higher in search results. Using keywords—whether in blurbs or elsewhere—to boost your searchability is a marketing strategy known as search engine optimization (SEO). Blurbs can also be persuasive. A few solid blurbs on your cover can go a long way toward convincing a potential reader to choose your book over another.

If you receive a particularly flattering review, you can use a line or two as a blurb, either on the cover or in marketing materials, such as a teaser or promotional copy. Note that professional reviews are different from customer reviews, such as those on Amazon or Goodreads. Both types of reviews are covered in chapter 16 and 17.

Blurbs can provide a compelling reason as to why a person should buy or read your book:

1. By offering social proof, meaning they tell readers that other customers have read and liked your book. (For more on social proof, see page 15.)
2. By underscoring your book's importance and relevance, thereby helping readers identify with the content.
3. By lending your book credibility, especially if the blurb is from a noteworthy source.

Where and When to Use Blurbs

When most people think of blurbs, they imagine them on the back of a book—which is indeed the most common place to find them—but blurbs can also be used elsewhere:

1. **Inside the book.** If you already have two or three blurbs on the back cover, you can include any additional ones in the front matter. The most common way to do that is to title a page "Continued Praise for [*Book Title*]." Including this section provides more space to use longer review snippets or even full testimonials.

2. **Online.** This includes on your website, in social media, and in newsletters.

3. **On your Amazon page.** You can include blurbs in your Amazon book description and in the Editorial Reviews section of your Amazon Author Page. When authors use blurbs this way, it is often as a placeholder until they receive professional reviews.

4. **In advertising and marketing materials.** If you decide to use a PR agency once your book is published, they will greatly welcome any blurbs you can provide, as they can use them in their own marketing materials, such as press releases and ads.

When you receive a blurb for a book, you can't just use it whenever and however you want. The blurb should be used in the context of *that book* only. If, for example, you plan to write a follow-up, you shouldn't use blurbs from your first book unless you provide context.

One of Sara's authors had written four other books before publishing with Redwood. He'd received some strong testimonials for those prior titles and wanted to find a way to include them in his new book, so Redwood added a couple of pages to the front, titled "Praise for Ritch's Previously Published Titles." This allowed him to garner credibility with new readers while being clear that those testimonials were for different works.

There is some debate as to whether you can use a blurb anywhere outside of on or in your book. To be safe, we recommend stating in your request letter that the testimonial and any resulting blurbs will be used in and on the book and potentially in marketing materials. We provide a template for a testimonial request letter in Appendix H.

Identifying Blurbers

Your blurbers (as we will refer to people who provide testimonials from which you can source blurbs) don't have to be household names. They just need to be relevant to your book, which will be evident by the descriptors you provide next to their names. You may not know the name of the head of Beyond Meat, but if you see their name and title endorsing a vegan cookbook, that's far more helpful than if that same person provided a blurb for a romance novel.

Stephen King once wrote, "I've seen the future of horror...and it is named Clive Barker." There's not a much better endorsement a writer of that genre could ever hope to get. But if King had reviewed *Goodnight Moon*, his endorsement most likely would have given the wrong impression of what is a lighthearted picture book for toddlers. So when you start thinking about blurbs, make a list of individuals and organizations that would be credible for your readers specifically.

A former NFL player turned family financial planner and life insurance expert was trying to decide whom he could reach out to for blurbs. Although his former coach and teammates were notable, he recognized that he needed names in his new industry, not his former one, as his book was intended to be a calling card that would earn him credibility. Fortunately for him, one of his clients was a descendent of the prestigious Vanderbilt family, who had changed her last name when she married. Her blurb focused on how appropriate the book's subject was for families looking to understand whether they needed life insurance, and the descriptor following her name mentioned her financial heritage. The author now had a strong, relevant name tied to his book—one that would mean something to his financial colleagues and convey to his prospective clients the level of wealth he managed. So aim high, but do so with relevant names.

Wrangling blurbs is another instance in which a robust author platform (discussed in chapter 2) can help. If you've been active on social media, you may now be following, or be followed by, people who are influential or well known to your target audience. Reach out and ask for a blurb.

Or you may just know someone pertinent. When Jenna was publishing her Depeche Mode fan memoir, she approached a friend who wrote about music for the *Huffington Post,* as well as an instructor from her graduate writing program. Although not well known in Jenna's genre, the instructor was also an award-winning writer, so having a blurb from her lent credibility to the quality of Jenna's writing.

If you're working with a publisher or PR agency, they may send out advance reader copies (ARCs) to journalists, professional reviewers, and even other authors. If the recipients like what they've read, they will often write a review from which you can source a blurb.

Blurbers don't even have to read your book. Instead, they can focus on you and your expertise. Some may skim the first chapter or two of your book to get an idea of the material. In such situations, the best approach is to provide sample blurbs that they then approve, which we will talk about more in a bit.

When setting off on a blurb-gathering expedition, many writers fear rejection. But of all the books we have ever helped get blurbs for, none of our authors were ever flat-out refused in an unpleasant way. The worst that has happened is that the blurber passed because they didn't have time or couldn't participate for contractual reasons, or they simply didn't reply. We recommend tracking all of your requests so you can follow up in a timely manner. To that end, we've created a worksheet to help you, which you can find on our Book-A-Go-Go worksheets page (bookagogo.com/worksheets). When compiling your list, order the individuals by importance so that you ensure you have time to contact the most important ones first and also have time to ask for a foreword, which we cover in the last section of this chapter.

Here's another strategy that can not only help you land a blurb but also build your business connections. One of Sara's authors was writing a book about how photography helped him gain focus in many areas of his life: He managed his ADHD, found a passion for business coaching, built a business from the ground up—the list goes on.

He spent a couple of months browsing LinkedIn for people he wanted to connect with and came across the CEO of Kodak and the publisher of *Inc.* magazine. He recognized some shared interests, so he wrote them each a personable LinkedIn message asking if they'd be interested in having a short conversation about photography and finding focus in life. He didn't mention the book at all. Both agreed to a conversation. In those talks, he made real connections with each, which made it easy for him to casually mention his book at the end of the call. About a month or so later, he reached out to those connections again, reminding them of their conversations and the book and asking if they'd be willing to provide a blurb. They both said yes.

Authors who have chosen to blog (see chapter 4) can write about their dream blurbers. If you're working on a book about baseball, for example, write a post about your favorite shortstop. When it comes time to ask for a blurb, you can send them a link to the post. There's even the possibility they'll find your blog before you send it to them.

Asking for Blurbs

When requesting a blurb, include a link to your website's book page (covered in more depth on page 29). This page should state the approximate publication date and allow visitors to subscribe to a newsletter to receive updates. It can also include a longer description of your book, the cover art (when you get it), and even blurbs, which you can add as you receive them. If a potential blurber sees other notable individuals providing blurbs, they might be convinced to provide one themselves.

Try to get blurbs that cover a variety of different aspects of your book—characters, humor, plot, writing style, etc. The more specific, the better. You don't want five testimonials that all say, "Great book!" or "Read it now!" The blurbs should cover the different potential questions readers may have when they first discover your book.

For nonfiction titles, these questions can include:

- What will I learn from this book?
- How will this book help or entertain me?
- Who is the person giving me this advice or information?

Nonfiction authors can include blurbs that are focused on you and your experience or credibility in the area you've written about, rather than the book's content.

For fiction, some of the questions your blurbs should answer are:

- What sort of storyline can I expect in reading this book?
- Will I connect to the main characters?
- What is the tone of the book? Is it similar to other novels I've enjoyed?

As you reach out to blurbers and track requests in the worksheet, suggest points you'd like them to mention so that your blurbs call attention to a variety of your book's aspects. The best way to do this is to provide an example blurb, which also allows you to include any keywords and to cover different aspects of the book. Just make sure you don't send the same sample blurb to more than one blurber or they both might choose it.

A critical part of your blurb request letter is the book synopsis. Believe it or not, this short paragraph might be one of the hardest pieces you ever have to write. But the synopsis is incredibly important, especially since you will be using it—or versions of it—in many, many places: on your website, on your Amazon listing, in press releases, on the back cover, and so on. So make sure you run it past several people in your book's demographic to see if it resonates with them.

If you receive a blurb that doesn't quite hit the mark—maybe it doesn't really say anything of value about you or the book, or maybe you just don't like the way it reads—don't be afraid to suggest changes to the blurber. It's very rare they will reject your edits. (One blurber for this book actually thanked Jenna for improving her quote by removing an exclamation point, Jenna's least favorite of all punctuation marks.)

Once both you and the blurber have agreed on the copy, make sure you get the blurber to also approve their name and descriptor. You don't want to print that your blurber is the author of a book that's out of print or, worse, misspell their name or get their title wrong. Always make sure that they approve the *full blurb.*

If, after all this work, you find yourself in the enviable position of having a ton of blurbs, know that this is a problem many writers would love to have. Unless you have a blurber with a huge household name (think Oprah or Stephen King), you don't need a blurb on the front cover. Some authors pick out the three or four strongest blurb snippets for the back and include longer versions of the original testimonials on the "Continued Praise" page, along with any additional testimonials that didn't make it onto the back cover. Any remaining can be used in other marketing materials, particularly the website and Amazon page.

Although this should go without saying, *thank everyone* who provides a blurb. Within one business day of receiving it, send a follow-up email that also asks for an address where you can mail a signed copy of the book when it comes out—and don't forget to send it. If you want to be extremely gracious, you can even send copies to those blurbers who turned you down.

Blurbs vs. No Blurbs

Don't get hung up on getting blurbs. Despite all the reasons to have them, blurbs are not critical, so you should not delay publishing just to wrangle them. Releasing your book so you can start collecting reviews from customers and professionals is far more important.

The content of your book isn't going to change whether or not you have a testimonial from your dream blurber. In fact, some experts say it's better not to have any blurbs than to have bad or irrelevant ones. If you're writing a book about space exploration, for example, it wouldn't be terribly helpful to have a politician provide a blurb unless they're a well-known NASA enthusiast. Once your book is published, you can still work on blurb-wrangling. And if you've decided to go the route of hybrid publishing or self-publishing (see previous chapter), you can add a blurb to your cover even if it comes in after your release date, so that it appears on the next run of your books—or immediately, in the case of print on demand.

There are also times when getting blurbs just isn't possible. When the 2020 pandemic hit, many authors rushed to get books to market and so didn't have time to wrangle blurbs. Sometimes a blurber promises to send one, only to back out at the last minute. It's okay—it's not always in the cards. Blurbs *can* help the success of your book, but they don't guarantee it. So don't let a lack of blurbs deter you from moving on to the next phase of your publishing journey.

Foreword Solicitation

The process of blurb-wrangling can be combined with asking someone to write a foreword. After you've compiled your worksheet of potential blurbers, identify the highest-profile individual and weigh whether their writing a foreword would benefit your book. Reach out to this individual first and, if they pass, move on to the next on your list. If they pass on writing the foreword, they might still be open to providing a blurb.

Since writing a foreword requires more effort than writing a blurb, be sure to express how much the potential contributor's involvement would mean to you and your book. Being asked to write a foreword is a compliment in itself, but gratitude goes a long way in the art of persuasion. Once a contributor agrees to furnish a foreword, provide a contract that states the extent of their involvement and compensation, such as whether they will receive credit in some form.

Forewords, including how they differ from prefaces and introductions, are discussed further in the next chapter.

Timing & Costs

Fortunately, blurbs are one of the areas you don't have to budget for, as you don't have to pay someone to provide a blurb. If someone asks for monetary compensation, thank them and move on.

Because blurb-wrangling can take time, we recommend you start early—at least three months before you plan to submit your manuscript to your proofreader or publisher. This might mean you begin while you're still writing the book. It takes time to identify whom to ask, tailor a letter specifically to them, wait for a response, and then send the book, whether it's a rough draft or just the first few chapters. You don't want to be scrambling at the last minute to get blurbs, especially since that means putting pressure on your blurbers, who are, after all, doing you a favor.

Next Steps

- Authors with BAGGs of Catharsis, Documentation, or Self-Expression can most likely skip blurb-wrangling, thereby moving up their publication date in the timeline in Appendix A.
- Keep a list of potential blurbers, keeping your BAGG front of mind. Make a spreadsheet of individuals and organizations you contact, and track their responses.
- Write your book synopsis, which you can use in blurb request letters, on the back of your book, and many other places.

- Create a variety of sample blurbs based on what you hope to receive from blurbers.
- Decide whether you will solicit blurbers for a foreword and, if so, include that in your blurb-wrangling process.
- Write your blurb request letter, including the book synopsis and, optionally, a sample blurb. Personalize each letter for the recipient.
- Thank each contributor as you receive their blurb and, when the book is released, send each a copy of the book.

Further Resources

Visit bookagogo.com/books/further-resources for the complete collection of all links in this book.

Companies, Individuals & Resources Mentioned in This Chapter

- **Testimonial/blurb request worksheet:** bookagogo.com/worksheets

Compiling & Organizing the Sections of Your Book

Many books, particularly nonfiction ones, have multiple sections, aside from the body copy and copyright page. Although not all books require each of the sections mentioned in this chapter, whichever ones are included in your book need to be compiled and completed before the interior is laid out. When trying to decide whether your book needs a particular section, ask yourself if including it would be helpful for readers, press, or reviewers. If not, you can probably omit it.

Book sections are compiled into three categories: front matter, main matter, and back matter. All sections that come before the body, or main matter, are referred to as front matter, while those that follow are known as back matter. In this chapter, elements for each section are listed in the order in which they most often appear in print books, although e-books are sometimes ordered differently (more on that near the end of the chapter). Refer to Appendix I for an infographic outlining the sections we are about to discuss.

Front Matter Sections

The front matter usually consists of testimonials, copyright information, metadata (such as ISBNs), and legal details. Often, it also contains some longer introductory material (usually written by someone other than the author). Although many readers skip through this section, it's important to include some of the elements for legal reasons and others to convey a professional impression.

Blank first page. Many authors leave the first page blank for signing, while others prefer a blank page for aesthetic reasons. It's your call whether to include a blank first page.

"Continued Praise" page. Use this section to share testimonials that don't fit on the back cover. Typically, this page contains a headline that reads "Additional Praise for [*Book Title*]," "Continued Praise for [*Book Title*]," or "Expanded Praise for [*Book Title*]." You can also use this page to display the full testimonials you've received, in the event that you use blurbs only on the back cover.

Other books by the author or series title. If you have written more than one book, particularly if they belong to a series, you can mention them here, along with their respective publishers and original release dates. Optionally, this section can instead be included after the half-title page or in the back matter.

Frontispiece. Used most often in books with illustrations, the frontispiece is artwork that is generally positioned to the left of the title page.

Title page(s). A book can have either one or two title pages. If two are included, the first is the half-title page, which is optional, and the second is called the full-title page. The half-title page includes only the title of the book, while the full-title page includes the title, subtitle, author name, and, optionally, publishing company name.

As of the writing of this book, the trend seems to lean toward forgoing the half-title page and going straight to the full. Alternatively, you could forgo the blank page and use the half-title page for signing books. The back of the full-title page is the copyright page.

Copyright page. Technically, any work receives copyright protection from the moment of its creation. (See chapter 8 for more about obtaining a copyright for your book.) Although a copyright page isn't required, we highly recommend you include it, as it makes the overall book look professional and can help readers, press, librarians, customs agents, and reviewers find out more about you and your work.

The copyright page should include:

- The copyright info (example: Copyright © [year] [name of copyright owner]).
- The rights reserved notice—i.e., "All Rights Reserved"—and some mention that no parts of your book may be reproduced, stored, or transmitted in any form without written permission from you or your publisher.
- Publisher information and their logo.
- The International Standard Book Number (ISBN), a unique thirteen-digit identifier assigned to each version of your book. If your book has multiple versions, such as a paperback and a hardcover, include the ISBNs for those as well. Although an ISBN is not always required for an e-book (it depends on the retailer), we recommend purchasing one so that you own all ISBNs associated with your title. ISBNs can be purchased through Bowker (bowker.com), although many publishers include this in their services.

- Contact information. Include at least an email address and a website, although some books also include a phone number. If your book is published by a traditional publisher, their contact information, not yours, typically goes here.
- Details on how a reader can order your book in bulk, if this is something you plan to offer.
- Any disclaimers (more below).
- Where the book is printed and distributed, if you are engaging a distribution company.
- Edition details (i.e., whether it's the first or second edition).
- Any copyright information for other works that you have used or cited. If you have several credits or permissions you'd like to list, you can always place them in the back matter and reference where on the copyright page, e.g., "For cited works and permissions details, see page 101."
- Designer credits, including who designed and/or photographed the cover, the interior, and any graphics or images. Although you might include this information in the acknowledgments section, which typically goes in the back matter, including it here gives you a more elegant way of also including the artists' websites.
- Library of Congress Control Number (LCCN), if you end up registering for one. This number acts as a unique identifier for libraries, including the Library of Congress. Apply for the catalog number at loc.gov, then once your book is published, send a printed copy, with the catalog number on the copyright page, to the Library, who then reviews your book to determine if it will carry it.

Registering for a catalog number does not guarantee that the Library of Congress will carry your title; the Library generally accepts only 20% to 25% of titles submitted. Obtaining an LCCN is free and easy, and even if the Library of Congress elects not to carry your title, having the number can add to the credibility of your book and allows libraries to easily find and reference it. Self-published authors can obtain their own LCCN by registering as an author or self-publisher and submitting their title.

"While having an LCCN is not the end-all-be-all to getting into local libraries, it definitely helps," says Tiffany Obeng, an author and owner of Sugar Cookie Books, which publishes educational and inspiring literature for children. "As self-published authors, we need all the help we can get. Plus, acquiring an LCCN is free! Not much in the self-publishing world is free, so let's take advantage when we can."

- CIP Data Block, if you are able to obtain one. Also called Library of Congress Cataloging-in-Publication (CIP) Data, this is a bibliographic record that helps libraries know where to file books. Although only traditional publishers can register for a CIP Data Block, some third-party companies sell them to self-published authors (in which case it is referred to as a P-CIP Data Block). You must first have an LCCN before you can receive a CIP Data Block. A book can be published with only an LCCN, but a P-CIP/CIP Data Block cannot exist without an LCCN.

Typically, this data block includes title, author name(s), publisher name, book description, LCCN, ISBN, and BISAC code(s) (discussed on page 182). It usually looks something like this:

Names: Robbins, Jenna Rose
Title: *Faithful and Devoted: Confessions of a Music Addict*
Description: Paperback edition. | Redwood Publishing, LLC, 2017.
Identifiers: LCCN 2017935109 | ISBN 978-0-9981760-6-2 (softcover)
Subjects: Autobiography -- Music. | Pop Culture Music -- Nonfiction. | Travel Writing -- Nonfiction.
BISAC: BIO004000

See Appendix J for an example of how to lay out a copyright page.

If you opt to include a disclaimer on your copyright page, which we highly recommend, here are suggestions of what it might include:

- Nonfiction book or memoir: Mention that some names or dates have been changed.
- Books that offer advice (such as medical, therapeutic, diet, or exercise): State that the book does not replace the advice of a professional in that field.
- Books with profanity or that talk about difficult subjects: Provide a trigger warning so readers are aware before they dive in.

Refer to Appendix F for sample disclaimers you could include in your book. As we mentioned when discussing legal compliance in chapter 8, a lawyer can suggest what disclaimers you need and will often include the wording as part of their legal review.

Dedication and/or epigraph. The vast majority of dedication pages are a mere line or two, but there's no steadfast rule on the length. You can even skip this page altogether.

Another option is to include a quote, one that exemplifies the theme of the main matter. If you go this route, this is called an epigraph page. You can include both a dedication and an epigraph, one or the other, or neither. If you include both, the dedication usually comes before the epigraph.

Table of contents. It's first important to note what is and what isn't included in the table of contents. To understand that, you need to know how to number the pages of your book. There are several book sections that may precede the main matter, such as a preface or foreword. These sections all take lowercase Roman numerals—i, ii, iii, etc. Pages in the main body of your book take Arabic numerals—1, 2, 3, etc.

The table of contents comes after all the front matter that does not get a page number. For example, you wouldn't include a dedication page in the table of contents, so the dedication should come before the table. Anything that follows the table of contents, including back matter, should be listed in the table.

Many fiction books can do without a table of contents, especially if the individual chapters have only numbers and not titles. You also may not need a table of contents if your book is on the shorter side, such as thirty pages or fewer. But for all other types of books, including poetry and short story compilations of any length, a table of contents should be included so that readers can easily find what they're looking for. Non-memoir nonfiction books can most benefit from a table of contents, especially when there are multiple sections and subsections. See Further Resources for a link demonstrating how you can automatically generate a table of contents using Microsoft Word.

Explanatory maps/charts. Examples of such material include the map of Middle-earth in *The Hobbit*, the satirical periodic table of the elements in *Shampoo Planet,* and the family lineage chart in the Game of Thrones series. For his young-adult series Once Upon a Time in the Texas Panhandle, one of Sara's authors included a map to show where the fictional town he'd created lay within the borders of a real-world county. Throughout the series, he references the map when he mentions nearby fictional towns and counties.

The explanatory section can go most anywhere in the front matter, although placing it before the introduction can assure that the reader doesn't overlook it. Since there's no hard-and-fast rule as to where such material should go, place it where you think it fits best with your story and where your readers can easily find it, particularly if you think they will refer to it often. For this reason, some books include it at the very beginning. Hardcovers often include maps and charts on the inside of the cover itself, although this is not usually an option for self-published books, particularly those who use print on demand.

The next few sections—preface, or author's note; foreword; and introduction—are often confused with one another, so be sure you understand the role each plays so you don't accidentally name your introduction a foreword, or vice versa. For more detailed information about the differences between each and the purposes they serve, see Further Resources.

Preface, or author's note. While the foreword is written by someone else, the preface is the author's chance to include a note to the reader, such as how the book came about or the inspiration behind a particular character. The section can also be a way to provide more information around the disclaimer from the copyright page: A writer may want to use the author's note to elaborate on why they chose to write in a particular style or discuss a controversial topic.

Although *preface* is the standard industry term for this section, some authors choose to title it "Author's Note," "A Note From the Author," or "An Invitation From the Author" to entice readers. Otherwise, as with the foreword, readers may see this section as extraneous and skip it.

Foreword. Typically written by somebody other than the author, the foreword acts as an extended testimonial for you and/or your book. As mentioned in the previous chapter, you can include asking for a foreword as part of the blurb-wrangling process. If no one offers to provide you with one, you can skip this section. It's not necessary, and many readers ignore it, even when it's written by someone noteworthy.

Introduction. Often written by the author, the introduction presents the main matter in one of two ways. If the introduction is critical to the reader understanding the book's content, the section should be included in the main matter. If the introduction is written by somebody else and/or presents the background story of the topic, the introduction goes in the front matter. For example, a book about yoga philosophy with an introduction about the overall concept and key terminology would include that section in the main matter.

However, if the introduction contains a history of yoga that is not required for understanding the rest of the book, it would go in the front matter.

Main Matter Sections

The main matter is the crux of the book, the part that justifies the existence of everything in the front and back matter. In many cases, it constitutes the whole of an author's completed manuscript: While content in the front and back matter could be created and compiled by others, the main matter is solely the work of the author or authors.

Prologue. Unlike the introduction or preface, the prologue is part of the main body of the manuscript, not the front or back matter. Think of it as an optional chapter 0, a way to advance the storyline, provide key background information, or tantalize the reader for the main show to come. This is typically done for works that follow a narrative arc, such as novels, biographies, and memoirs, and is rarely used in nonfiction.

Body/story. The heart of the book begins with chapter 1 and continues through to the final chapter. Some authors additionally organize their content into parts or sections, which are in turn separated by chapters. Parts are often used to denote the passing of time, major plot milestones, or even a change in point of view, such as switching to another character's perspective. When parts are used, they are often laid out by having a single page announcing the part number and, if used, part name.

Epilogue. The counterpart to the prologue, the epilogue is the same in every way except it comes directly after the main matter, often to tie up loose ends or provide concluding thoughts within the universe you've created. In that sense, the prologue and epilogue act as bookends to the body, although neither is required.

Back Matter Sections

Back matter is composed mainly of supplementary and/or reference material, although sections such as acknowledgments and the author biography also belong here when included.

Conclusion. This is the author's last chance to get any final statements across to the reader as well as provide a summary of everything the reader has just learned. Similar to an introduction, if this section is pertinent to the content, rather than related reflections, it is included in the main matter.

Afterword. Similar to the author's note in the front matter, an afterword is a statement from the author and may include background on the book's origins or updates to the material, which is common in classic works of literature. You might consider including an afterword instead of an author's note if the information contains spoilers or might somehow influence the reader in their experience of the main body of the manuscript. It is rare for a book to have both a conclusion and an afterword, and even rarer for one to have both a foreword and an afterword.

Acknowledgments. Thank everyone who helped you in the book-writing process, from the professionals you hired to the friends and family who supported or inspired you. Here's a quick checklist of people often thanked in the acknowledgments section:

- Editors
- Designers
- Publishers
- Agents and/or managers
- Any other contributors to your book
- If you worked with a ghostwriter, acknowledge them by thanking them for their editorial expertise. Check your legal agreement to make sure you meet any contractual obligations.

Remember that in the U.S., the word *acknowledgments* is most often spelled without an E after the G.

Discussion Questions. Many authors now opt to include a list of questions or prompts about the book. These can also be posted to the author's website and are useful in media kits or for book clubs and academic settings.

Appendix. Any supplemental information, such as recommended reading, citations, charts and diagrams, etc., should be included in an appendix, which itself can contain multiple sections. For researched nonfiction works, an appendix both bolsters the credibility of your manuscript and helps readers further explore the topic. In some cases, you might want to include full original source materials, such as correspondence, photos, or supporting documents.

Glossary. Although many books, even nonfiction ones, don't require a glossary, if your manuscript uses many unfamiliar terms, we recommend you include one, as we did in this book. As discussed in chapter 6, if you choose to work with an editor, you might find it worthwhile to ask them to compile a list of entries to include. As someone new to the material, the editor would be well suited to identifying terms that readers might want to easily look up. Then either you or the editor can write the definitions for the compiled list.

It's not just nonfiction books that can benefit from a glossary. Novels with unusual or newly coined wording often include a list of definitions. Perhaps the most famous example can be found in *A Clockwork Orange*, which relied heavily on Slavic-influenced vocabulary created by the author. Although the first edition of the book did not contain one, when the "restored" version of the book (containing a twenty-first chapter not included in the first U.S. printing) was released, author Anthony Burgess also opted to include a glossary.

Endnotes. If you decide to cite sources or provide annotations in your manuscript but prefer not to clutter your pages with footnotes, you can always create an endnotes, sometimes simply called notes, section. The material within the main text is noted with a superscript character, usually a numeral, just like a footnote would be, but the supporting citation goes at the back of the book rather than at the bottom of the page. Many authors prefer endnotes, as they believe they are less distracting to the reader. Your endnotes section can be a part of the appendix or its own section.

Bibliography. Include any and all references and sources used in the book, both to provide credibility and to allow readers to research further on their own. As with endnotes, the bibliography can be a part of the appendix or its own section. Unlike endnotes, a bibliography cites only sources, which are not referenced (e.g., via superscript characters) elsewhere in the book.

Index. If you are writing a nonfiction book, particularly one about a complex subject, consider including an index to help readers easily find information. Creating an index is a highly specialized task, although it's not impossible to do yourself, especially since Microsoft Word has an indexing feature.

When our first choice of an indexer was unavailable, Jenna decided to try her hand at it and discovered that it helped her notice some editing issues she might have otherwise overlooked. In preparation for creating the index, she reviewed several similar books to determine a style and rubric for entries, and also consulted the relevant section of *The Chicago Manual of Style*.

The most efficient way to create an index is to compile it as the absolute last task before your book is sent to press—after proofreading and interior design. Ted Goodman, a professional indexer who has worked as an editor and indexer for publishing companies Hachette Book Group and Sterling Publishing, advises not to make any changes to the manuscript once indexing has begun, as an index is based on a book's pagination. "Any edits or added material could change the flow of the book," says Goodman, "thereby requiring an indexer to start from scratch."

However, you might find the indexing process to be a good exercise for reviewing your book's content, as Jenna did. Just be aware that you may have to update the page numbers after the book has been laid out, which could require your indexer to charge an additional fee.

If you decide to handle indexing yourself, plan for this in your timeline, including time to learn how to use the feature in Microsoft Word, researching other books, and reviewing the manuscript multiple times while compiling the entries. Hiring a professional costs $25 to $40 hourly or $2.50 to $4 per page, with total costs averaging $300 to $1,500.

Author biography. This can be as short as one line or run for a few paragraphs, but the author bio usually doesn't run longer than one page. A headshot is optional. If you plan to include an author biography on the back cover of your book, you can skip this page altogether. Some authors use this page to continue their author bio from the back cover.

We recommend you have at least a few versions of your biography ready to go at any given time for use in press and marketing materials, bylines when guest-blogging or contributing articles, and numerous other purposes that will arise during the course of your publishing journey. When writing your bio, keep in mind that you'll likely be using the copy, or some version thereof, multiple times in multiple places.

You can also use this section to include links to your social media and website and to remind readers to rate and review your book.

Cited works and permissions page. Include any information that did not fit on the copyright page, if necessary.

Colophon. This brief text section contains the technical information related to your book, including details about the typeface, publisher, and/or printer. Although this is a somewhat archaic practice, some books still carry one, particularly if the design elements are special in some way, such as the use of a medieval font relevant to the book's subject matter. The most common place to find the colophon is on the last page of the back matter, but you could insert it in the front matter on the copyright page, if you so choose. An example colophon might read:

The text of [*Book Title*] is set in [interior book font]. The book cover was designed by [name of cover designer]. Interior design by [name of interior designer]. Manufactured by [printer] on [paper type and/or weight] paper. Limited edition of [number] copies.

You can include any or all of the above information, as you so choose and is relevant.

Organization of E-Books

In many cases, the e-book can be organized exactly as mentioned above, which is convenient because then you can use the same design files for both print and e-books. However, there are some reasons for organizing the e-book differently from the print version.

Length of free samples. Many retailers, including Amazon and Barnes & Noble, allow users to download a free sample of a book before purchasing. If you have a lot of material in the front matter, the sample won't include any main matter, the part that will hook readers and entice them to buy your book. If this is an issue, you may want to move some of your material to the back matter.

Promo pages. In an e-book, it's quite common for the page directly after the main matter to contain a call to action, such as signing up for your newsletter, rating the book, or learning about other books you've written. Such a page might not even exist in the print book, or this content might be rolled into About the Author or another page. But in an e-book, it's crucial that this page be included here since you risk having readers stop once they get to the end of the main matter.

Don't delay publishing your book just because you think you *need* to have any particular one of these sections, but don't rush the process if the section would truly elevate the quality of your book. Weigh the advantages of speed to market versus quality of product. If you cover the basics—title page, copyright page, table of contents—you're good to go. You can always add sections to future editions of your book, and can even call out the new material in future marketing. For example, if you land a foreword from somebody well known, the next edition can include a note on the cover that reads, "With a New Foreword by [Person's Name]."

If you still have a question about book sections, leaf through recently published books for ideas, with a focus on books in your genre, as this is the format readers of that demographic are accustomed to seeing. Every year, Sara makes it a point to buy the most talked-about *New York Times* bestsellers and flip through the pages to look for any new styles or trends. For example, just a few years ago, many of her clients wanted their acknowledgments at the front of their books. But since 2020, she's noticed this section being placed in the back matter, and now her authors are following suit. By doing your research, you're also ensuring that your book will look professional, which in turn makes *you* look professional.

Next Steps

- Write your author bio, as well as any variants you might need. (See Further Resources below.)
- Decide which sections your book will include and which will require hiring help so that you can get started creating the content.
- Create an outline of your book's sections to act as a checklist and begin work on completing them.

╪ Further Resources

Visit bookagogo.com/books/further-resources for the complete collection of all links in this book.

Companies, Individuals & Resources Mentioned in This Chapter

- Bowker (ISBN and barcode purchase): myidentifiers.com/identify-protect-your-book/isbn/buy-isbn
- Library of Congress Control Number (LCCN): loc.gov/publish/pcn
- Sugar Cookie Books: sugarcookiebooks.com

Additional Books on the Subject

- *Handbook of Indexing Techniques: A Guide for Beginning Indexers* by Linda K. Fetters: amazon.com/Handbook-Indexing-Techniques-Beginning-Indexers/dp/1573874612

How-Tos

- Creating a glossary: bstaveley.wordpress.com/2013/03/14/the-fuck-you-method-glossaries-in-speculative-fiction
- Creating an index in Microsoft Word: klariti.com/2018/01/28/how-to-create-an-index-in-ms-word-beginners-tutorial
- Creating a table of contents in Microsoft Word: support.microsoft.com/en-us/office/insert-a-table-of-contents-882e8564-0edb-435e-84b5-1d8552ccf0c0
- Creating free samples of your book:
  - ○ Amazon: kdp.amazon.com/en_US/help/topic/G200644250
  - ○ Barnes & Noble: help-press.barnesandnoble.com/hc/en-us/articles/5357648612763-Custom-Sample-FAQs
- Writing an author bio: bookbeaver.co.uk/blog/write-author-bio

Preface, Author's Note, Foreword & Introduction

- Difference between: laeditorsandwritersgroup.com/preface-foreword-introduction-vs-authors-note

CHAPTER

12

Designing Your Book Cover

When paired with the right title, the cover is your most impactful marketing component, as it's usually the reader's introduction to your book—whether it's on the bookshelf of a brick-and-mortar store or in an online search, where the cover is often displayed as a very small graphic, called a thumbnail. That initial interaction can be a make-or-break moment: If the cover doesn't entice, a potential reader might pass it by and choose a competitor's title.

A well-designed cover accurately reflects the book's content, using visual cues to convey the genre, tone, and even quality of the writing. If a cover looks cheap or unprofessional, a reader might decide the book isn't worth their time or money. This is one reason why, if you have a limited overall budget, we recommend you reserve much of that to hire a professional to design the cover. You can always use a junior designer for tasks such as resizing and creating marketing materials with the designs your more seasoned professional creates.

It's important to start your cover design after you have a finalized title, subtitle, and a somewhat finalized manuscript so you have a clear idea of how you want your book to represent its contents. As mentioned in chapter 7, even changing one word in your title could throw off your entire design.

If you have signed with a traditional publisher, they—not you—dictate the design, using their own team and budget. Although the publisher will usually run the cover by you, you most likely will not be very involved in the design process, unless they agree to a clause stating otherwise in your contract. It's not that the publisher doesn't value your input; it's that they see your book as their product, not your art.

As companies that sell products often do, publishers sometimes put the covers through market research, testing designs with potential readers before ultimately deciding which one will drive the most sales. Even if you aren't involved in the publisher's design process, you can still run cover ideas by your editor while you're working on the manuscript. Your editor may be able to help pinpoint specific scenes that are cover-worthy and narrow down a set of ideas to float by your publisher.

As mentioned in chapter 9, which covers the different publishing options, self-published authors have complete control over the look of their books. That said, there are still industry rules and guidelines that you should be aware of. For example, your acceptance into certain distribution channels, such as some airport stores, relies on a specific look for your cover. If having your book carried by one of these outlets is a priority goal, you should partner with a book distributor who works with those retailers so they can advise you on creating a design that meets these guidelines. (More about distribution in chapter 15.)

Working With a Designer

As with most creative processes, designing a book cover can take many forms. Sometimes an author pictures their cover right from the start, gives direction to a designer, and receives a design that reflects precisely what they envisioned. But more often than not, authors go through several rounds of creative exploration and multiple design iterations before landing on a cover that best conveys their book to the target audience.

Before signing a contract with a designer, find out how they work: what the process looks like, how long it will take, how many mockups the fee includes, etc. Request to see books they've designed, particularly those within your genre, and clarify the following:

- If the developer allows for revisions once the design is fully laid out and, if so, how many.

- If they can design the book for both print and digital formats and if they are familiar with requirements for different outlets, such as Amazon. If you plan on offering an audiobook, send them the cover requirements for this format, and ask if they can create this as well.

- If your budget allows, ask if the designer can provide imagery for marketing materials, such as an image of your book lying flat on a table, your book standing on a shelf, a stack of your books, etc. You may also want to ask if they can assist with creating marketing assets, such as ads, one-sheets, etc. It's not necessary that your cover designer be able to perform these additional tasks, as you can always hire a junior designer to handle them, but it does make it more convenient to work with just one person.

Many designers present three to five front-cover mockups as part of their fee. After you submit feedback, they tweak and edit the designs until you arrive at a final front cover. The designer then mocks up the full cover—front and back. See Appendix K for a diagram of the elements of a book cover.

If you do pay for a selection of front-cover concepts, you may want to ask your author platform for feedback. Post three of your top cover choices on your social media channels and ask your followers to weigh in by commenting and voting on their favorite. Just remember to take it all with a grain of salt.

You don't have to give every comment equal weight—or even listen to them all. But if a comment resonates with you or sounds like something you've been feeling but haven't been able to articulate, don't ignore it. Also look for patterns, such as several comments saying the cover conveys a different genre. If multiple sources are saying the same thing, take the time to consider whether the issue needs to be addressed.

One of Sara's designers once told her that designing a book cover without guidance feels like being blindfolded, given a bow and arrow, and told to hit a bull's-eye on a moving target. It's almost impossible to hit the mark if the author doesn't first do some of the legwork and provide specific direction. All too often, authors simply say they want their cover to "pop" and then lay all the responsibility in the designer's lap without any guidance. Designers, as talented as they may be, can't read your mind, so you need to convey what your book is about and provide background about your aesthetic likes and dislikes.

In Appendix L, Michelle Manley of Graphique Design Co. describes the steps an author should take before they provide guidance to their designer. The appendix also includes a template and tips for developing a creative brief (a document that explains in detail your preferences, audience, and goals), including how to identify your book's genre and what specific design options you should consider, such as fonts and colors. We used this very creative brief, crafted by creative director Lluvia Arras, when developing the cover of this book, which was also designed by Arras. In the creative brief, include the elevator pitch you developed in chapter 7 to provide more direction.

Although the tips in the appendix apply mainly to self-publishing authors, you can keep them in mind if your traditional publisher is willing to include you in the creative process. If you are hybrid publishing, your publisher will walk you through these steps and then handle the conversations with the designers. Any fees your hybrid publisher charges should include design costs.

Cover Structure

The structure of a book cover can be just as important as the design. Ensuring that each piece is properly placed and executed is essential for marketing and sales.

Front cover. This should include the title, the subtitle (if you have one), and your author name. If you have a rock-star foreword or book blurb, you may want to include this as well.

Spine. This also carries the title and author name and also sometimes the logo of the publishing company. Include the subtitle if space allows. The text of the spine should run from top to bottom, so that if your book is lying face up on a table, the title on the spine is right side up. This is the opposite of the format in Europe, where the title on the spine is upside down when the book is face up.

Back cover. This section varies, depending on whether the book is paperback or hardcover. On a print book without a dust jacket, the back cover is the only real estate you have for marketing copy. A typical back includes a headline (an eye-catching hook), a synopsis, and around three blurbs, if you have them. (See chapter 10.) The back cover should also include the ISBN, barcode, and the full name and logo of your publishing company. You can purchase both the barcode and ISBN directly from Bowker, who then attaches the book metadata to both. There are resources that offer barcodes for free, but Bowker is the industry standard and won't break the bank. Some online publishing companies, such as Amazon KDP (kdp.amazon.com) and IngramSpark (ingramspark.com), generate free barcodes if you use their services. For a more in-depth dive on barcodes, see Further Resources.

If you like, you can also list the BISAC categories of your book and the book price above or below the barcode. However, as we mention in the chapter 15 section titled "Codes, Categories & Prices," we advise not including the price on the cover. Some back covers also include an author bio and photo, but if you don't have enough room, you can include these in the back matter.

In addition to these three sections, some hardcover books have additional space for content on the flaps of the dust jacket, allowing you to dedicate your back cover to a catchy headline, your blurbs, and/or an abbreviated book synopsis. The front flap then contains a longer synopsis, while the back flap usually contains the author's bio and photo—just make sure the bio and photo appear in only one place on the cover, not on both the flap and back. If you included your biographical information in an interior book section, as we mentioned in chapter 11, you can instead use this flap for more blurbs or a continuation of the synopsis. We've included a diagram of a hardcover dust jacket in Appendix K.

Reviewing the Cover

It's generally more efficient to design the cover of your book before the interior. Once you have a final cover, provide that to your interior designer, who can then incorporate the cover's design elements—fonts, colors, imagery, iconography, etc.—into the interior to achieve a coherent overall book, rather than two independently designed pieces. (Cover designers and interior designers are often separate contractors, as the skill sets are quite different. Interior design is discussed further in the next chapter.)

On rare occasions, your cover design might cause you to rethink some of your book's contents. Over the years, Manley has worked on projects where the cover design conversation gave the author a renewed perspective on their book or inspired them to write new content, which in turn resulted in their changing the storyline to better fit the look of the cover.

Manley was once approached by an author who had already completed the writing and editing process for his memoir. As he was a new client, she asked many questions: *What do you like to do? What are your interests?*

What is the purpose of the book? Why did you write the book? Do you have any goals for publishing? As the two got to know each other, he told Manley that he came across some of his old journals while cleaning out his garage, and it struck him that his children and grandchildren might be interested in some of the stories. This gave Manley the idea to design the book to look like one of his journals, inside and out. The author loved the concept, as he felt it would make the book more authentic and personal, giving his family a glimpse into his everyday thoughts and feelings. However, the design also meant the manuscript, which had already been copyedited, would have to undergo drastic changes—requiring additional time and money. In the end, the concept was important enough to the author that he decided to make that investment.

Because of this experience, Manley prefers to speak with authors as early in the writing process as possible. Even if she doesn't start the design process for months (or even years), having a talk sooner rather than later can help shape the overall end product and alleviate wasted time and/or effort. Beyond that, she finds that such a conversation motivates authors and gives them extra time to plan and budget.

Once the cover is laid out, it is critical to proof it or hire a proofreader to do so—and proof it more than once:

1. After it's been laid out
2. Before you send it to the printer
3. When you get the printed proof
4. Before you go to print

Refer to Appendix E for a design proofreading checklist, which includes items specific to covers. Both Sara and Jenna have, on numerous occasions, caught last-minute cover issues right before a book was set to print.

The last step in the cover design process is to get a physical proof, or printed copy. Although this is done after the interior is laid out, we mention it here because it also affects finalizing the cover. Many authors get impatient and want to bypass this step, but we strongly urge against it. Having a proof is incredibly important because sometimes things just look different once you're holding the actual physical book. In particular, colors often differ from what you see on a computer screen, so much so that it's not uncommon for an author to change the cover's color once they see the proof copy. This color variation can occur for many reasons, from the calibration of the computer monitor to the printing process to the type of material the cover is printed on. With so many variables, your best bet is to review the proof.

One of Sara's authors had a cover design that was mostly one color: turquoise. After receiving the first proof, she saw just how different the printed turquoise was compared with the color she saw on the computer. Sara and the author sat for hours reviewing shades of turquoise to get the color of the book cover as close as possible to the version she liked. She eventually decided to invest in four separate printed proof copies—each with a different shade of turquoise. And it's a good thing she made that investment, as the chosen color proved to be integral in her branding: It dictated her website design, business cards, and every single piece of marketing collateral.

Once your cover is finalized, have the designer turn over all source files (e.g., fonts, images, and raw design files) in addition to a front cover JPEG and a print-ready PDF. (Make sure this step is stated in your contract.) Because you will most likely need these for designing other marketing materials, you want to secure them now so that you don't have to hunt down your designer at a later date.

Timing & Costs

How long the cover design takes depends on how quickly you and your designer settle on a direction. This is one of those instances where being decisive can speed up the process and often save you money.

Expect a full cover design to take anywhere from two weeks to two months, depending on how many changes you have and the design style. Manley says she spends an average of six to eight weeks on a cover for fiction or nonfiction, while children's books can take upwards of six months, depending on the complexity of the illustration. Rushing the process can introduce unnecessary errors, and when you get this close, you want to ensure a smooth finish.

Your budget might dictate the kinds and quality of your design. Authors with limited funds should do as much of the design research themselves as possible so that they can communicate very specifically what they want. Doing this exploration with your designer, rather than on your own, could inflate your costs by hundreds or even thousands of dollars.

Also note that different types of designs command different costs. Asking for a custom-illustrated cover is going to be much more expensive than a simple one-color cover with bold type. Be honest with your designer and tell them how much you can comfortably afford to spend. Then ask if what you're looking for can be achieved within that budget. If not, ask what types of ideas could be executed within your price range.

If the designer you first interview doesn't seem like the right fit, feel free to explore other options. Just as with assembling your editing team, you want to ensure your designer "gets" you and doesn't just interpret your book the way they feel is best without taking your ideas into consideration.

Next Steps

- Decide if your book will be sold in any specialty outlets, such as airport bookstores, and research the requirements so you can provide them to your designer.
- Complete the steps in Appendix L and fill out the creative brief, then submit these to your designer.

- Research and interview cover designers.
- Get feedback on cover designs from your demographic, author platform, and any marketing professionals you will be working with.
- Choose a cover design that speaks loudly and clearly to the audience identified in your BAGG.
- Have the designer turn over all source files, as well as a front cover JPEG and a print-ready PDF.

Further Resources

Visit bookagogo.com/books/further-resources for the complete collection of all links in this book.

Companies, Individuals & Resources Mentioned in This Chapter
- **Michelle Manley of Graphique Design Co.:** graphiquedesignco.com
- **Lluvia Arras:** lluviaarras.com
- **Bowker:** myidentifiers.com
- **BISAC Categories:** bisg.org/BISAC-Subject-Codes-main

Barcodes
- "All About Barcodes for Books": thedietitianeditor.com/barcodes-for-books

Find a Designer
- **99designs by Vista:** 99designs.com
- **Fiverr:** fiverr.com
- **Reedsy:** reedsy.com
- **Upwork:** upwork.com

CHAPTER

13

Designing Your Book Interior

O nce your manuscript has been proofread and your cover is nearly done, you can begin working on the interior design, sometimes referred to as the interior layout. The cover and interior are two parts of the same whole, so they need to look as such.

An interior book designer often uses the same or similar fonts as those on your cover to design elements such as chapter and text headers, subheaders, and title pages. For this reason, be sure you are happy with the elements of the cover design so that once your interior designer begins, they can ensure a complementary look. Note that the interior designer will most likely *not* be the same person who designs your cover, as their skill sets are quite distinct and often involve the use of completely different software.

Interior design involves such tasks as setting the margins, manipulating the text to avoid awkward spacing issues, and making design choices such as fonts and placement of page numbers. Appendix M includes a diagram of some of the most common interior design elements. Note that although *typesetting* refers to an antiquated method of arranging type for print, some graphic designers still use the term to refer to the word-based portion of their work, so you may still hear someone refer to a book as being "typeset."

Manuscript Changes

It's crucial that you sign off on the final manuscript before you give it to an interior designer. If you start to rewrite entire paragraphs, move sections around, insert new imagery, etc., it can greatly delay the time it takes the designer to complete the layout—not to mention what it could do to your budget. Smaller changes, such as editing a few words or fixing a typo, most likely won't be a problem. However, every designer has a personal limit as to how many of these adjustments they'll make before they start to charge for their additional time.

Even a seemingly small change can have a domino effect. Further Resources contains a link to a video that shows how minor changes can shift all the following text of a chapter, requiring it to be redesigned. This information isn't intended to dissuade you from making changes. If something *has* to be changed, it has to be changed. Just make sure the overall contents are as finalized as possible before you begin the interior layout process, to better ensure that your designer can easily manage any necessary modifications.

If you're considering creating an audiobook (discussed more in the next chapter), you may want to record it before you begin the interior design process, as reading and/or hearing it aloud might bring to light changes you want to make. So, by recording the audiobook at this stage, you might save yourself some headache during interior design. If you're not planning to publish an audiobook, consider reading your manuscript out loud to catch any such issues.

Interior Design Considerations

When choosing the designer for your book interior, make sure to hire one proficient in Adobe InDesign, the industry standard for book layout. Although you could use other software, such as Microsoft Word, few offer the advanced features of InDesign, which was created specifically for desktop publishing. As with hiring any professional, ask to see samples of other books the designer has worked on, then ask about their process.

Although interior design is usually simpler than designing the cover, you can use many of the same exploratory tips we provide in Appendix L, although there are others to consider, listed below. As with the cover, take note of what you do and don't like, and relay these preferences to your interior designer. These considerations include the following:

Interior formatting. Review other titles in the same genre as your book. Flip through the pages and notice what you like—and don't—about the design, such as the size of the font and how tightly paragraphs are spaced. Your readers will be spending a lot of time within these pages, so you want them to look as inviting as possible.

Chapter heads. The beginnings of chapters have their own unique style. Any content that precedes the actual chapter (such as the chapter name and number, an illustration, or a quote) is known as the chapter head. The design of chapter heads varies, such as starting halfway down the page or using drop caps (overly large first letters of the first sentence, often spanning several lines). A visual representation of some of the more common style options is provided in Appendix M.

Layout of additional materials. If you plan to include photos, graphics, or illustrations, research ways other books handle such materials for ideas on how these elements can be laid out. When interviewing interior designers, communicate which, if any, elements you want to include, such as charts, diagrams, or photos alongside text. Not only do some book designers feel more comfortable than others with such layouts, but there could also be a large difference in price for the design and printing.

If your main matter includes photos or images, find out what your prospective printer requires to print these. Will they print only on glossy paper and, if so, what does that cost? Do they print low-resolution images, or must every image meet a specific DPI requirement? Will they require printing to be done in signatures (see next paragraph)? A designer needs to know all of these requirements before they begin. For example, glossy paper is usually thicker and might require your cover designer to adjust the size of the spine, while printing in signatures means your interior designer must carefully plot where pages with images need to be placed within the book.

Printing in signatures is when a printer uses a configuration to lay out pages on a single large sheet in such a way that, when the sheet is folded, the pages appear in the proper order. (See Appendix O for a visual as to how books with signatures are laid out.) When a printer uses signatures, the final page count of the book must be divisible by a certain number. While a signature can be as low as 2 or 4, it is more common to have signatures of 8, 16, or 32 pages. Any inserts, such as photo spreads, must comprise a number of pages that can be divided into the signature. For example, if a printer says they print in signatures of 32, a photo section could be 4 or 8 pages, but not 5 or 6. The section could then go between any of the main signatures, so that a sample layout might be: 32 pages of text + 32 pages of text + 8-page photo insert + 32 pages of text + 32 pages of text. In this scenario, the photo insert could potentially land in the middle of a stream of text, rather than at a natural stopping point, such as the end of a chapter. Although some authors might find this undesirable, it's actually quite common, even in traditionally published books.

Note that the photo pages do not also have to fall within the total signature printing requirement, meaning a photo page doesn't have to be 32 pages long but does have to be divisible by 8. That means that the insert should be, at a minimum, 8 pages. It's also worth noting that photo inserts are typically not included in the total length of the printed book, meaning that they are not taken into account when the printer calculates the signatures. For this reason, when receiving a printing quote, you have to be clear that you need a quote that accounts for "X total text pages" + "X total photo pages." For example, a 320-page book could be printed in 10 text signatures of 32 plus 1 photo insert of 8.

Kathy Leingang of Forum Communications Printing suggests that authors have a conversation with a potential printing partner before they get too far into the project. "I can't stress this enough: You are not alone in this process," Leingang says. "A printer can give you suggestions before you get started with design, which can improve the overall look and quality of your book and possibly even provide cost-saving options."

In the course of his decade designing books, Ghislain Viau of Creative Publishing Book Design has compiled a slew of tips to help authors prepare for working with an interior book designer. The following are a selection of the most common pitfalls to avoid when designing the interior of your book:

- When requesting a quote for an interior design, send the designer your manuscript in the most final form possible. Be upfront about your need for charts, images, or graphics, as including these can change the interior designer's timeline and, thus, quote. If you receive a quote too soon and end up adding text or imagery, your designer may provide a drastically different estimate once you submit the final manuscript.
- Perform all proofreading prior to submitting your manuscript for design so that your interior designer does not have to navigate a multitude of changes once the manuscript has been laid out. As mentioned in chapter 6, if you have the budget to perform a proofread *before* your book is designed, it may save you a lot of headache (and even some money) versus proofreading everything after the book

is designed. The money you think you're saving by skipping this proofread may end up going to the designer if the final proof of the designed book requires many changes.

- Be open to potential layout modifications. If you have a chart formatted in a Word document, for example, it may jump to another page or need to be split across two pages once the manuscript is properly laid out. Your designer can advise on the best look for graphics once layout begins.

Designing an E-Book

The tips given thus far apply mostly to print interior design. Authors who decide to move forward with only an e-book design may not need to hire a professional interior designer, as many of the above-mentioned elements are likely not available for that format. Viau refers to such situations as "e-book conversion projects" rather than interior formatting. However, the quality of the final e-book layout depends heavily on how well the Word document is formatted, so it might still be worth hiring a designer to work their magic, even if it's just in a few key locations, such as chapter heads. This is one reason that Viau prefers to format a print version before he tackles an e-book.

While the design of an e-book is not as complex as that of a physical book, it does have its own set of considerations, such as linking of references or maintaining the same design elements as the print version, such as drop caps in chapter heads. Keep in mind that no matter the style you choose, some design elements may not translate well, depending on the device used to read your e-book. Therefore, it's important to adjust your expectations, as the print and digital versions of your book may look quite different. In addition to that, some interior designers are more skilled at formatting e-books than others, so be sure to ask for samples before you sign the contract.

There are two types of e-book formatting: fixed and flowable. In a fixed layout, the interior is consistent across all devices: It looks the same whether viewed on a Kindle, tablet, mobile phone, etc. This option is better suited for a book with a lot of images, graphs, or charts, such as cookbooks, children's books, or coffee-table books. While you should always consider what's best for your particular book, there are several disadvantages to publishing a fixed-format e-book, including:

- They are typically more expensive to produce and update if changes need to be made.
- Some retailers do not accept fixed-format e-books from self-publishers. Even if they do, not all e-readers support this format, so you'll face limited distribution regardless of whether the retailer allows you to list the title on their site.
- Text might be difficult to read or even illegible on a smaller device, such as a phone, as the only way to read the page would be to zoom in; the device will not adjust the page to your screen. On an e-reader, such as a Kindle, zooming might not even be an option.

A flowable format, on the other hand, is one in which the content is responsive: The pages adjust according to the device and its orientation. Because of this responsiveness, a flowable format can handle only a limited number of font selections and design elements. You also have little control over the text display, as the purpose of the format is to cede this control to the reader. As with the fixed format, there are some disadvantages to a flowable e-book:

- It is not a desirable option for books with a lot of artistic elements, images, or charts.

- As mentioned above, limited font options are available. Even if you are able to use the same font as in your print book, readers can override that option.
- Because the content adjusts to the device of each screen, you cannot have complete control over the layout.

Despite these disadvantages, the majority of e-books are designed with a flowable format due to the more economical pricing and the compatibility across devices. Please see Appendix N for a side-by-side comparison of the layout of an e-book versus its print counterpart.

Beyond flowable versus fixed, you may also want to ask your designer which file format they will convert your book (.epub, .mobi, or both) into. As of the writing of this book, Amazon announced it would no longer accept the .mobi version of books (their former long-time preference) and suggested that authors convert their files to .epub and reupload to their KDP account. Since some services, such as OverDrive (overdrive.com) and Draft2Digital (draft2digital.com), still accept the .mobi format, it might make sense to have both on hand from your designer. Although you may come across other file formats, the only one you really need is an .epub file, as it is the most professional-looking, universally accepted format and the file size is smaller.

Proofing the Interior

Once your interior is finalized, the next step is to hire a design proofreader, a professional with a completely different skill set than any of the other editors you may have worked with to date. A design proofreader reviews such details as:

- Consistency in page numbers and chapter titles in the table of contents and throughout the book

- Correct use of blank pages
- Making sure there are no widows, orphans, or bad breaks

Authors who opt to proof their own book layouts can refer to our design proofreading checklist in Appendix E.

If you plan to publish a hard-copy version of your book, as opposed to just an e-book, now is the time to order the proof copy mentioned in the previous chapter. As with the cover, the interior might have a different appearance in the print version than it does on the computer screen. Your font might be smaller than you'd expected, your margins could seem too close to the edge of the paper, or your interior colors could look entirely different due to the paper being used or style of printing, such as digital printing versus offset, which can change the brightness of colors on the page. (More about printing and distribution in chapter 15.) Plus, holding a real-life version of your book is quite an experience. It puts the whole journey in perspective and lets you see that the end is now within sight.

Timing & Costs

As far as overall timing, interior design can take anywhere from two to six weeks, depending on how long or complex your manuscript is, while receiving a proof copy can take anywhere from a few days to a week. Take time to review and sit with the proof before you give the printer the green light.

If you've given yourself enough time before you release your book to the public, usually two to three months, you might choose to send out advance reader copies, or ARCs, before you finalize the printing. This is commonly done by traditional publishers, and many self-published authors do it as part of their PR and marketing strategy. Advance readers often include book reviewers, celebrities, librarians, journalists, and any other experts in the author's field who can provide testimonials or feedback.

ARCs can also be used for submissions to book contests. After the entire book is designed, ask your designer to create an ARC copy by adding a disclaimer stating, "Advance Reader Copy—Not for Resale," either on the front cover or on the interior front page. Alternatively, you could put a sticker on the book with the same disclaimer or include a note stating the enclosed book is an early review copy, not meant for circulation. You can then print a short run, usually twenty-five to fifty copies, and send the ARCs to beta readers, reviewers, friends, and family members. This strategy can help you wrangle blurbs (discussed in chapter 10) and give you the opportunity to make any last-minute changes found by your advance readers.

⌁ Next Steps

- Read your manuscript out loud, or have your computer read it while you listen, to help catch any errors.
- Ensure your manuscript is finalized before sending it to the interior designer.
- Decide if your layout will include elements beyond text, such as charts and photos.
- Research other books and review the illustration in Appendix M to decide on design elements, such as chapter heads.
- Review Appendix M for tips on preparing to work with an interior book designer.
- Research and interview interior designers.
- Make sure your interior reflects your BAGG as much as your cover does.
- Send ARCs to advance readers if this is part of your marketing strategy.
- Hire a design proofreader or refer to our design proofing checklist in Appendix E.
- Review the printed proof of the entire book.

Further Resources

Visit bookagogo.com/books/further-resources for the complete collection of all links in this book.

Companies, Individuals & Resources Mentioned in This Chapter

- Ghislain Viau of Creative Publishing Book Design: creativepublishingdesign.com
- Kathy Leingang of Forum Communications Printing: forumprinting.com
- Video showing small edit affecting interior design: Watch at bookagogo.com/books/further-resources

Producing Your Audiobook

When planning your book journey, you may not have even considered an audiobook. But we highly recommend you do, as audiobooks are becoming increasingly popular. Consider some of these impressive facts:

- In 2019, audiobook sales increased by 16% in the United States and generated more than $1.2 billion.[34]
- The global audiobook market is predicted to grow to $15 billion by 2027, almost quadruple that of 2020.[35, 36]
- When the 2020 pandemic hit, print-book sales actually plunged due to store closures and lack of distribution infrastructure.[37] Having e-books and audiobooks available for download allowed some stores and authors to keep their heads above water.
- In 2019, the Audio Publishers Association (APA) reported that 50% of Americans twelve and older had listened to an audiobook.[38]

All of these stats point to a trend: Audiobooks are a growing segment of the publishing industry. However, certain genres aren't well suited for audiobooks. Cookbooks, reference books, travel guides, or even books that rely heavily on imagery, such as children's picture books, often don't work well in an audio format. Narratives, on the other hand, are perfect for the medium. Memoirs, novels, romance, self-help, professional development, motivational, and business are all genres that often find success as audiobooks.

Benefits of an Audiobook

Although creating an audiobook isn't a requirement, there are several reasons you might want to invest in one:

1. **Simplicity.** It's not terribly difficult to create. You've already done the hard part (writing the book), so you might as well get more bang for your buck.

2. **Cost.** Even if you outsource the whole project, it's not very expensive, relative to other costs associated with publishing. However, if you have more time than money on your hands, you could produce it yourself. Narrating and editing the files requires a bit of a learning curve but not much in terms of equipment. Just keep in mind that not all authors' voices lend themselves to narration. If DIY doesn't work out, hire professionals to get you over the finish line. You can even take a hybrid approach: Pay a couple hundred bucks for the equipment, which you could also use for a podcast or future audiobooks, and then hire an audio engineer to mix and master the files.

3. **Sales.** Not offering an audiobook could cause you to miss out on a potential audience. Some readers just prefer to listen, while others' lifestyles make listening a more viable choice. Many drivers and travelers prefer books to music, while other bibliophiles enjoy the efficiency of working out their body and mind at the same time.

In addition to those reasons, if someone has a disability such as dyslexia, being able to listen to your book is a more accessible way for them to enjoy your content.

4. **Repeat purchases.** You might get individual readers to buy multiple copies, particularly those who use Amazon's Whispersync feature, which allows users to read or listen to a book on different mediums seamlessly. You can finish chapter 2 on your Kindle, and when you open the book on Audible (audible.com, the app for Amazon's audiobook division), the app will pick right up at chapter 3. Having Whispersync enabled for your book could potentially mean more sales, as readers would need to buy two formats to use this feature.

5. **Marketing.** As with an e-book, having an audiobook gives you more options for freebies and giveaways. If you plan on making podcasts part of your marketing strategy, giving away audiobooks to listeners is the perfect complement for such an audience.

6. **Competition.** Audiobooks are still a growing market, and many authors don't want to invest the time or money to produce one. That means if you do, you could grow your audience larger and faster than the authors in your category who opted out of an audiobook release.

Working With Audiobook Professionals

As of the release of this book, it takes ACX (acx.com, Audiobook Creation Exchange), Amazon's service for creating audiobooks, ten to thirty days to review audiobook files, so if you're thinking about producing one, we recommend getting started as soon as your manuscript is final so you can release it at the same time as the print version.

If you don't plan to produce the entire audiobook yourself, you may need to hire the following professionals: a narrator, a sound engineer to mix and master your audio, and somebody to upload the completed files, such as yourself, your narrator, or a self-publishing expert. As we mentioned in chapter 12, you'll also need files of your cover formatted specifically for audiobook sites, which your graphic designer should be able to provide.

Before you begin, your sound engineer and narrator should discuss each other's requirements so there are no surprises. Different audiobook distribution services may have their own technical requirements, so be sure to visit their sites ahead of time and download any pertinent information to share with your production team.

Whether or not you are the narrator of the audiobook, you should read your book out loud, as mentioned in the chapter on designing book interiors, as doing so may lead you to make changes based on how the manuscript sounds. There may also be parts of the book that don't translate to audio, such as charts, images, or notes for the reader to refer to other sections of the book. Listen to a variety of audiobooks within your genre to see how each handles these situations. Remember, you can likely borrow audiobooks from your local library without even leaving the house, so you don't need to spend a lot of money for this research.[39] For example, you may choose not to include a preface or acknowledgments in the audio version, although ACX requires you to at least record credits that state who contributed to the production.

Narrating Your Own Book

If you do decide to narrate the audiobook yourself, follow these tips from Dave Margalotti, who has more than thirty years of commercial voiceover experience. Margalotti has been heard on-air in New York City, Boston, Long Island, and other markets around the country, and has done freelance audiobook narration for Cherry Hill Publishing, Beacon Audiobooks, and ACX.

- **Know what you're getting into.** Recording an audiobook is not as easy as it sounds, and you want to strive for a professional-sounding final product. Ask yourself: Do you have the equipment and the environment to create a professional-sounding recording of your book? Are you the right person to bring your book to life? Be honest with yourself—you might be a great writer, but that doesn't mean you're equipped or have the skill to give your manuscript a voice. All too often, Margalotti hears from authors who thought they could just sit down in front of a microphone and read through their book—only to discover it was far more difficult and time-consuming than they'd expected.

- **Rehearse, rehearse, rehearse.** Your recording environment should be noise-free with good acoustics—no echoes or reverberation. Make practice recordings and listen with high-quality headphones or speakers. Listen to it in the environment in which your audience is likely to listen (in the car, on a walk, etc.). Don't just listen to the words but the recording as a whole: Is there background noise? How is your pacing? Are there extraneous sounds from breathing, lip smacking, mouth clicking, keyboard tapping, etc.? Any of these noises will negatively impact the quality of your audiobook by distracting the listener and drawing attention to the amateur production values.

- **Don't just read—narrate.** Narrating an audiobook and bringing it to life does not simply mean reading it out loud. Unless you have honed your skills, you'll sound like you're reading, which can be tedious to listen to. You need to be able to hold the listener's attention and pull them into the narrative with nothing more than just your voice. That means understanding the nuances of pacing and inflection and making sure you come across as authentic, relatable, warm, and engaging.

If you are set on narrating your own book, record a small sample and ask a trusted friend, family member, or colleague to give you an honest and independent evaluation. It's okay if narration isn't your gift, but if that's the case, consider working with an experienced professional.

Production Styles

Audiobooks have traditionally been treated as books, not as productions or podcasts, meaning little use is made of music, sound effects, or other audio theatrics. Aside from the extra cost, the inclusion of music and sound effects renders your book ineligible for Whispersync, mentioned above. But if Whispersync isn't a priority, feel free to include any production values that might enhance your book.

Michele Cobb, executive director of the Audio Publishers Association (APA), has said she has started to see "full-cast performances with sound effects and music [becoming] a larger part of the landscape." [40] As a case in point, at the 2020 Audie Awards, the Oscars of audiobooks, the award for Best Audio Drama went to the recording of Tony Kushner's *Angels in America,* a full-blown oracular spectacular complete with musical score. That doesn't mean you have to hire a full Broadway cast and orchestra, but it does show the range of production values—and budgets—out there.

Audiobook Copyrights

If you are working with a traditional publisher, make sure to discuss your audiobook rights before you sign a contract. If your publisher owns the audiobook rights, they often license the book to a number of audiobook publishers, who then decide whether or not to publish it. This means that you could be waiting a while for the audiobook to get picked up, and you won't even have the option to publish it yourself if the publishers give it a pass. However, if you own the audiobook rights, you have complete control over how to handle this version of your book. (Again, we are not legal experts, so be sure to have an attorney review any contracts, including those with narrators and sound engineers.)

Many hybrid publishers operate the same way: They negotiate the audiobook rights in the contract and, when it comes time to publish, they record and release the audiobook. However, they may have their own in-house narrators or production teams, as opposed to licensing the book. Remember to review their audiobook process and abilities when negotiating your contract.

If you are self-publishing or hiring a company like Redwood Publishing, the audiobook falls more into the do-it-yourself category. Most of Sara's authors record the book on their own at a professional studio, hire the studio to produce the files, and pay Redwood to upload the files and make the audiobook available for sale.

ACX

Love it or hate it, no discussion of audiobooks would be complete without discussing ACX, the marketplace for narrators and authors to connect and record books. ACX is the back-end name of Audible, Amazon's audiobook app, which is where most readers—some 90% of the market—find and purchase audiobooks.[41] Owing to this monopoly and other issues, some authors, including journalist Cory Doctorow, do not agree with ACX's policies and so do not publish their audiobooks there.

For those who decide to go the ACX route, it's very convenient to have so many resources available in one place. For authors eager to get the job done and who know what they want, ACX could be the ticket. However, this is an Amazon product, so the company keeps tight reins on the interactions. For example, all communication between you and your potential narrator is done within the ACX messaging system.

When you prepare to launch your title, ACX gives you the option of receiving royalties under either their exclusive or nonexclusive royalty program. Once you have made your selection, it cannot be easily changed. If you are caught breaking the exclusivity agreement—and, trust us, Amazon always finds out—they can discontinue your audiobook. If you decide to go nonexclusive, there are other non-Amazon services to release e-books, some of the most common of which are Rakuten Kobo (kobo.com), Voices by INaudio (voicesbyinaudio.com), OverDrive, and Draft2Digital. For more about the pros and cons of ACX exclusivity, see Further Resources.

Timing & Costs

Audiobooks take time to produce—from the actual recording to the sound mixing and editing to the upload process. ACX approval times also vary: Before the pandemic, turnaround took approximately six weeks; at the time of this book's publication, the ACX site says that the approval process should take around ten to thirty business days. However, if your files are flagged for problems during the review process, you must start from the beginning. For this reason, we recommend that authors producing their own audiobooks start by uploading a test chapter for an ACX quality-control check. This can help identify any issues that need to be fixed before you push the completed file through for a full review.

Outside of the ACX review timeline, you should factor in one to two months for the creation of your audiobook. This allows time for you to find a narrator or, if you decide to narrate it yourself, to procure equipment, record, and work with an engineer to master the files. As always, anticipate delays and challenges—even mundane ones. One author Sara worked with had to postpone the start of his audiobook narration by two weeks due to his allergies acting up.

ACX reports that one finished hour of audio—the standard for calculating rates in the audiobook industry—is the result of about six hours of work.[42] A good rule of thumb is to calculate 9,000 words as one finished hour.[43] ACX estimates that it takes about two hours to narrate what will become one finished hour, which then requires an average of three hours to edit and master. At that point, you should review the final recorded file to ensure you are satisfied with the quality and to determine if anything needs to be rerecorded or remixed.

Audiobook editors charge an average of $75 to $100 per finished hour to edit and master an audiobook, so a six-hour audiobook would run $450 to $600. Narrators, who often build editing into their fees, run $150 to $250 per finished hour, which amounts to $900 to $1,500 for a six-hour audiobook. Note that not all narrators are editors, and vice versa, so you either have to hire someone for each task or find someone who can perform both as part of their fee (some narrators, for example, already have teams of editors).

When interviewing potential hires, ask about their previous audiobook experience, if they have voice samples for you to listen to, and whether or not they have formatted audiobook files. And, as always, confirm what services their fee includes.

Next Steps

- If you chose Income as your BAGG, producing an audiobook is a must; you more than likely should produce one if you chose Reputation. For all other goals, go with your gut.
- Read your book out loud to catch any changes you want to make before sending the manuscript to your interior designer.
- Identify which professionals, if any, you need to hire.
- Make sure you begin the audiobook process early enough that you can release all book versions simultaneously.
- If you decide not to produce an audiobook, you can move up your publication date in the timeline in Appendix A.

⧧ Further Resources

Visit bookagogo.com/books/further-resources for the complete collection of all links in this book.

Companies, Individuals & Resources Mentioned in This Chapter

- **ACX:** acx.com
- **Amazon Whispersync:** audible.com/ep/wfs and everyday-reading.com/whispersync
- **Dave Margalotti:** dmproaudio.net

Pros and Cons of ACX Exclusivity

- **From the Alliance of Independent Authors:** selfpublishingadvice. org/audiobooks-and-exclusivity-a-comparison-of-acx-and-findaway-voices
- **From Steve Bremner:** stevebremner.com/why-not-go-exclusively-with-acx-for-your-audiobook
- **From Libro.FM:** blog.libro.fm/the-harmful-impact-of-audible-exclusive-audiobooks

Audiobook Distributors at a Glance

- Includes comparison chart: deborahjacobs.com/2018/04/03/audiobooks-audible-acx-amazon

Requirements for Common Audiobook Distributors

- **ACX:** help.acx.com/s/article/what-are-the-acx-audio-submission-requirements
- **Draft2Digital:** draft2digital.com/digital-narration
- **Rakuten Kobo:** kobowritinglife.zendesk.com/hc/en-us/articles/360 059385511-How-to-Upload-Your-Audiobook-Directly-on-Kobo
- **Voices by INaudio:** voicessupport.inaudio.com/en/articles/3548096
- **OverDrive:** company.overdrive.com/publishers/faqs

CHAPTER 15

Printing & Distributing Your Self-Published Book

A t this point in the publishing journey, you need to consider how you want to print and distribute your physical book. In chapter 9, we covered the three main kinds of book publishing: self-publishing, traditional, and hybrid. The type of publishing you select may affect what types of printing and distribution are available, although there is a wide range when it comes to self-publishing.

Most printing options fall into two categories: offset or digital. The former is still the industry standard and the option that many professional authors choose.

Offset Printing

Used by all major traditional publishers, offset printing is the process you'd probably imagine if asked to picture your book rolling off the presses. It involves relatively large ink rollers transferring your book's image to paper in mass quantities. In addition to its high quality, offset printing has several advantages:

1. **More control over the per-book rate.** Most offset printers require you to purchase a minimum number of books with each print run. Because offset printing usually comes with a flat setup fee, the more books you purchase, the lower the per-book rate, which allows for better control of sales margins.

2. **One-on-one customer service.** You can speak to the same rep or team throughout the entire process and typically contact the print facility directly, as opposed to contacting a random representative via phone, chatbot, or email.

3. **Lower costs with local printers.** If there's a printer in your area, you can save money on shipping charges since you can pick up the books yourself.

4. **Better quality control—and more customization.** Before you print a run of your books, some printers provide cover and paper samples for review, allowing you to choose from different weights, colors, etc. They can also help you make decisions about printing materials, explaining the benefits and costs of each, as well as how such decisions might affect your printing timeline.

5. **Streamlined process.** Most print facilities have staff with the skills to make minor tweaks to your book files, so you don't have to wait on your designer for small changes.

Some disadvantages of using an offset printer are:

1. **Longer lead times.** The lead time for an offset printer is generally at least several weeks longer than if you opt for print on demand. Add to that the fact that offset printers often have jam-packed schedules and you're looking at a much longer lead time.

2. **Proof copies.** Instead of providing a bound book for your proof copy, many offset companies print the cover on glossy paper and secure it with a rubber band around the loose interior pages—a presentation that requires some imagination as to what the final printed book will look like. As mentioned in the chapters on cover and interior design, you should give yourself time to review your printed proof copy, in whatever format it comes.

3. **Use of printing plates.** Offset printers use metal plates to apply ink to paper. Custom plates are produced for each printing project, which means changes made after a proof copy has been printed can be very difficult (and expensive). If you plan on publishing revised editions of your book frequently, offset printing may not make financial sense.

4. **Warehousing needs.** Many offset printers ship bulk orders on pallets, which need to be unloaded by someone other than the delivery driver. You also need somewhere to store this mountain of books. Note that if you use a distributor, they handle warehousing and delivery matters.

Using an offset printer might mean you also need to hire a distributor, but not always. Authors who chose Promotion or Documentation as their BAGG probably do not need commercial distribution. Instead, they might want to print a finite number of copies for their clients or relatives and be done. If you're writing your book for Catharsis, you might not even need to print your book at all—although if you can afford to print just a single copy, holding your published book in your own two hands is an incredible feeling.

Anyone whose BAGG is Reputation, Education, or Satisfaction most likely needs to consider a distribution strategy. In addition to warehousing your books and handling fulfillment of orders, a distributor ensures your book is available through all of the appropriate distribution networks, from Amazon to bookstores of all sizes. Your only responsibility is ensuring they always have enough copies of your book on hand to manage inbound requests. In addition to their fees for storage, administration, shipping, and maintenance, a distributor also takes a percentage of your royalties.

Finding a professional and reliable printer and distributor can take its share of research, which is another way a self-publishing concierge such as Redwood Publishing can be helpful. Self-publishing concierges usually have relationships with numerous printers and distributors and can either refer you to ones they've used or help you screen and compare any you've found through your own research.

Digital

The other common printing option is digital, which is what's most commonly used for print on demand (POD), and thus the two terms are often used interchangeably, even though some traditional printers also offer digital. Because POD can usually fulfill both your printing and distribution needs, it's a popular choice for many self-published authors. By far the most popular POD option is Amazon's Kindle Direct Publishing (KDP) service, but there are several others of note, such as IngramSpark, Lulu (lulu.com), and BookBaby (bookbaby.com).

Print on demand is just as it sounds: Your book is printed only when a customer orders a copy, so you don't have to worry about many of the fees associated with traditional distribution, such as warehousing. What fees do exist are instead taken out up front, straight from your royalties. POD companies allow you to upload your book files to their site, where your book is then made available to Amazon, Barnes & Noble, and a handful of other book retailers, both online and off, for distribution. Some POD companies, including IngramSpark, also allow authors to distribute e-books to digital retailers such as Apple Books (apple.com/apple-books), Barnes & Noble, Rakuten Kobo Plus, and OverDrive.

As discussed in chapter 9, hybrid publishers generally publish titles under their print-on-demand account. Because a hybrid approach can vary from one publisher to the next, the points below apply to an author who is publishing their own title through their own POD account.

Here are some reasons you might opt for POD:

1. **No printing minimums.** You can order as many as 1,000 books for yourself—or as few as one.

2. **No distributor required to be carried by major book retailers.** When printing with IngramSpark, for example, your book also gets added to the Ingram book catalog, which is made accessible to almost all bookstores, so even small brick-and-mortar shops can order your book to stock on their shelves.

3. **Control over the suggested retail price for your book.** Although bookstores can sell it at whatever price they want, your royalties are based on the price *you* set. Note that *list price* is often used interchangeably with *retail price.*

4. **Lower discounts for retailers.** Retailers always take a cut of the royalties—that's not an option. When you distribute through a print-on-demand service, that rate is usually 40% to 45%, far less than the standard 55% when using a traditional distributor. Although offering a larger discount can increase the chances of your book being carried by a wider range of retailers, many Redwood Publishing authors have been able to set a 45% rate and still be carried by Amazon and Barnes & Noble.

5. **Competitive per-book rates.** Print-on-demand companies now offer very reasonable per-book printing rates, often on par with those of offset printers.

6. **Ability to change your book's content on the fly.** You can upload new files anytime you'd like to make a change. If, for example, you finally receive a coveted testimonial from a well-known celebrity and want to add it to your front cover, you can easily update your files and upload them to your account. The new version of your book becomes

available as soon as the print-on-demand company approves the changes. Note that there are some details of your book that you cannot change once your book is published, such as the title, type of printing (color or black-and-white), and book size. See Appendix P for a chart detailing what can and cannot be changed once a title is published.

7. **Easy royalty tracking and payments.** Royalties are paid automatically, usually every sixty to ninety days, and are deposited directly into your bank account. Because you, not your distributor, have your own account with the POD company, you maintain total control over your title and have visibility into all of its metrics and data. You can access sales reports anytime and, if you publish future books down the road, use the same account to track all your books in one place.

8. **Ability to offer preorders.** With Amazon's KDP program and IngramSpark specifically, you can offer your title for sale before it's officially released. (Note: As of the publication of this book, KDP offers this feature only for e-books, not for print.) Traditional publishers use this tactic so that they can market books in advance. More about preorders in chapter 16.

Overall, print on demand is a low-risk, relatively low-cost way to start your publishing journey. However, that doesn't mean it has more advantages than offset printing in all areas. Here are a few points that might make you reconsider using a POD company for printing and distribution:

1. **Limited customization options.** There are far fewer choices for paper thickness (usually just one or two), color (generally cream or white), and cover finish (matte or glossy). Options such as embossed covers or frayed-edge paper are rarely offered. However, the overall print quality is now often equal to that of offset printing, which wasn't always true in the early days of POD.

2. **Expensive color printing.** Color printing is expensive no matter what technique you use, but with print on demand, it's even more so.

3. **Inflexibility with large print runs.** If you're planning a book tour to potentially drum up thousands of sales in a short amount of time, POD may not be equipped to handle such a load. A sudden deluge of orders could result in Amazon temporarily listing your book as out of stock—which not only results in you missing out on sales but might cause potential readers to purchase something else in the meantime—and then forget to come back.

4. **Few, if any, bulk rates.** While some print-on-demand companies offer bulk-printing rates for their authors, most do not. So although you might have secured a reasonable price-per-book for a low quantity, you'll likely overpay once you hit the 750-copy threshold.

5. **Inferior customer service.** You're just one customer in a sea of thousands, so you'll likely have to wait for help with any issues. We've also seen instances—with a few different publishers—where a book cover is printed with the incorrect interior file and gets shipped to the customer without a quality-control check. (One such high-profile incident saw a customer order his friend's financial book, only to find content about Nazism inside the cover.[44]) Although the customer can request a corrected copy from the company, some customers won't realize this was not *your* mistake and could leave a poor review.

6. **Potential for costly/timely mistakes.** For those not familiar with the process of uploading files, it's easy to make a small slipup—such as uploading the wrong file or choosing the option for a 6″ x 9″ book when the layout is 5.5″ x 8.5″—that will cause the printer to reject your file. This causes not only delays but also great expense: Since some companies charge a fee for each revised file uploaded, this part of the process could cost as much as hiring a professional to do it for you.

While there are several print-on-demand companies to choose from, they each have different services and advantages, such as the ability to review reports in real-time, preorders, and print quality. To compare the features offered by the most common print-on-demand services, see Appendix Q.

You may even consider using more than one POD company. For example, Redwood Publishing often uses both Amazon KDP and IngramSpark to ensure a book is released to as many retailers as possible. The benefit of publishing directly with Amazon opens some additional doors: It's easier to run ads through Amazon Ads (advertising.amazon.com, formerly Amazon Marketing Services), you can usually reach their customer service department at any time of day, and you can participate in KDP Select, which offers wider distribution options to select countries, as well as some free and easy-to-use marketing tools (such as Amazon A+ Content, mentioned in chapter 17).

Amazon also offers expanded distribution—if you opt in and your book meets certain size requirements. (At the time of this book's publication, this option is offered only for e-book and paperback versions, not hardcover.) With expanded distribution, Amazon also makes an author's title available outside its platform, such as in bookstores, libraries, and other online retailers. However, titles listed through Amazon's expanded distribution are not eligible for distribution through other services, such as IngramSpark.

If you skip Amazon's expanded distribution and use only the POD platform to distribute solely through Amazon.com, you can then opt to use another POD company, such as IngramSpark. IngramSpark partners with a number of retailers outside of Amazon, including Barnes & Noble, Books-A-Million (booksamillion.com), Bookshop.org (bookshop.org), Alibris (alibris.com), and even Target and Walmart. Authors can utilize IngramSpark's platform to reach a wide net of retail outlets while still reaping the above-mentioned benefits that come when publishing with Amazon. This means authors can add links to the other outlets on their website and social media pages, allowing them to cast a wider net when attracting customers. Plus, bookstores can find and purchase an author's book through the Ingram book catalog, which bookstores regularly use to make book-buying decisions. Many Redwood authors have had success in contacting local mom-and-pop bookshops to entice them to order a box of their books through the Ingram catalog. Other authors have worked out deals with bookstores in areas where the author will be for a conference or seminar, letting the stores know they will send attendees to buy a copy. The bookstore then orders the book via IngramSpark for the conference time frame.

Book Distributors

Just as with writers, editors, and designers, the role of a book distributor varies greatly, with some performing many more services than others. Some distributors take on a sales role and actively work with retailers to get them to carry your book, while other distributors are simply wholesalers who store your book and ensure it's in stock at retail outlets. So before hiring a distributor, decide which level of services you want and have the distributor list theirs in writing. Other questions to ask include:

- What other books they've handled distribution for
- What those books' distribution looked like, such as whether the author started off on Amazon and then grew into other retailers and, if so, how many and in what amount of time
- If they handle distribution into airport bookstores and what that process looks like or requires of you (if having airport bookstore distribution is important to you).
- If there's a limit to how many books they warehouse for each author
- Whether they have a time limit for storage without sales
- How often they report sales

You can also ask to speak to authors they represent so you can get a better feel for the distributor's work style.

Since offset printing and distribution generally go hand in hand, the advantages and disadvantages are also the same. Specific to the distribution end is the benefit of working with a professional who specializes in fulfillment. Provided you supply enough books to your distributor for the launch and sales, you likely won't ever run into delays or out-of-stock issues, as can happen when a print-on-demand title suddenly receives an influx of orders.

Some disadvantages specific to using a distributor are:

1. Distributors are not necessarily salespeople, so they don't have a vested interest in whether your book sells and won't be proactive in moving units.

2. You are charged monthly for storage, administrative fees, shipping, etc., on top of the percentage the distributor takes from your book sales.

3. You need to be able to quickly replenish your stock of books whenever the distributor is running low.

4. You generally have little or no visibility into sales other than quarterly reports.

5. If books are not selling, a distributor will eventually want to return the books to you, at which point you'll have to find a new storage facility, pay to have the remaining books shipped to the new facility, and develop a new sales strategy.

Most self-published authors today rarely need a distributor and so should opt for print on demand.

But there is another option: a hybrid approach. You can use an offset printer to print a limited customized run of your book and POD for a broader release, including Amazon. This way, customers can find your book on any site, for a reasonable price. The logistics of printing and shipping are all taken care of at a low cost to the author, who can then show off their more luxurious print job to friends and family or at special events, such as book signings and speaking engagements.

Alternatively, you could explore becoming your own distributor, which would allow you to print your book exactly as you want and share the profits solely with the seller. In such a scenario, the most common seller authors choose is Amazon. Through services such as Amazon Advantage (advantage.amazon.com) and Amazon Seller Central (sellercentral.amazon.com), authors can create their own selling profiles to sell their books. While you do make more profit per book, this approach is very hands-on, as you are responsible for the fulfillment of every order—and Amazon has strict expectations for its sellers.

Amazon Advantage works much like consignment: Amazon places orders directly with the author, who ships books to Amazon warehouses across the country, where they are stored until sold, at which point a royalty is paid to the author. Essentially, your book becomes part of Amazon's inventory. With this program, Amazon buys the book from you at a 55% discount on your retail price, paying you the remainder.

Another distribution option is Amazon Seller Central, a marketplace for anybody who wants to sell anything—books included. Vendors on this platform are labeled as third-party sellers, and while you might make slightly more per book (as Amazon takes a much smaller percentage), you are responsible for shipping and customer service, and your book's listing shows as sold by you (or whatever name you register on the account) versus by Amazon. This can cause confusion as to whether your book is available as a newly distributed title or as a resale copy. It's also important to note that Amazon does not allow certain Seller Central products—including books— to be marketed via their paid-click advertising campaigns, so that may be a consideration if such ads are part of your marketing strategy.

Codes, Categories & Prices

No matter how you decide to distribute your title, you should first determine which BISAC (Book Industry Standards and Communications) codes are most applicable to your book. Essentially a genre code, the nine-character alphanumeric BISAC code tells book retailers, distributors, and librarians which categories and subcategories your book belongs in. Visit the Book Industry Study Group website (bisg.org) to review the complete category list and identify the top three for your title. Then provide them to your distributor or keep them at the ready for when you need to enter them into any relevant forms.

After you choose the BISAC codes, browse the book and Kindle categories on Amazon. While many of these categories mirror those on the BISAC website, there are also more niche ones, as Amazon is continually adding to its lists. In addition to that, there are often completely different categories for the different formats of a book. For example, within the Health, Fitness & Dieting category for physical books, Women's Health is listed as a subcategory and has several additional subcategories underneath it (ranging from Breast Cancer to Lupus to Pregnancy), whereas Kindle's Health, Fitness & Dieting category only displays two subcategories within the Women's Health category—Menopause and Pregnancy. Another example is Short Reads, which categorizes e-books only—no print books—that can be read in anywhere from fifteen minutes to two hours. Amazon, as well as most other print-on-demand distribution sites, lets you select up to three categories for your book. Previously, Amazon allowed more than three, but that changed in 2023.

Redwood Publishing released *The Prosperity Loop* by Chris Lautenslager, a book geared toward business leaders who wish to create a socially conscious life, organization, and community. While the Business & Money category and the Economics category fit the title perfectly fine, Redwood identified even more specific categories, such as Income Inequality and Workplace Culture.

Rather than having to compete against tens of thousands of titles in the more generic category of Business & Money, where it didn't even crack the top 100, *The Prosperity Loop* broke into the top five for Workplace Culture.

Depending on your publisher, your book may be placed into a catalog, which is how many bookstores and libraries identify which books to carry. At some traditional and hybrid publishers that use them, sales teams then use this catalog to sell your book to retailers. Even some self-publishers, such as IngramSpark, create catalogs, although you are responsible for selling the book. When approaching bookstores, make sure to provide them with the names of all the catalogs where your book can be found, along with the ISBN and title.

As you browse through these categories, take note of the prices of comparable titles so you have an idea of how you should price your book, which you need to do *before* you publish. The following are some factors to consider when setting the price of your printed book:

The printing and distribution costs. If you opt for nonbasic options, such as printing with gold-trimmed pages, or use a distributor to store and ship your book, you have to factor in the additional associated costs into the per-book price. Even if you act as your own distributor, there are still costs such as shipping, which you must decide whether to charge for separately or roll into the retail price. Using a POD distributor for a standard, noncustom paperback (e.g., black-and-white interior with regular paper and a glossy cover) usually runs around $3 to $5 per book, affording much more wiggle room on price. However, each nonstandard option you choose drives up costs, meaning you need to price your book accordingly.

If using offset printing, you can provide your printer with an estimate of the page count and other relevant details (trim size, interior paper, cover material choice) to get a rough idea of the per-book cost, then build in your profit from there. If taking the POD route, use the calculator available on most printers' websites to plug in your details and get a cost estimate.

Links to the calculators for Amazon KDP and IngramSpark are included in Further Resources.

The wholesaler's discount. In traditional publishing and for authors using a distributor, the required wholesaler's discount is 55%. This means that every retail partner working with that distributor expects to buy an author's book for 55% off the retail price. The distributor then typically takes their cut, leaving you with the remainder. These costs, in addition to those for printing, must be factored in when calculating your book's price if you wish to turn a profit (which is especially true if your BAGG is Income).

Authors using the IngramSpark POD service originally had the option of setting a wholesaler's discount as low as 30%, although that's not recommended, as you want to make your book as attractive to retailers as possible. In fact, many bookstores flat-out reject titles that do not offer "traditional" discounts. Most of Redwood Publishing's authors have been able to set the discount at 40% to 45% without issue. (As of the printing of this book, IngramSpark requires all authors to choose at least the 40% discount option.) Some services set the wholesaler's discount for you—40% in the case of KDP. The author then receives royalties for the remaining percentage *less* the print fee. For example, a $14.95 paperback on KDP would have a wholesale price of $8.97 (40% of $14.95). If it costs KDP $4.25 to print and distribute the book, the author nets $4.72 on each book sold.

The retail price of your competition. When researching your categories, make a list of competing books and their prices for hardcover, paperback, and e-book. Take note of any specialty printing that might cause these books to be priced higher. For example, cookbooks often command a higher price due to color printing and photography. So it wouldn't be uncommon to see a cookbook selling in hardcover for $44.99, paperback for $24.99, and e-book for $14.99. But those prices might not be feasible in genres where the average costs run far lower. You don't want to price yourself out, but you also don't want to appear too cheap, as that may make customers question the credibility of what you have to offer.

Pricing your e-book and audiobook is a little different, as there are no printing costs to consider. With traditional publishing, authors generally do not incur costs for services such as e-book formatting and book narration, as the publisher covers these. Typically, traditionally published authors receive royalties of about 20% on e-books and anything from 5% to 25% on audiobooks.

For self-publishers of e-books and audiobooks, royalty rates vary by company. Amazon KDP, for example, has two royalty rates for e-books: 35% and 70%. With the 70% royalty rate, Amazon charges a fee to deliver each e-book (at the time of this book's publication, the fee is $0.15 per megabyte). The rate also requires the book price be between $2.99 and $9.99 and that the book is in the KDP Select program (more on this on page 178). With the 35% royalty rate, you can price at any rate you choose, no delivery fee is charged, and your e-book is made available to more marketplaces outside of the U.S. You cannot select the 70% royalty program for certain countries, such as India, Brazil, and Mexico; you are automatically locked into the 35% rate. Selecting the royalty rate is up to you, and you can experiment in your Amazon KDP account by entering different prices to see how much you will receive with each.

If you use ACX to release your audiobook, you earn 25% to 40%, depending on the distribution agreement you select and whether you choose to pay your narrator a portion of the royalties. Although offering a revenue share with your narrator can help save some costs up front, you should discuss this option with your narrator, as some feel they would not be adequately compensated for their work, in which case they might require full payment up front or ask that their revenue share continues in perpetuity. Under the latter arrangement, the narrator will benefit greatly if your book sells well, while you would end up paying more than if you had paid them a flat rate.

Some self-publishing platforms offer free royalty calculators on their websites, a few of which we have included in Further Resources. Even if you haven't yet finalized your book's printing details, you can use these tools to get a sense of the cost and your subsequent royalty. Doing this sooner rather than later can help you move ahead on certain print-related decisions, such as whether to have a color or black-and-white interior.

Keep in mind that just because you set a retail price does not mean that retailers will adhere to it. For example, you may decide to list your hardcover at $26.95, only to find Amazon selling it for $24.95. There's really nothing you can do about this—retailers use your stated price as a suggestion but reserve the right to set the price as they see fit. However, you will always be paid based on *your* retail price ($26.95 in the example above), but because retailers purchase books wholesale, they can afford to offer the book at a discount. This is why including the price in your book's barcode could pose a challenge, as a retailer might want to update the cover with the price they choose. Other retailers don't mind if the price on the book differs from their list price. If you want the flexibility to change your retail price often—such as when you run promotions—you might want to consider not including the price anywhere on your cover.

Timing & Costs

Depending on the style of printing and type of publishing you select, it can take anywhere from one to six months to get your book on the shelf. The time of year may also play a factor, as many printers and publishers do not take on new clients during the holiday sales season of October through December and are often booked for these months as early as May. Publishing and distribution costs are so variable that it's very likely these will have changed by the time you read this book. As of the time of publication, Amazon KDP and IngramSpark are free. However, the latter does charge a nominal fee to upload revisions after the title has been live for sixty days and also tacks on a distribution fee of one percent of the local list price.

Although Lulu is also free, they charge a much higher distribution fee than other services do.

If you decide you want to order copies using the POD company you chose, you can do that at an author's rate—meaning you don't have to pay full retail price for your own book. A standard black-and-white paperback costs about $3 to $5, depending on the page count, while a color version costs $7 to $10.

A hardcover book is a different story: The cloth linen and dust jacket can add considerable costs. A black-and-white hardcover may run $9 to $12, while a color version costs upwards of $15. Some POD companies that offer a premium color print job with higher-quality materials charge as much as $24 per book. The difference in cost for color is because print-on-demand companies don't typically print black-and-white pages and color pages separately and then bind them all together. Instead, if you have any color in your book, even on just one page, the entire file—every single page—is run through the same color-ink digital printer. If you are intent on printing in color or want a hardcover book, make sure you run the numbers. Most print-on-demand services have cost calculators on their websites, allowing you to plug in factors such as size, page count, color versus black-and-white, and matte versus glossy. That can help you determine early on whether POD or offset printing is the more affordable option for your book.

For standard print jobs, offset printing is typically more aggressive in price. If you plan to order thousands of copies of a black-and-white paperback, you might be able to get the cost down to less than $2 per book. An overseas printer might even do it for far less, although the shipping times can take months. Once you start adding in premium options, such as embossing or heavier paper weights, your per-book cost begins to rise. You then need to factor in shipping costs and, if using a distributor, the storage and fulfillment fees. Distributors can charge anywhere from $15 to $30 per month, plus between 5% and 15% of your royalty.

Since there are so many cost factors to consider, our worksheet in Appendix B can help you better gauge which printing and distribution options are most beneficial for your book.

▶ Next Steps

- Make a list of any special requirements (e.g., paper weight, black-and-white vs. color) for your book.
- Complete the worksheet in Appendix B to see whether offset printing, print on demand, or a hybrid approach makes the best financial sense, particularly in relation to your BAGG.
- Research the types of printers for the approach you've chosen and determine which can provide the special requirements you are seeking.
- If you choose offset printing, research distributors and compare their services and prices.
- Choose three BISAC codes by reviewing the list at bisg.org.
- Research your competition to help determine your price for hardcover, paperback, and e-book.

≡ Further Resources

Visit bookagogo.com/books/further-resources for the complete collection of all links in this book.

Companies, Individuals & Resources Mentioned in This Chapter
- **Amazon Ads:** advertising.amazon.com
- **Amazon Advantage:** advantage.amazon.com
- **Amazon KDP:** kdp.amazon.com
- **Amazon Seller Central:** sellercentral.amazon.com

- **BookBaby:** bookbaby.com
- **IngramSpark:** ingramspark.com
- **KDP Select:** kdp.amazon.com/en_US/select
- **Lulu:** lulu.com

How-Tos

- **Selecting categories on Amazon:** kindlepreneur.com/how-to-choose-the-best-kindle-ebook-kdp-category
- **Setting your royalties:** danieljtortora.com/blog/self-publishing-royalties

List of Offset & POD Publishers

- **From Reedsy:** blog.reedsy.com/book-printing-services

Lists of Book Categories & Codes

- **Amazon:** amazon.com/gp/browse.html?node=283155 (Once on the Amazon page, choose the "Categories" dropdown to view all the top-level category options. Toggle between "Kindle eBooks" and "Print Books" to see the categories for each.)
- **BISAC:** bisg.org/complete-bisac-subject-headings-list

Print-on-Demand Calculators

- **IngramSpark:** myaccount.ingramspark.com/Portal/Tools/PubCompCalculator
- **Amazon KDP:** kdp.amazon.com/en_US/help/topic/GSQF43YAMUPFTMSP

Marketing & PR for Your Book

As we mentioned early on, each of the topics in this book is discussed at a very basic level to provide a jumping-off point so you know where to begin your research. This is especially true for marketing and PR, as entire books have been written on the subject. We've included a few of the more prominent ones in Further Resources.

Just as your BAGG is about your overall book journey, you should also have in mind a goal for book promotion, such as becoming a bestselling author, gaining exposure for your business, or receiving recognition in your area of expertise. Many of the goals we discussed in chapter 1 also apply here, such as:

1. **Promotion.** Using your book as a calling card for your business, such as being able to say, "I wrote the book on producing podcasts" or "Here's my proven system for retirement planning."

2. **Reputation.** Establishing yourself as a professional writer or an expert in a given field.

3. **Education.** Conveying a new idea and educating others on it.

Identifying a marketing goal helps you measure ROI (return on investment), which we discussed briefly in chapter 1. There's no sense in spending advertising dollars or hiring a PR firm to market a family history intended only for your relatives, for example. But if you're looking to establish yourself as an authority in your field so that you can book more speaking engagements, you can easily calculate your ROI, whether you handle the marketing yourself or hire professionals.

Your ROI might not be tied to book sales. If your BAGG is Promotion, for example, you might calculate your ROI based on whether the marketing helped you attract new clients. Decide early on how you will calculate your ROI and set reminders to readjust at key milestones.

If you're going the DIY route, this is where that author platform we discussed way back in chapter 2 will prove to be indispensable. If you've been diligently plugging away at it, DIY promotion will be a whole lot easier. If you haven't, you should probably consider hiring marketing and/or PR help.

"If all goes well, you'll spend more time marketing and promoting your book than you spent writing it," says Anne Janzer, a nonfiction book coach and author of *The Writer's Process* and *Subscription Marketing.* "So choose a sustainable approach: promotion strategies that play to your strengths and help you grow, rather than drain you. Your strategy may not look like everyone else's, and that's fine."

Choosing a Release Date

One of the first steps in promoting your book is choosing your release date. You might want to opt for a relevant time of year, such as spring for a travel book or January for books related to fitness or healthful cooking. For PR purposes, you could choose a specific holiday, for example, World Vegan Month in November for a vegan cookbook, or an anniversary, such as that of a historic date related to your subject matter.

Although many PR professionals use the terms *release* and *launch* as synonyms, that's not always the case. "When the words *launch* and *release* are used before the word *strategy,* they're interchangeable," says Burke Allen, owner of the public relations firm Allen Media Strategies. "A *book launch,* on the other hand, encompasses a number of factors: marketing, PR, book tours, virtual appearances, book clubs, etc. The *book release* is more finite, a date or short window of dates on a calendar. A release date comes and goes as part of the strategy, but it's not the whole blueprint for success."

Although a release date doesn't have to have relevance, it should be strategic—and that alone could be a reason to work with a professional, as they'll have insight as to what time of year works for different genres, as well as when *not* to launch your book. In fact, despite what many people believe, the holiday season is generally *not* a good time for a book launch— so much so that some indie book marketing and PR companies shut down between Thanksgiving and Christmas. While Redwood Publishing works on books during this time, the company usually doesn't release anything between October 15 and the new year, due to the increased competition. So, if you're considering making your book available in time for the holiday gift-giving season, set a release date no later than mid-October.

If you come up with a particularly strategic date, even if it means a tight turnaround, you might want to run with it. Jenna had originally planned to publish her book about her fanaticism for the band Depeche Mode a few months after the release of their new album and several months before their tour, as she knew fans would be looking for more material about them. However, when she received forty-eight hours' notice that she'd won the chance to take over the band's Facebook page for a day, she rushed to get the e-book online so that she could share news of it with the band's seven million Facebook followers.

Common Marketing Strategies

There's almost an unlimited number of ways to market your book, some more tried and true than others. The following are among the more common strategies:

- Printing ARCs to collect reviews and testimonials
- Book tours (either virtual or in person)
- Online marketing campaigns
- Publicity campaigns (such as print and podcast interviews)
- Taking part in a panel, seminar, and/or webinar (or organizing your own)
- Achieving "bestseller" status on Amazon
- Preorders

Preorders allow readers to purchase your book before its official release and receive it on or slightly after the release date. There are many marketing benefits to preorders, including maintaining control over your launch and having a URL to use in marketing efforts. Preorders can also help generate buzz and interest in your book far in advance of its release date. In some cases, collecting sales throughout the preorder period can significantly help your book gain visibility and potentially even rank on one of the coveted bestseller lists (*New York Times, Wall Street Journal, USA Today, Publishers Weekly,* etc.). Because each list operates under its own rules and algorithms, the sales and other criteria required to climb to the top of one list may be completely different from that of another list, and these algorithms change often and without notice. If making it onto a bestseller list is important to you, you need to either research each list's criteria or hire a professional whose job it is to stay on top of such knowledge.

Samantha Kaiser, one half of the blogging duo the Lifestyle Travelers, self-published her book, *Become a Better You Abroad: Ditch Your Comfort*

Zone for Self-Growth Through the Ten Skills You'll Gain by Studying Abroad, through Amazon. One month before the release date, Kaiser offered the book to interested readers for free in exchange for an honest review on Amazon. Then, upon its publication, the book was promoted at a discount to encourage buyers.

"Both of these strategies led my book to rank number one in my chosen Amazon category within the first week," says Kaiser. "This led to more visibility right away, with twenty-five strong reviews that, in turn, led to more book sales in the long run."

Build in at least three months for a proper preorder strategy so that you can stockpile the orders in anticipation of launch, retailers can have time to process and accept those orders, and distributors can fulfill and ship. If you're using an offset printer and distributor (as discussed in the previous chapter), you also need sufficient cash flow to print more books quickly, should the preorder go gangbusters.

In 2019, one of Sara's authors printed 500 books for his launch. He gave himself about three months to market the book while on preorder, sending out ARCs and promoting on social media. Redwood provided Amazon with 150 copies per their preorder requests, but a couple of weeks before release, Amazon submitted a request for an additional 310 copies—while the author's prelaunch strategy had already burned through most of the original 500. The author had to pay for a rush printing of another 500—at a cost of about $2,500—to ensure Amazon had enough books for the release date, as well as more for a buffer, in case another large order came through.

When researching marketing ideas, you'll most likely come across sources that recommend you use private label rights (PLR) books as free giveaways to those who sign up for your newsletter. When you purchase a PLR product, you're buying permission to brand it as yours. While this is similar to paying for a work-for-hire or hiring a ghostwriter, the voice of a PLR book won't be yours, as it was written without your input. Most PLR books can be purchased by numerous customers, meaning that other people are likely using the same book in their marketing strategy. On top of that, we've found that most of the sources that suggest using PLR books are get-rich-quick schemes that advocate shortcuts, meaning there's no emphasis on quality. Instead of considering a PLR product, invest in creating your own assets that are unique to you and maintain the voice you've worked so hard to hone and develop.

Media Kits

In preparation for your release date, create a media kit to provide to interviewers, reviewers, podcast producers, etc. Here are the most common elements of a book media kit:

- **Press release.** Writing a killer press release is an art form in itself—and can be very different from writing a book. Make sure you follow the proper format or hire a PR professional to write one for you. Check Further Resources for more information about how to properly structure a press release.
- **Bio.** Many media outlets ask for an author bio. We recommend having three different versions prepared: a short version of one or two lines, a fifty-word version, and a full page. These will come in handy when you guest blog, schedule speaking engagements and book signings, etc. Journalists and reviewers can cull the information from the full-page bio that is relevant to their particular outlet. If your book will be used to promote your business, you should also prepare the same three versions for your company. Include only the full-page bios in the media kit, but it will be useful to have the others ready to go at a moment's notice.
- **Images.** In addition to high-resolution files of the front and back of your book, consider including headshots of yourself or photos of the

topic, where relevant. Make sure you have the rights and permissions to use them. (Revisit chapter 8 if you need a refresher on the subject of copyright and fair use.)

- **Book trailer.** Not every book needs one, but there are some authors who swear by their effectiveness. Book trailers have waned in popularity over the last few years, but it doesn't hurt to check the trend's current direction.
- **Book excerpt.** Include the first chapter of the book in the media kit, but also offer journalists and reviewers access to the full e-book version.
- **Sample Q&A.** Having this makes it easier for journalists to come up with story ideas that might feature you or your book.
- **Questions for book clubs.** Some book clubs specifically seek out books that have questions written for them, so having these could increase your chances that a group will buy your book and discuss it.

Once your media kit is prepped, include it as a page on your website so that you can easily send the link to journalists and reviewers. Even if you only have the bare bones at first, you can add to it over time.

In the early days of computers, it was common for two types of media kits to be produced: hard copies and electronic (digital) copies. The latter were known as EPKs (electronic press kits). While this term is still in use, assume that any press kit today is digital unless stated otherwise.

Working With a Publicist

One of a publicist's first tasks is writing the press release for the media kit. Most publicists like to get started in the months leading up to the launch of your book, and many prefer to work on a book that has been made available via preorder so media outlets can link directly to your book when they feature you.

Keep in mind that a publicist's primary goal is to get you publicity, which includes interviews, media appearances, and reviews. However, publicity doesn't always translate into sales. As mentioned in chapter 2, every time Coca-Cola posts on Facebook, only a small percentage of their 108 million followers purchase their product.

A publicist can also help organize a book tour, which was a much more common marketing strategy in pre-pandemic days. This entailed lining up a series of in-person appearances at various bookstores and other places where your book can be sold. Typically, the venue buys your book in advance and you read an excerpt at an event—after which you sign copies. *Writer's Digest* has tips on how to organize a DIY book tour.

In the post-pandemic era, many publicists are organizing virtual book tours, where their authors participate in online events hosted by the same venues they would typically visit during an in-person tour. Also gaining popularity are podcast tours, in which authors appear as guests on shows whose audiences align with their own. If you're more comfortable with the written word, set out on a blog tour by reaching out to website owners and offering to write a guest post for each site.

If you decide to hire a book promotion professional, ask other authors in your genre for recommendations, as some promoters—publicists in particular—focus on a specialized area, such as sports or business, so they have contacts in those fields.

Publicists can be relatively expensive, especially when compared with other expenses on your self-publishing journey. Some act as a one-person operation, so your book is often all they work on for however many months you hire them, while others may balance a couple of authors at once. Still other publicists have full teams, with each member specializing in a particular role. Some publicists charge a monthly fee, while others charge a set fee for a certain volume of work.

Other Promotional Strategies

A relatively simple way to get free PR is through the website Source of Sources, or SOS (sourceofsources.com). Three times each weekday, subscribers receive a newsletter of media leads from authors, journalists, podcast hosts, and other media outlets looking for sources to cite or have on as guests. The SOS service is free, both for journalists and sources, and we've had pretty good luck getting our clients and ourselves quoted in SOS outlets, so we recommend checking it out.

Many authors don't have a budget for publicity and instead focus on paid advertising, both traditional and digital, which can be more cost-effective and easier to measure in terms of ROI. If your marketing budget is on the smaller side, you may want to focus your efforts on paid advertisements, sponsored ads, and anything else that drives potential readers to places they can purchase your book. A subset of digital marketing, social media marketing is one of the most common ways authors promote their books today—especially if they've already spent a considerable amount of time building their author platform. As the name suggests, social media marketing involves interacting with potential readers on services such as Facebook, TikTok, and Instagram to increase awareness and sales and drive website traffic. Visit Further Resources for more guidance on social media marketing.

Of course, there are professionals who can do it all: social media, advertising, and publicity. An all-in-one firm is an efficient way to go, but it's certainly more expensive. Most charge by the hour for social media maintenance, and monthly for PR and advertising work. Some other services they might provide, which you could also handle yourself, include:

- **Getting customer reviews.** Amazon reviews are critical to your book's success. Most bibliophiles head straight to Amazon when looking for a product, so having positive reviews can make all the difference when somebody is on the fence about buying your book. This is another opportunity to tap into your author platform: You can let your fans and followers know how important reviews are for your book and politely ask them to write one. You can do this all at once—in a newsletter, for example—or on a one-on-one basis, as readers contact you. Just remember that many sales sites, Amazon especially, have some pretty strict guidelines about how you can request reviews, so make sure you go about this the right way. More on Goodreads reviews in the next chapter.

- **Getting professional reviews.** You can have a professional reviewer or organization write a review, which you can then use in marketing materials, or on social media. Some of the most common places that provide reviews are Kirkus Reviews, *Publishers Weekly*, Midwest Book Review, BlueInk Review, Clarion Reviews, and *Foreword Reviews*.

- **Book awards.** The potential prestige of winning an award isn't the only reason to submit your book to award contests. Some entry fees also include a critique or review, a description of your book on the contest's website, and/or a link to purchase. Then there are some of the intangible benefits: "Although my book sales have remained steady since receiving awards, the greatest advantage I've gained is a surge in speaking engagements through various channels such as news outlets, social media, podcasts, and live events," says Karla J. Noland, a certified self-discovery coach and author of *The Day My Heart Turned Blue: Healing After the Loss of My Mother*. "The number of speaking opportunities has skyrocketed since winning the book awards."

Some of the most common indie-book awards are the Next Generation Indie Book Awards, IPPY (Independent Publisher Book Awards), the *Writer's Digest* Self-Published Book Awards, and the BookLife Prize (run by *Publishers Weekly*), although there are also genre-specific competitions. Always research a contest before entering, especially if there's an entry fee, as some offer perks—such as feedback from judges—while others are in it purely for the money. You can verify a contest's reputation by checking the database of either Poets & Writers (pw.org) or the Alliance of Independent Authors (allianceindependentauthors.org), both of which can be searched by date, genre, and several other criteria.

- **Kindle price promotions.** E-books published on Amazon KDP and through the KDP Select program have a few additional marketing tools at their disposal. While these have varied over the years, they're generally in the form of special promotions in the Kindle Store or temporary price discounts. (Note that if you sign up for KDP Select, you are agreeing to make the digital format of that book available exclusively through KDP, which means you can't distribute it outside of Amazon Kindle.)

- **Amazon bestseller and category assignment.** Some marketing companies, especially those specializing in Amazon, work with you to identify the most granular categories and subcategories for your book. Part of their strategy is to find categories with less competition and whose existing titles are not selling well. This way, if your book gets added to that category and can outsell the existing books, yours could shoot to the top of that category's bestseller list. In such cases, Amazon updates your listing with an orange tag reading "Amazon Best Seller," "Amazon New Release," or "#1 New Release." You can mention this achievement in future marketing, such as sharing a screenshot of your book at the top of the Amazon charts on your website or in an email blast.

- **Book subscription services.** To find their next read, many bibliophiles rely on book-discovery sites such as BookBub (bookbub.com) and Buck Books (buckbooks.net), which serve both the reader and the author. The demographics for these sites can vary widely, so do your research before you pay for a promotion.

- **Blogging.** As discussed in chapter 4, blogging is an important part of your author platform—whether you blog for your own site or guest-blog somewhere else so you can get discovered by a whole new audience.
- **Giveaways.** The chance to receive something for free is always a draw, so consider running giveaways. Although you can run such a promotion through the author platform you've built, you may want to consider using an established service such as Goodreads, which not only has a larger reach but also covers all the legal aspects of such a promotion.

  Individual giveaways can also boost your marketing reach. "Don't be afraid to give your book away, even to people who are in your primary audience and would be most likely to purchase it," says Jonathan Ferry, author of the children's chess book *Across the Battlefield: A Pawn's Journey.* "Giving your book away is a great way to fail fast—meaning that if the people who get it for free aren't interested, then you know you either need to change your book or let it die. However, if it does gain reader interest and starts to garner good reviews, then giving your book away can help to accelerate your sales by building awareness of your book within the marketplace."

- **Corporate speaking.** If your book is business-related and you enjoy public speaking, consider offering a complimentary talk in exchange for purchasing a certain number of copies. Karen Catlin used this strategy to sell more than 3,000 books in the first few months after publishing *Better Allies*, which she bills as a practical guide for how to be an ally in the workplace. "I contacted my network of former co-workers, told them about my new book, and asked if they were interested in hosting me to share some of its key concepts," Catlin says. "I offered to waive my speaking fee if they purchased 150 paperbacks or 100 hardcovers at the list [retail] price. It was a win-win. I sold books, and they provided a unique employee development training session."

For more info on the above points—and even more ideas for marketing strategies—see Further Resources.

Social media is teeming with author communities, particularly on Facebook Groups, Reddit, and Goodreads. Since the marketing space changes so rapidly, you can ask other members if, say, BookBub is still relevant or if anyone knows a book publicist who specializes in science fiction.

As your marketing strategies shift into gear, remember to thank those who've been with you since the beginning. Show your gratitude to your author platform by providing exclusive content and news, giveaways, and other members-only offers. Thanking your followers doesn't have to be a costly line item. Just remember to be genuine and grateful.

"My personal book marketing mantra is this: Be generous and strategic," advises Janzer. "If you are generous without being strategic, you will burn out. If you are strategic and never generous, no one will want to talk with you."

Timing & Costs

Budgeting for marketing and PR is not a requirement. How much you allocate to that line item and which strategies you choose are entirely up to you. You can hire a specialist in a specific strategy mentioned above, or you can work with a professional who has a broader reach and can handle several strategies.

The average rates our authors have spent on hiring a publicist range from $2,500 per month to $10,000 for eight weeks, although several of our authors have paid far more than that, with mixed results. If you know you want to hire a PR or marketing company, reach out to them early on so you can gauge how much lead time they require and so you can get on their calendar, as many agencies handle only a limited number of clients at a time.

In our self-publishing timeline, found in Appendix A, the length of the marketing segment is intentionally vague—and that's because the time depends on which marketing strategies you choose. For example, if you decide to print ARCs (see chapter 13), plan on scheduling a minimum of three months to print and circulate copies so you can collect reviews and testimonials. If reviews aren't as critical but you want to ensure you have a certain number of followers on Facebook before launch, you may want to consider spending more time with a social media marketing company before you begin promoting your book.

"Be prepared to promote your book for at least three years," advises Melanie Choukas-Bradley, a traditionally published author and naturalist. "I'm the author of seven published books, and I'm still promoting a book that's been in print for forty-two years."

Next Steps

- Decide on a strategy for showing appreciation to your fans, followers, and subscribers.
- Identify your marketing goal and calculate your target ROI. Schedule regular intervals to monitor ROI.
- Choose a release date and decide which book marketing strategies you will use.
- Create a media kit.
- Decide whether you will hire a marketing/PR professional.
- Calculate and list the wholesale price for your title.
- For authors whose BAGG does not require marketing, you can remove this step from your timeline in Appendix A, thereby moving up your publication date.
- Update the Appendix B worksheet to reflect any changes based on the information in this chapter.

Further Resources

Visit bookagogo.com/books/further-resources for the complete collection of all links in this book.

Companies, Individuals & Resources Mentioned in This Chapter

- **Amazon's KDP Select:** kdp.amazon.com/en_US/select
- **Karen Catlin:** betterallies.com
- **Melanie Choukas-Bradley:** melaniechoukas-bradley.com
- **Jonathan Ferry:** chesstalesbooks.com
- **Source of Sources (SOS):** sourceofsources.com
- **Responding to SOS Queries:** siteseeingmedia.com/marketing/how-to-respond-to-a-haro-query
- *The Day My Heart Turned Blue: Healing After the Loss of My Mother* **by Karla J. Noland:** amazon.com/Day-My-Heart-Turned-Blue/dp/1737498111

Additional Books on the Subject

- *How to Market a Book* **by Joanna Penn:** amazon.com/dp/B071NPVK28
- *How to Market a Book: Overperform in a Crowded Market* **by Ricardo Fayet:** amazon.com/dp/B08TZJQ1FB
- *How to Sell Books by the Truckload on Amazon* **by Penny C. Sansevieri:** amazon.com/dp/B08N5FR99T

Discount Book Services

- **BookBub:** bookbub.com
- **Buck Books:** buckbooks.net

Marketing Ideas

- **Book launch checklist:** scribemedia.com/book-launch-checklist
- **Choosing a launch date:** davidwogahn.com/5-considerations-book-launch-date

- Organizing a book tour: writersdigest.com/whats-new/the-diy-book-tour-how-to-organize-a-book-tour-yourself
- Writing a press release (with template): blog.hubspot.com/marketing/press-release-template-ht
- Finding a publicist: fauziaburke.com/blog/6-steps-for-finding-the-best-pr-firm-for-you-your-book

Getting Reviews

- Customer reviews: writtenwordmedia.com/how-to-get-book-reviews
- Amazon reviews: scribemedia.com/amazon-book-reviews
- Outlets to submit your book for a professional review:
  - BlueInk Review: blueinkreview.com
  - *Foreword Reviews*: forewordreviews.com
  - Kirkus Reviews: kirkusreviews.com
  - Midwest Book Review: midwestbookreview.com
  - *Publishers Weekly*: publishersweekly.com
- Book contests:
  - BookLife Prize: booklife.com/about-us/the-booklife-prize.html
  - IPPY (Independent Publisher Book Awards): ippyawards.com
  - Next Generation Indie Book Awards: indiebookawards.com
  - Poets & Writers: pw.org/grants
  - *Writer's Digest* Self-Published Book Awards: writersdigest.com/writers-digest-competitions/self-published-book-awards

- Lists of other contests, awards, & grants:
  - ○ **Alliance of Independent Authors:** selfpublishingadvice.org/author-awards-contests-rated-reviewed
  - ○ **IndieReader:** indiereader.com/2018/01/self-published-book-award
  - ○ **TCK Publishing:** tckpublishing.com/book-awards-contests

Where to Find Author Communities

- **Facebook:** facebook.com/groups/explore
- **Goodreads:** goodreads.com
- **Reddit:** reddit.com

Author Service Accounts

Self-publishing can require a bevy of accounts to get your book on the shelf and manage its content and sales. Jenna and Sara refer to these core book resources as author service accounts, as they are required for some aspect of book publishing, usually distribution. Not all of the accounts mentioned in this chapter are required, but they are by far the most common ones among the many dozens you'll likely run across. Unless otherwise noted, all of the author service accounts we mention are free to set up, although additional services or functionality may come with a fee.

Note that in order to set up many of these accounts, you first need to have an ISBN for your book (see chapter 11). Once the ISBN has been registered, your book automatically appears in Google search results, so whoever is in charge of ISBN registration, whether that's you or your publisher, should add as many book details as possible. Further details, such as a final front cover, can be added as they become available.

Note that Google search results are different from those on Google Play (discussed later in this chapter). Publishers usually handle the ISBN registration, so ask if they need anything from you to fill in all the details about your title.

Amazon

At the very least, most authors want their book on Amazon, so it's often one of the first accounts to be set up. Publishing your book's listing requires providing all of its metadata—i.e., title, subtitle, whether or not it belongs to a series, author name, book description, etc. Unlike some other service accounts, Amazon gives you the ability to use HTML in your book description, meaning you can include formatting such as line breaks, boldface, and font size.

Some print-on-demand companies let you enter more metadata than Amazon does. On IngramSpark, for example, you can include info such as the table of contents, author biography (discussed as part of your media kit in the previous chapter), and editorial reviews. These details are then made available to any retailer looking to carry the book.

Wherever you decide to list your book, you should keep all of your metadata details compiled in one place so that when it comes time to enter them, you can easily copy and paste the details as needed. See Appendix R for a template you can use to keep all of your book's details in one place. Keep it updated as you finalize information so that it always contains the most accurate details about your book.

If you own the Amazon and KDP login for your book (see chapter 15), you can easily make changes to your listing whenever you want—although there are a few bits of data you cannot change. For example, once a title is published and sales are registered to it, you often cannot change the size of your book, the paper type, or the interior details, such as whether it's in black-and-white or color. These details are locked into the title and ISBN of your book. To change them, you'd have to unpublish your title and republish it with a new ISBN, so be sure you're satisfied with the overall look and feel of your book by thoroughly reviewing your proof (see chapter 13). If you only wish to adjust details such as editing your synopsis or adding reviews, you can typically do that without much hassle. Most changes do not appear immediately. Amazon's print-on-demand service says changes can take up to seventy-two hours to process, while other service accounts, including those that use a distributor, can take anywhere from one to four weeks, depending on the level of change. Refer to Appendix P for a cheat sheet on what can and can't typically be changed after you publish a book.

Some changes may *never* occur. Depending on the third-party company used, authors are able to make changes to their book's metadata, and the third-party company then sends the book's information to all of their retailers. Unfortunately, while many third-party companies do allow authors to control the book details on their listing, they cannot guarantee the change is processed correctly—or even at all. In fact, in 2015, when Sara helped publish a client's book, the third-party POD company she used merged with a larger company, which then required all titles to be transferred from the original company to an account with the new parent company. In the process, the book's imprint name somehow reverted to the name on the client's account (his author name), rather than Redwood Publishing, as it had been with the first company. Once the title was picked up by Barnes & Noble, the error stuck, and no matter how many times Sara reached out to the print-on-demand company, she was unable to correct it. The listing was finally rectified after Sara submitted a claim directly to Barnes & Noble's quality-control department, which required showing proof that her company was the publisher and ISBN owner.

Making changes may be more difficult if you publish your title through a traditional publishing house or self-publish through a midsize or hybrid publishing company. You first have to communicate the desired changes to your publisher, who then submits the changes to the retailers. The length of time this chain of communication takes can vary greatly, from a few days to several weeks—if ever.

No matter how you publish your book, once it's listed on Amazon, you should claim your Amazon Author Profile and fill it out completely. Note that an author profile cannot be created until you have at least one book live. The name on the profile must exactly match the author name on the book. So if you publish books under a different name, you need an author account for each one.

Go to author.amazon.com and log in either via the same login you used to set up your book or through your personal Amazon account. Unless you know for certain that you will be the only one who needs to access your author account, you should set it up under a different login from your personal Amazon account so that anyone you might hire to help with Amazon marketing or to maintain your listing will not have access to your personal shopping info.

Next, search for your book via the title or ISBN and then follow the steps to claim it. Once your profile is approved, which usually takes about twenty-four hours, you can build out the details, such as uploading an author photo and adding editorial reviews.

Some of the benefits of building out an Amazon Author Profile are:

1. **Improved search results.** The more robust your page, the more likely it is that Amazon will place your book higher in search results than those books of authors who aren't selling and don't have author profiles.

2. **More personal connection with readers.** By adding more details about yourself, readers can better get to know you and your expertise, and thus may be persuaded to buy your book

3. **Ease of tracking sales.** You can track how your book is selling in each market, which at the time of this book's publication includes the United States, Canada, Australia, Japan, and several European countries. This is especially helpful if you're working with a distributor who sends out quarterly reports.

You only have to complete the process for setting up your author profile the first time you publish a book. For subsequent books, you can add them to your profile as they are published. Note that once your author profile is created, it cannot be deleted and the name you set as your author name cannot be changed.

When publishing through Amazon's KDP Program, authors can now add A+ Content to their books, a feature that was previously offered only in their Seller Central Program or to traditional publishers but is now open to all. A+ content gives authors a chance to enhance their book page beyond the simple text description. Through images and videos, authors can utilize the feature to share unique points or benefits about their book, which may further sway potential buyers. Having A+ content not only breaks up the text on the book page with eye-catching imagery but can also sell more books—it's been reported that Amazon listings with A+ content receive 10% more in sales.[45] In order to post A+ content, authors must make their book available in the KDP Select Program.

Goodreads

As a social media hub for bibliophiles as well as one of the most prominent and thorough repositories of published books, Goodreads is a great resource for book clubs, librarians, and avid readers, who are always on the hunt for the next book to stick their nose in.

Although Goodreads is owned by Amazon, it can have its own login and account for author profiles, where you can upload a headshot and fill out basic information. Because the site pulls most of their metadata from IngramSpark and Amazon, once your title is up on one of those, you should be able to find your book on Goodreads and update the details accordingly. If you cannot find your title, you can manually add the details, although it's highly recommended you wait for the listing to become searchable on Goodreads so that you don't inadvertently end up creating a duplicate.

Goodreads is also a great place to get customer reviews for your book. As on Amazon, readers can write critiques and rate books on a scale of one to five stars. The site also has a feature that allows you to highlight quotes from books and post them to your profile, which you can do with your own book, highlighting noteworthy selections and providing behind-the-scenes details. Other ways to promote your book on Goodreads include organizing book giveaways and hosting discussions.

Google Play

Google Play (play.google.com) handles only e-books and audiobooks, not print books. You need an ISBN to complete the listing, but all authors are eligible to add their titles. If you want to fully use Google Play to your advantage, consider signing up for the Google Books Partner Program (play.google.com/books/publish/u/0). You have to prove that you own the copyright to your title, but doing so will afford you a few additional benefits, such as getting paid for book sales made through Google Play, the ability to add links to your website and other online bookstores, and viewing detailed sales reports, the last of which can be especially helpful if you decide to run Google Ads.

There's a good chance your publisher is already part of the partner program and will add your book there, so ask if they are willing to share the data about your book with you. And, of course, make sure you are receiving the royalties from any book sales that come through Google Play if your publisher sells via that service. Should you ever decide to remove your book from Amazon or elsewhere, you can always keep your book live on Google Play and even add it as an out-of-print edition to their Library Project (books.google.com/intl/en-GB/googlebooks/library.html), which will ensure perpetual access to your book so it can live on forever.

OverDrive

While you won't make any money through this free service that libraries and schools use to allow clients to borrow digital content, OverDrive (overdrive.com) is still a worthwhile distribution option to consider, as it provides your book a wider release and gives libraries more incentive to carry physical copies. For this reason, it's highly recommended you include OverDrive links on your website and in other marketing materials.

While these are the most popular websites for book promotion and management, there are many others, some of which are more appropriate for specific genres. To find those in your niche, perform a web search for authors in your genre or try to find books similar to yours and see if they are on any other websites or distribution services that might be beneficial to you.

It's important to remember that once you're done, you're not done. Both Jenna and Sara have revisited book sites after several months, only to find incorrect formatting, missing or irrelevant categories, and numerous other issues. We have no idea why these problems crop up, but they do, and they can be difficult and time consuming to fix, so set a reminder to review your profiles and listings at least every couple of months. Or, maybe you got a rockstar testimonial from a well-known individual that you've since added to the cover of your book. By having these accounts in place, you can upload the new cover to all the sites and post an update to your reviews page. Just try to keep yourself relevant.

Next Steps

- Claim your author profiles on Amazon, Goodreads, Google Play, and OverDrive. Even if you don't fill them out completely, you can prevent squatters from sitting on your desired handles.
- Research other sites where authors in your genre are listed.

Further Resources

Visit bookagogo.com/books/further-resources for the complete collection of all links in this book.

Companies, Individuals & Resources Mentioned in This Chapter

- **Amazon A+ Content:** kdp.amazon.com/en_US/help/topic/GHL7P99B7AA543CN
    - **Example of book with A+ Content:** amazon.com/Ends-Us-Novel-Colleen-Hoover/dp/1501110365
- **Amazon Author Central:** author.amazon.com
- **Goodreads Author Program:** goodreads.com/author/program
- **Google Library Project:** support.google.com/websearch/answer/9690276
- **Google Books Partner Center:** play.google.com/books/publish
- **OverDrive:** overdrive.com

CHAPTER

18

You're Published! What Next?

I t's time to pop the cork! After you've cleaned up the confetti from your launch party and reveled in post-publishing bliss, take some time to revisit your BAGG and take actionable steps to ensure your goal is met, if you haven't done so already. Or perhaps, upon review, you'll find your BAGGs have even changed.

Calculating ROI

Now's the time to refer back to the ROI discussed in chapter 1. In terms of your BAGG, did you have a positive or negative ROI? How far off were you from your initial calculations? Can you still do anything to improve the ROI? The basic ROI calculation is:

revenue (R) ÷ the cost of the investment (C) x 100 = ROI%

That second variable, C, includes all the costs you tracked in the spreadsheet in Appendix B. Depending on where you spent your budget, this number will vary wildly. R, on the other hand, is based on your BAGG. Let's go through some examples, using $10,000 as the total cost of investment in each (not including time spent).

Example 1: Promotion. You decided to calculate ROI based on increasing your business, so you assigned a value of $500 to each new prospective client. During the six months following the publication of your book, forty new clients tell you they booked an initial consultation after hearing of your book. In that case, your calculation would be:

$$20,000 \div 10,000 \times 100 = 200\%$$

Not a bad ROI! You can improve further by continuing to track performance for months after the book's release. If you have book sales in addition to new clients, you can throw those into the calculation, improving your ROI even further.

Example 2: Reputation. Your goal was to book more speaking engagements, for which you charge an average of $5,000. In the first year after your book is released, you finally get signed with a speaking agency, which books you for three engagements.

$$15,000 \div 10,000 \times 100 = 150\%$$

And that's just the first year! Now that you're on a roll in your new career, you're getting booked more often and your speaking fee has increased to $10,000. You already have an incredible ROI, so anything you earn after that is icing on the proverbial cake.

Example 3: Persuasion. Some things can't be quantified in terms of money. When Rachel Carson wrote her 1962 book *Silent Spring*, about the harm caused by pesticides, she greatly swayed public opinion on the subject for the first time. The book is credited with getting the U.S. to ban the use of the chemical DDT and to enact stricter regulations on pesticides in general, as well as spurring the grassroots environmental movement. That's not to mention the numerous awards it garnered and the enduring impact the book still has to this day. How would Houghton Mifflin, the book's publisher, have quantified such successes against ROI?

Maintaining Momentum

There's plenty you can do to support your title after it's been published, much of which falls under the marketing and publicity umbrella. This includes continuing to pursue reviews and/or testimonials and submitting it to contests. Note that some awards organizations have a limit as to how old a submitted title can be, so make sure to review the criteria and prioritize the time-sensitive contests.

Not long ago, you could easily see how many new titles were being released on Amazon. When that feature was disabled sometime around 2018, Amazon was releasing between 30,000 and 50,000 e-book titles each and every month.[46] That number has likely grown over the past five years, which means there's exponentially more competition today.

So, no matter how well written your story or eye-catching your cover, if you aren't actively promoting your book, your title probably won't cut through the clutter on its own. If Income was one of your BAGGs, you need a regular and steady marketing and promotion schedule that extends well after your release date.

Stay up to date on the developments in technology, publishing, and advertising in the book world, because you may be able to make changes to your book to accommodate these new advancements. For example, in early 2021, Amazon's print-on-demand publishing service began to roll out a beta version of their hardcover publishing program. Many authors jumped at the opportunity to publish their titles in a POD hardcover format, as the new version gave them a fresh reason to market their titles to their followers once again. Kindlepreneur, Jane Friedman, the Book-A-Go-Go podcast, and the author communities mentioned in chapter 16 are good sources for such news.

Another way to stay up to date on the latest in publishing and book news is by following trade publications. While we don't consider the Book-A-Go-Go podcast a news source, we will make it a point of covering any major new developments as soon as we hear about them. If you learn of a new change or advancement in the publishing world and would like us to cover it, drop us a line at bookagogo.com/contact or info@bookagogo.com.

Many authors ask if books have an expiration date. Some marketing folks recommend that authors give it their all for about a year before calling it quits or trying a radically different tactic. While that may be true for timely topics covered in some books, we firmly believe that with the right strategy, you can continue to grow your audience for years after your original publication date. It may take a year, it may take five—it depends on the time and money you are able to funnel into your book after it's published.

You may even develop new BAGGs that will start you down an unexpected path. Perhaps your original goal was to educate readers about a topic you're passionate about, but, after the book is published, you shift your BAGG to Reputation and seek out speaking engagements. It's fine for your goals to evolve with you.

If your BAGG is Self-Expression or Satisfaction, you might decide you want to keep writing and publishing, even if your first outing isn't a blockbuster success. Numerous now-famous books were self-published or initially rejected by publishers, only to go on to reign at the top of the bestsellers charts. Stephen King's debut novel, *Carrie,* was rejected dozens of times before being picked up by a traditional publisher. *The 4-Hour Workweek* by Timothy Ferriss was rejected by twenty-five publishers, while it's reported that Jack Canfield's *Chicken Soup for the Soul* was passed over by a whopping 144. Colleen Hoover's first novel was self-published and netted her $30. She has since gone on to sell more than twenty million books. The bottom line is: Don't throw in the towel.

Download individual episodes of our Book-A-Go-Go podcast for a refresher on any of the topics discussed in this book, or subscribe to hear interviews with industry experts and authors with success stories to share. Tune In, Write On, Get Published!

Next Steps

- Revisit your BAGG and, if relevant, calculate its ROI to see if you've achieved your goal. If not, refine your previous strategies accordingly.
- Set a schedule to maintain marketing objectives such as pursuing reviews and/or testimonials and entering contests for book awards.
- Identify sources (websites, author communities, etc.) for staying current on self-publishing trends.
- Celebrate! You've earned it.

Further Resources

Visit bookagogo.com/books/further-resources for the complete collection of all links in this book.

Reach Out to Us

- **Contact:** bookagogo.com/contact or info@bookagogo.com

Acknowledgments

Numerous people were instrumental in helping with this book—some of whom we met after we began this journey.

On the editorial side, Marilyn Oliveira and Kate Zentall provided valuable feedback on both structure and copyediting that helped us fine-tune the manuscript. Their eagle eyes caught numerous issues that we would have otherwise overlooked. Feedback from Justin McKinley and Drew Clayton, who both read the manuscript in preparation for publishing their own books, helped us recognize key areas that needed expanding, as did our many beta readers.

The advice from Andrew Barcello of Feig Finkel LLP helped us to both shore up our legal chapter and make it timelier, particularly with the addition of information on the still-nascent area of artificial intelligence. Expertise from Lluvia Arras, Michelle Manley, and Ghislain Viau was used not only as tips in the design chapters and to create two of the appendices but also to create the book itself.

When it came to cover design, we knew there was only one person to turn to. As she had with Jenna's memoir, Lluvia created an eye-catching cover that perfectly embodied the look and feel we were going for, while Jose Pepito masterfully incorporated the cover's motifs in our interior design. We're always confident when our work is in their capable hands. A special thank you to Sara's husband, Chris Bielinski, for lending his design eye and

Photoshop skill to bring several appendices to life (and for putting in time after his own 8-5 job, moving graphics around one keystroke at a time, until Sara and Jenna were happy).

Numerous individuals submitted quotes, tips, and anecdotes sprinkled throughout this book, helping us to better illustrate concepts and give them more urgency. While there are too many names to mention here, we want to give special acknowledgment to Bree Barton, Ted Goodman, Kathy Leingang, and Dave Margalotti, who provided not only content for the book but also their services and feedback on our work.

Lastly, we'd like to thank our friends and family for their patience and support over the last four years. Thank you for going on this adventure with us.

Self-Publishing Timeline

While every book project varies, the timeline below can give you a rough idea of how long certain parts of the process may take. Keep in mind that some steps, such as design, may take longer depending on your project's specific requirements. Once your book is released, marketing can be an ongoing process that lasts months or even years, depending on your book's success. Visit bookagogo.com/infographics to view a larger version of this infographic.

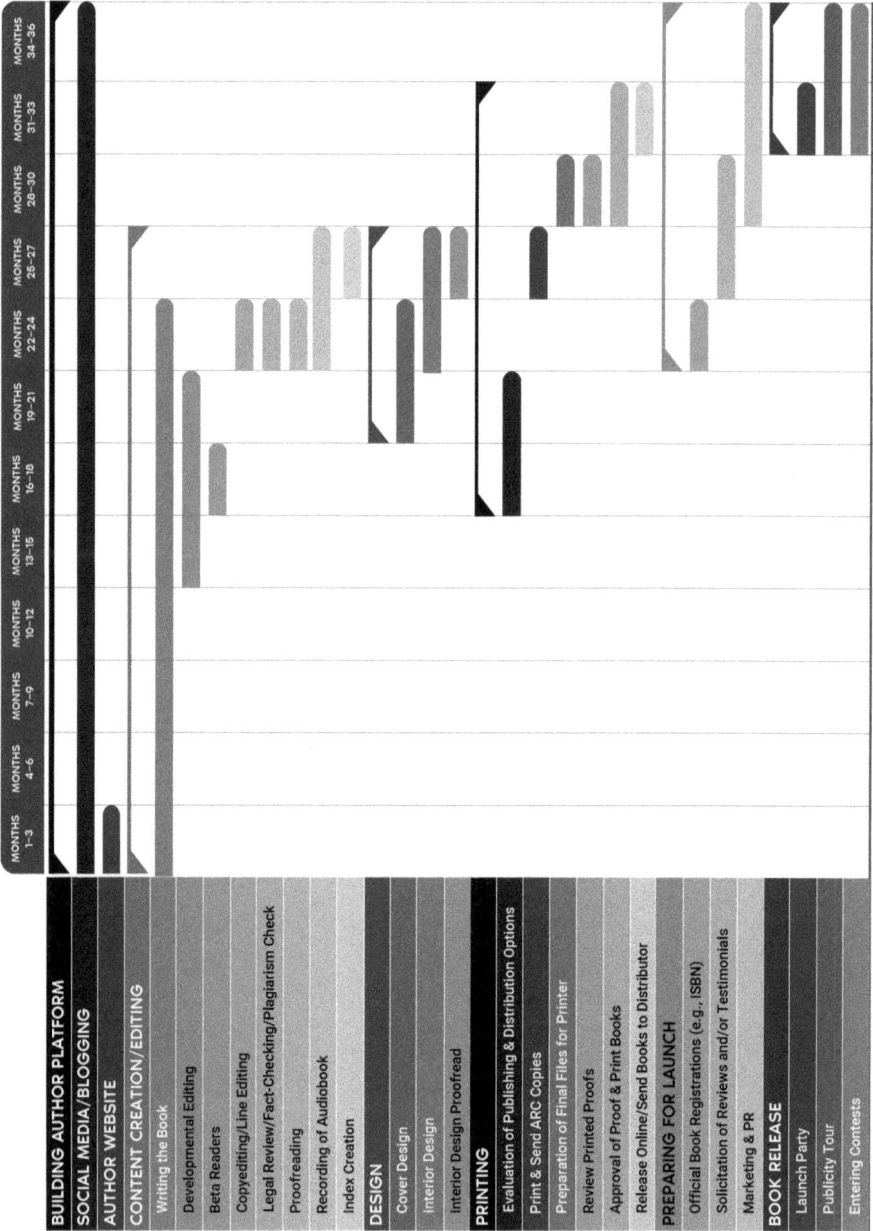

	MONTHS 1-3	MONTHS 4-6	MONTHS 7-9	MONTHS 10-12	MONTHS 13-15	MONTHS 16-18	MONTHS 19-21	MONTHS 22-24	MONTHS 25-27	MONTHS 28-30	MONTHS 31-33	MONTHS 34-36
BUILDING AUTHOR PLATFORM												
SOCIAL MEDIA/BLOGGING												
AUTHOR WEBSITE												
CONTENT CREATION/EDITING												
Writing the Book												
Developmental Editing												
Beta Readers												
Copyediting/Line Editing												
Legal Review/Fact-Checking/Plagiarism Check												
Proofreading												
Recording of Audiobook												
Index Creation												
DESIGN												
Cover Design												
Interior Design												
Interior Design Proofread												
PRINTING												
Evaluation of Publishing & Distribution Options												
Print & Send ARC Copies												
Preparation of Final Files for Printer												
Review Printed Proofs												
Approval of Proof & Print Books												
Release Online/Send Books to Distributor												
PREPARING FOR LAUNCH												
Official Book Registrations (e.g., ISBN)												
Solicitation of Reviews and/or Testimonials												
Marketing & PR												
BOOK RELEASE												
Launch Party												
Publicity Tour												
Entering Contests												

Costs Associated With Writing & Publishing Your Book

Rates quoted are the industry average, where applicable, at the time of publication and are subject to change; in most cases, you also have the option of performing these tasks yourself. Specialty manuscripts (e.g., medical texts) often command much higher rates. Books that are long and complex, such as ones that contain a lot of charts, images, and footnotes, can also command different costs and timelines. Visit bookagogo.com/worksheets to download this worksheet. Use the last (blank) column to track your book's estimated budget.

GENERAL INDUSTRY RATES	YOUR ESTIMATED COST
AUTHOR PLATFORM (SEE CHAPTER 2)	
Social Media — Ranges based on needs/desires; can be anywhere from $400/month to thousands	
Blogging — See Writing Team section for costs to hire professionals	
Website — Initial development starts around $300 and can go up to $4,500, depending on functionality and number of pages. Annual fees: $100–$300, depending on functionality (e.g., shopping platform)	
WRITING TEAM (SEE CHAPTER 5)	
Co-Author — $60K flat rate or $200/hour	
Ghostwriter — $75K–$150K flat rate or $200/hour	
Writing Coach — $200/hour	
EDITING TEAM (SEE CHAPTER 6)	
Developmental Editor — $200/hour, $15/page, or $.09/word	
Line Editor — $75–$150/hour, $12.50/page, or $.07/word	
Copyeditor — $50–$75/hour, $4–$7/page, $.02–$.04/word	
Proofreader & Design Proofreader — $35–$50/hour	
LEGAL (SEE CHAPTER 8)	
Legal Review — $3,750 flat rate or $250–$750/hour	
Fact-Checking — $5K–$25K flat rate or $30–$40/hour	
MARKETING (SEE CHAPTER 16)	
Publicity/PR — $2,750–$4,500/month or flat rate for set time frame. (Rate varies based on campaign needs, length of engagement, etc.)	
Amazon Marketing — $4,500–$6,500 for 6-week campaign to get title to the top of bestseller charts	
Reviews/Contests — $35–$1,000/professional review $50–$300/contest	

GENERAL INDUSTRY RATES	YOUR ESTIMATED COST
REGISTRATIONS	
ISBN — $125 for each version of your book	
Barcode — Only need for print versions ($10 each)	
U.S. Copyright — $65 covers all versions	
Library of Congress Cataloging Number (LCCN) — Free for all versions	
DESIGN (SEE CHAPTERS 12 & 13)	
Interior — $500–$6,500; $100–$500 (interior e–book conversion)	
Interior Illustrations — $10–$500 per illustration, depending on complexity	
Cover — $1,500–$4,500	
PRINTING & DISTRIBUTION (SEE CHAPTER 15)	
Printing — $2–$10 per book, depending on color/B&W, paperback/hardcover, quantities/type of paper/cover material/page count, etc.	
Distribution — Maintenance fee: $15–$25/month; Warehouse/storage fee: $10/month and/or per–book fee; Amazon royalties: typically 55%	
Print on Demand — Depends on company selected; some are free while others charge per-title setup (~$50) and/or annual fee.	
E-Book — Typically free to upload title, although some charge a nominal fee (~$50)	

AUDIO BOOK (SEE CHAPTER 14)	YOUR ESTIMATED COST
Narrator — $150–$250/finished hour, or $900–$1,500*	
Audio Editing & Mastering — $75–$100/finished hour, or $450–$600 total*	

*BASED ON A 10K HOUR BOOK

Website Development Checklist

The following is a generic checklist of terms that you can include in your contract with your website developer. This is not a comprehensive list, but it does cover a lot of issues that many first-time site owners are unaware of. Many of these terms may be unfamiliar to you, but they will be clear to any developer and assure a high level of functionality and stability. Although quite a few of the items below are standard on some website builders, they may not be on others. Each builder (WordPress, Squarespace, Wix, etc.) has its own quirks, so your needs may vary.

Overview

Developer will be responsible for all items below unless otherwise noted. If Developer needs assistance from Client on an item, Developer will inform Client within the first week of the project.

Pre-Development

- Review Client's existing hosting company and make sure it is compatible with new site, or work out a transfer process.
- Ensure you have all required logins before beginning so there is no holdup when the go-ahead is given for launch.
- Back up old site and provide files to Client. If site is only undergoing minor updates, screenshots of current site will be taken and stored in a location where all can access (e.g., Google Drive, Dropbox).
- Understand the website goals (e.g., newsletter signups, scheduling appointments, etc.), which will be provided by Client.

Design, UI & UX

- At least one website goal is promoted on each page, preferably as a sidebar module or in the footer. For example, if one of the goals is newsletter signups, a signup form is available on all pages in the sidebar and/or footer.
- Social media icons are included in header of every page.
- Social sharing buttons are included on every blog post.
- Landing page for newsletter signup (for social media, campaigns, etc.). This does not need to be in the nav, but it would be preferable if it could go in the footer.
- Site-wide favicon.
- Copy is consistent across site, e.g., always use the word *comment* instead of *message*.
- Font formatting is consistent, e.g., all hyperlinks are the same color sitewide, and nowhere is nonhyperlinked text the same color as hyperlinked text.
- Any links that point off-site open new tabs/windows.
- Provide graphic and/or code-based button that can be edited.
- Blog landing page, category/tag landing pages, and search pages have same formatting/layout.
- Photo captions are left-aligned and designed to be distinct and separate from body copy, either through color, size, or a border that separates the caption and photo from the body copy.

Functionality

- Website to follow standard best practices as followed by all the major websites (i.e., logo links to homepage, search box searches entire site, general UX behavior, navigation elements behave consistently on each page, etc.).
- Replies to existing comments are nested/threaded.

- Website is optimized for Google AMP.
- Any forms can be tabbed through in a logical order and have the necessary auto-fill data (e.g., state box has a dropdown menu of states) and expected field types (e.g., date fields have calendar to choose from).
- All forms, including those for comments, have CAPTCHA or similar security method to reduce spam.
- Press page is a single page with a listing of press mentions that can be updated as new mentions occur. Brand imagery on these pages is for media to download, so high-resolution versions must be made available, along with captions and credits. Photos for download do not have credit burn-ins.
- Customized 404 page, which contains links to other recommended areas of the site (e.g., recent blog posts, store, search).
- All pages load in under 1.5 seconds.
- All events and other content items with a limited life expectancy can be scheduled to expire and automatically move to the appropriate location (e.g., archive, past events).
- Developer will redirect individual pages from the old site to the new site under direction of Client.
- Client does not need to use HTML to update any major portions of the website, e.g., rotating hero, homepage promo spots. All such content can be edited in standard CMS fields.

Compliance

- Website will be compliant with ADA (with a minimum Level AA rating) and (for those sites that will have an EU presence) GDPR laws, including, but not limited to, a popup cookie disclaimer.
- Client to provide copy for Privacy Policy and Terms of Use page, as well as overall disclaimer, where applicable; website will have links in the universal footer to these pages.

Google Analytics

- Internal site search is set up for tracking in Google Analytics.
- Internal IP addresses are blocked from tracking.
- Google Analytics tracking is installed on every page; Google Search Console set up and enabled.
- Goals are confirmed with Client and set up.

Search

- Copy in internal search results is editable and can be independent of the main copy on the page it points to (e.g., uses Excerpt or Meta Description fields). This copy is also used on content-list pages, such as blog and category landing pages.
- Site-wide search enabled (for websites with more than twenty pages and those with a blog or dynamic pages). Search box is always in upper-right corner or as close to that as possible; must be above the fold.
- If no search results are found, alternative links (homepage modules, recent blog posts) show in addition to the search field and a CTA to search again.
- At launch, all items in search results will have an SEO-friendly excerpt and featured image.
- Search results show term that was searched for, e.g., "You searched for: calico cats."
- Ideally, layout for search results page is the same as a blog landing page, so that photos and copy can have same dimensions and length; this is also good for UX.

Blog

- Editable categories (that appear as a sub nav, if they are not in the main nav). Client can add/delete categories as they wish, and the navs will be easily edited or respond appropriately.
- Tags and categories appear on each post.
- Unless otherwise noted, each blog post should have the widget for author name and bio. Any steps needed on the part of user to have their bio and photo set up should be relayed to them at least two weeks before launch. Developer to include author setup in site documentation.
- Non-post pages show excerpts (using Excerpt field) of blog posts (not the whole post).
- Date posted on all blog pages.
- Ability to subscribe to blog via RSS feed.
- Bottom of each post has recommended/related posts.
- Must have landing page of most recent posts; can be blog landing page.
- CSS for blog posts properly formats bullets (including second hierarchy and inline images).

SEO

- H1 and H2 tags used to maximum efficiency.
- XML sitemap.
- Ability to modify SEO content for all pages.
- SSL certificate installed.
- Images are uploaded according to SEO standards and have naming conventions that allow users to find them easily in the CMS. For images that are uploaded solely for beta testing, please include FPO (For Production Only) in the Description field so that they can easily be found and deleted.

Security

- Sitewide backups are enabled to occur automatically—at least biweekly—and are stored in a third location, such as on Dropbox, that is accessible by Client at all times. Site owner is sent email confirmations each time backup is completed.
- Recaptcha installed in all relevant places.

E-Commerce

- Shopping cart shows that payment is secure (SSL certificate).
- Links to return/satisfaction policy (to be provided by Client).
- Ability to offer coupon codes.
- Ability to sign in or checkout as guest. Signing in allows a user to create an account that can be accessed on subsequent site visits.
- Client to provide required payment options (e.g., Apple Pay, Venmo, credit card).
- Abandoned shopping cart has ability to later remind user to return.
- To minimize distraction and cart abandonment, no other CTAs for goals should appear on shopping cart pages.

Testing & Delivery

- Documentation provided to Client on how to add, edit, and delete all editable content (if beyond basic CMS interface).
- Budget includes all costs, including photos and templates.
- Site to be tested on the following operating systems and browsers:
  - PC: Firefox, Chrome, Edge
  - Mac: Firefox, Safari, Chrome, Edge
  - Mobile: iPad, iPhone, Android
- Developer to provide Client with all logins and design info (website and font hex colors and font faces and styles).

Before Launch

- Developer to review hosting environment at least [TBD] days before launch to ensure host can handle all aspects of the site.
- Any existing email accounts are kept live throughout the process. If any downtime is anticipated, Client must be given at least five business days' notice and downtime should neither exceed three hours nor be during working hours.
- Site is not visible to users until it has been QA'd by Developer and Client. QA includes but is not limited to:
  - Testing site search to make sure it provides accurate results and looks correct.
  - Testing any forms and buttons, including e-commerce.
- All test copy and images are removed/replaced before site goes live.
- All URLs, including photos, should be relative to main site (i.e., photo URLs are www.newsite.com/this-photo.jpg, not www.devsite.com/this-photo.jpg).
- If site has moved hosts, make sure that all email files and addresses are also moved over. If previous host will no longer be used, confirm that account has been closed and send any confirmation documentation to Client and/or project manager.
- Ensure Google Analytics is set up.
- Before launch, Developer lets Client/project manager know if/when they will no longer have access to old website. Any new content is imported into new website, either by Developer or Client (TBD).

Review & Changes

- For items that require review during the development cycle, Client has two business days to review or schedule may get pushed.
- Upon completion, Client has two weeks to review site and request changes that fall within the original scope of the project.

Sample Beta Reader Letter

Below is the template of the letter Jenna and Sara sent to their beta readers for this book. Feel free to edit to meet your needs.

Hi, [Name of Beta Reader],

Thanks for agreeing to be a beta reader for my book, [*Book Title*]. We greatly appreciate your taking the time to provide your feedback and expertise.

As many of you know, this book has been a labor of love for more than three years. What began as a few blog posts quickly blossomed into a podcast (also forthcoming) and then this book. It's been a truly remarkable journey.

A few notes before you begin reading:

- If you send any notes, please refer to pages as they are numbered in the document (as opposed to the Word or Adobe page number).

- You are seeing the e-book version, which is why there are hyperlinks. The print version will be formatted differently.

- There are places we know are awkward. In some cases, we've left in sections we were unsure about to see if you felt strongly about them.

- None of the back matter has yet been finalized, but we wanted to include the placeholder copy and images to give you an idea of what these sections will include.

Feel free to send notes in whichever way you prefer—as Word comments, in a separate email, or however is most convenient for you. We appreciate any and all feedback! We'll also be sending an anonymous survey soon. The big-picture questions we have are:

- Is our information accurate?
- Is our information complete? Although we know we can't include everything in one book, we've included the most important evergreen information and directed users to online sources (many our own) when the information would get dated too quickly in a published document. (Ex: Information on how to set up an Amazon Author Page is included in a link, as this process changes every few months.)
- Is the content clear for those new to the subject?

Even if you read only the chapters that cover your expertise and no others, we're insanely grateful. We look forward to hearing your thoughts, which we appreciate receiving by [Date] (but please let us know if you need more time).

Again, thank you so much!

Sincerely,
[Your Name]

APPENDIX E

Design Proofreading Checklist

The following list contains some of the high-level design issues to check when reviewing your book's proof (usually a PDF, although it may be an actual print copy) after your designer completes the design. While this list is not comprehensive—depending on the complexity of your book's design, there may be other items you want to check—it does contain the most common issues to review. If changes are made to the interior during the design proofread, such as an edit to the book's title, the cover content may need to be updated to reflect those changes. This list covers design issues only and assumes that all content, including names of people and companies, has been copyedited and fact-checked.

Title Page(s)

- Title, subtitle, and author name match those of the cover and page headers, including the capitalization.
- The publishing company name is included on the full title page, under the author name (optional).

Copyright Page

- The year of copyright is accurate and the copyright name matches what was registered with the U.S. Copyright Office.
- A rights reserved notice and disclaimer are included and copyedited.
- The ISBN and Library of Congress Control Number are accurate.

- The Library of Congress Control Number matches the digits that were provided and the city/state of publication matches what was submitted to the Library.
- Credit to your cover and interior designers is included and copyedited.

Table of Contents

- Each chapter title is consistent with that of its respective chapter head.
- Page numbers accurately reflect the start of each corresponding chapter.
- All chapters, appendices, etc., are included.

Front and Main Matter

- Each chapter starts on the recto (right-hand) page. (Although this is standard for most books, very long books and novels may have chapter heads on either page.)
- Chapter heads are consistent and copyedited.
- The chapters are correctly labeled in order and follow consistent style (e.g., Chapter 4 versus Chapter Four).
- Page headers contain the correct chapter or part title, book title, and author name and are displayed in a consistent manner (e.g., author name is on all verso pages, book title is on all recto pages). Section pages and first pages of chapters do not have headers.
- Page numbers are correct and all odd-numbered pages are rectos.
- Any blank pages or pages containing only photos/tables do not contain text of any kind, including page numbers.
- Hyphenated words:
  - No more than three successive lines end in hyphens.
  - The hyphen is in the proper location within the word.
  - No hyphenated words appear across a turned page (i.e., recto to verso).

There are no orphan sentences and as few widows and stacks as possible.

- Paragraphs, bulleted lists, headings, and other section types (e.g., excerpts, written correspondence) are indented and formatted consistently.
- Page depth, gutter, and margins are consistent, where needed.
- Cross-references, including endnotes and footnotes, to other sections of the book are accurate and consistent (e.g., you don't tell a reader to see Appendix A when you mean B).
- If using images, confirm your designer has used high-resolution (300 DPI or higher) versions. If the proof is a low-resolution file, confirm that your designer will ensure all images are high-resolution in the final file submitted for print.
  - Images have captions and credits where necessary.
  - Captions and credit lines are copyedited and formatted consistently.

Back Matter

- Contact information in the About the Author section is accurate.
- Page numbers in index are correct.
- Entries in glossary and index are listed alphabetically.
- As a final step in reviewing the text portion (front matter, main matter, and back matter), review all pages of the formatted PDF, scanning each from top to bottom to ensure it looks exactly as it should.

Cover File(s)

- Title, subtitle, and author name match those of the title page and page headers, including capitalization.

- Spine has title, author name, and publishing company logo, in that order. Text runs from top to bottom, so that if the book is lying face up on a table, the title on the spine is right side up.
- Spine is correct width for final page count of book.
- Blurbs are properly credited and surrounded by smart (curly) quotation marks.
- Back cover has correct ISBN and barcode for that particular format (e.g., hardcover, paperback).
- Price is inserted into barcode (or left blank, if not using price for printing). See Appendix K for sample barcode.
- Categories (if listing) are placed above the barcode.
- Any Latin or placeholder text has been removed.
- Author photo has appropriate credit underneath the photo or is listed on the copyright page.

Sample Disclaimers

The following are some sample disclaimers that you can use for your book. For more about disclaimers, see chapter 8. While these samples have not been vetted by an attorney, you can use them as a jumping-off point in creating one for your own book.

Fiction Novels

Often, writers create fiction stories based on people or events from their past. Here's the typical disclaimer you might see in a fiction novel:

> This is a work of fiction. Names, characters, businesses, events and incidents are the products of the author's imagination. Any resemblance to actual persons, living or dead, or actual entities or events is purely coincidental.

Memoirs

If you have written a book about your life, you might want to clarify that the topics discussed are as you remember them.

> This book is a memoir. It reflects the author's present recollections of experiences over time. Some names and characteristics have been changed, some events have been compressed, and some dialogue has been recreated.

Nonfiction

If you are writing a nonfiction book that gives advice, you might want to consider a disclaimer specific to your field:

- **Financial**

  This book is not intended to be a source of financial advice. Making adjustments to a financial strategy or plan should only be undertaken after consulting with a professional. The author makes no guarantee of financial results obtained by using this book.

- **Fitness/Nutrition**

  No guarantees are made about the results of the information applied from this book. This is intended to be an educational and informational resource to help you succeed in [area of focus of book]. Your ultimate success or failure will be the result of your own efforts, your particular situation, and innumerable other circumstances beyond the author's knowledge and control.

- **Self-Help/Life Coaching**

  While the purpose of this book is to share insight and successful strategies in building a happy life, there is no promise or guarantee of success.

Publishing Flowchart

Note that hybrid publishing is not listed in this chart, as there are too many variables among the different companies. See chapter 9 for more information. Visit bookagogo.com/infographics to view a larger version of this infographic.

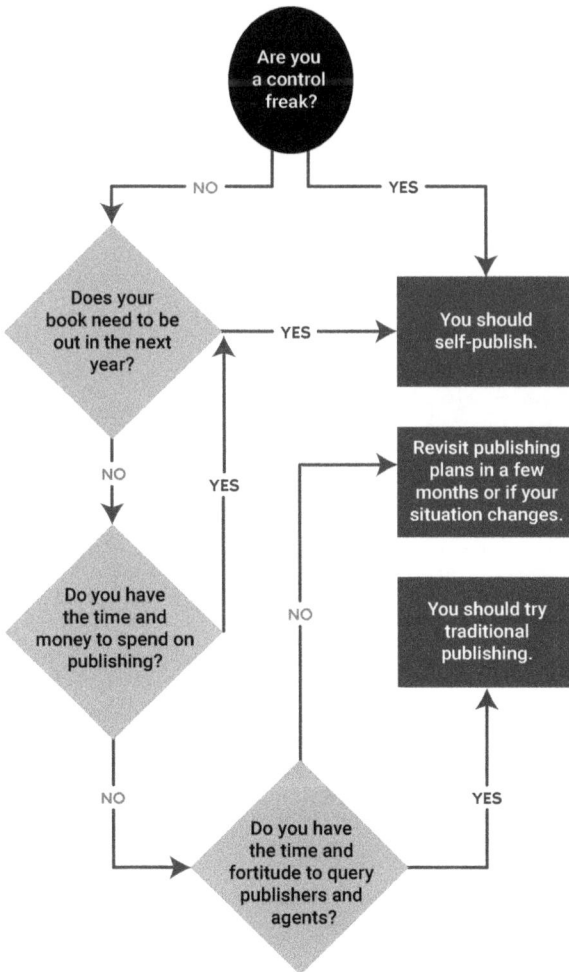

Testimonial/Blurb Request Template & Worksheet

The following form letters can be used to give you a head start on requesting testimonials. When customizing for yourself, make sure to personalize the letter for the recipient as much as possible. Visit bookagogo.com/worksheets for a worksheet to track the status of your requests.

Subject Line: Request for Book Blurb

Hi, [potential blurber's name]. I'm writing to ask if you'd provide a blurb for my upcoming book, [*Book Title*]. [Mention how you know each other or if you are an admirer of some sort. Appeal to their ego but remain sincere. Mention books or articles of theirs you've read, interviews you've watched, and what resonated most with you, especially if it is relevant to your book.]

It would mean a great deal to me if you gave an endorsement. [Insert specific reason why, based on your relationship.]

Here's a synopsis of my book: [Two to three lines maximum.] You can learn more here: [Link to the book page on your website.]

Here is a link where you can download a PDF and/or .epub version of the manuscript so you can read it if you'd like: [Include link]. [Provide a shorter version, if possible, or highlight key sections that might appeal to them. The latter shows you put in effort and *get* them. If they request a print version, you may have to print it out and mail it, which can be expensive, but some blurbers will read only hard-copy versions.]

Since I know your time is valuable and you may not be able to read the full book, I'm providing two example blurbs that [Explain what you're hoping their particular blurb will accomplish e.g., appealing to a certain demographic, attesting to how knowledgeable they are on a topic, etc.]. Feel free to edit them in any way you'd like.

[Insert example blurb #1]
[Insert example blurb #2]

Since the book will be published on [date], I would appreciate if you would provide the blurb by [date].

Thank you for your time. It would mean so much to me to be able to use your blurb for my book and marketing materials, as my readers really look up to you!

With gratitude,
[Your name]

APPENDIX

I

Sections of a Book Infographic

The following graphic shows the many parts that may comprise a book. Not every book has or needs all of these sections, and whether to include them is often at the discretion of the author. Use this graphic, along with the information provided in chapter 11, to determine the correct order of those sections you decide to include. Visit bookagogo.com/infographics to view a larger version of this infographic.

SECTIONS OF A BOOK INFOGRAPHIC

For more information, read chapter 11 of our book, *The Self-Publishing Roadmap: Everything You Need to Know About Becoming an Indie Author*, or listen to episode 11 of the Book-A-Go-Go podcast.

1. FRONT MATTER

a. Blank page
b. "Continued Praise" page
c. Additional books/series title page
d. Title page(s)
e. Copyright page
f. Dedication page
g. Table of contents
h. Explanatory maps/charts
i. Introductory pages
   i. Preface
   ii. Foreword
   iii. Introduction*

2. MAIN MATTER

a. Prologue
b. Body/story
c. Epilogue

3. BACK MATTER

a. Concluding pages
   i. Conclusion*
   ii. Afterword
b. Acknowledgments
c. Ancillary materials
   i. Appendix
   ii. Glossary
   iii. Endnotes
   iv. Bibliography
   v. Index
d. Author biography

*See chapter 11 for more specifics on how the location of an introduction or conclusion can vary within a book.

Sample Copyright Pages

Copyright pages can be as simple or complex as you need them to be. Self-published authors just need to include their copyright information (copyright year, copyright name) and ISBN(s). The following are templates of copyright pages that you can use to get yours started.

Simple Copyright Page

Copyright © [year] [name of copyright owner]

All rights reserved. No part of this publication may be reproduced, distributed, or transmitted in any form or by any means, including photocopying, recording, or other electronic or mechanical methods.

NO AI TRAINING: Without in any way limiting the author's [and publisher's] exclusive rights under copyright, any use of this publication to "train" generative artificial intelligence (AI) technologies to generate text is expressly prohibited. The author reserves all rights to license uses of this work for generative AI training and development of machine learning language models. (Text courtesy of The Authors Guild.)

ISBN: _____ [hardcover]
ISBN: _____ [paperback]
ISBN: _____ [e-book]

More Advanced Copyright Page

[Disclaimer]

Published by [Publishing company name]
[Publishing company address, or just the city and state]
[Publishing company website and/or email]

ISBN: _____ [hardcover]
ISBN: _____ [paperback]
ISBN: _____ [e-book]

Library of Congress Control Number: _____

Most Advanced Copyright Page

Copyright © [year] [name of copyright owner]

[Disclaimer]

Published by [Publishing company name]
[Publishing company address, or just the city and state]
[Publishing company website and/or email]

Printed by [Name of printing company and any other details you'd like to add about them]
ISBN: _____ [hardcover]
ISBN: _____ [paperback]
ISBN: _____ [e-book]

Library of Congress Control Number: _____

[CIP Data Block]

Cover Design: [cover designer name/company]
Interior Design: [interior designer name/company]
Photo Credits: [name of photographer/s for photos used on front and back cover]

To contact the author directly or order copies in bulk: [author contact info]

[edition number]

Infographic of Book Covers

The graphics in this appendix were designed as we were in the midst of the book-writing process, so the version of the book you see in the designs may vary from the final print copy. Larger versions of these images are available on the Book-A-Go-Go website at bookagogo.com/infographics.

Lines with larger dashes indicate a fold, such as on the spine or the dust jacket flaps. Lines with shorter dashes indicate a trim (where the book is cut to the size desired by the author), so no pertinent information or design should be included outside those lines. We also enlarged the barcodes for you to get a better understanding of the information usually presented on book covers.

EXAMPLE BARCODE WITH PRICE

LAN027000 / LAN005020 ◄———————— BISAC codes
ISBN 9781956470956 ◄———————— ISBN
51999 > ◄———————— Price ($19.99); "5" = U.S.

9 781956 470956

EXAMPLE BARCODE WITH NO PRICE
If you don't want to include a price in the barcode, use the default value of 90000—or remove the smaller, right-hand barcode altogether.

LAN027000 / LAN005020 ◄———————— BISAC codes
ISBN 9781956470956 ◄———————— ISBN
90000 > ◄———————— "9" = No price indicated

9 781956 470956

HARDCOVER DUST JACKET

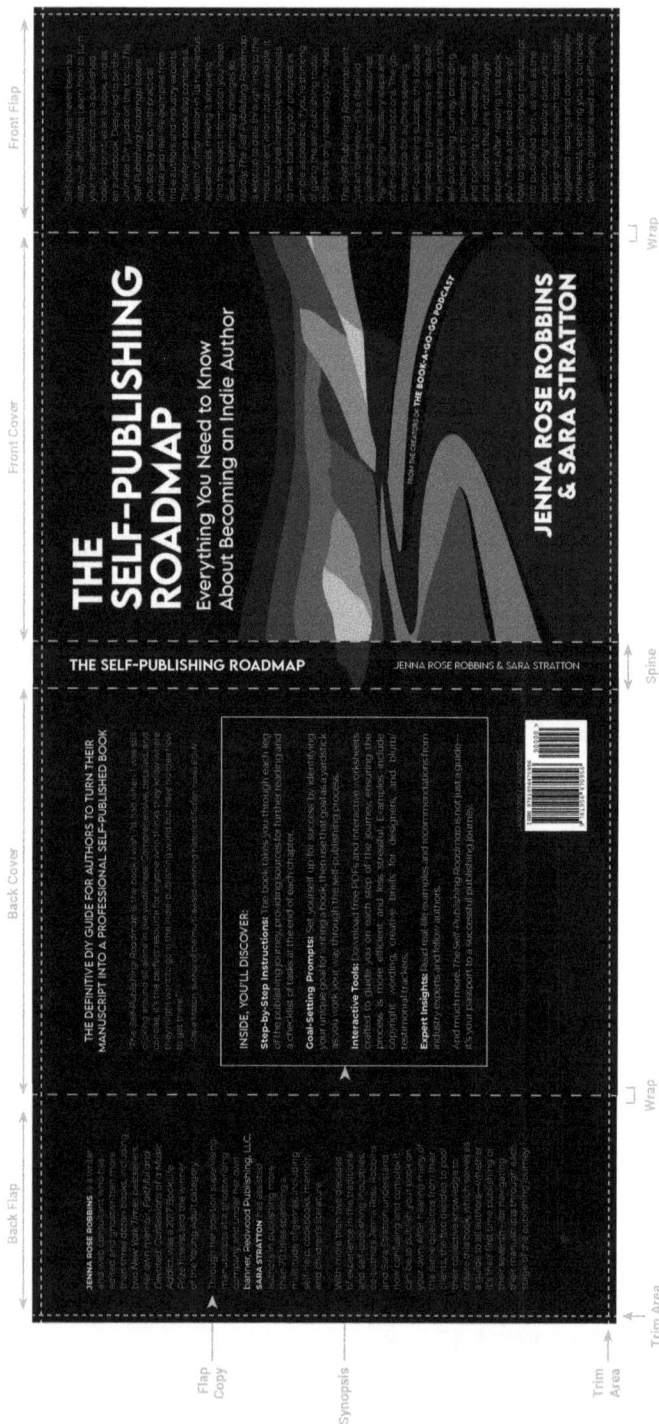

THE SELF-PUBLISHING ROADMAP

JENNA ROSE ROBBINS & SARA STRATTON

THE DEFINITIVE DIY GUIDE FOR AUTHORS TO TURN THEIR
MANUSCRIPT INTO A PROFESSIONAL SELF-PUBLISHED BOOK

The Self-Publishing Roadmap is the road map to take your manuscript and turn it into what others will call a professional self-published book. Covering everything from editing and cover design to formatting and marketing, this book will walk you through each step of the process with easy-to-follow instructions that have been proven to get results.

INSIDE, YOU'LL DISCOVER:

Step-by-Step Instructions: The book takes you through each key step of the publishing journey, providing sources for further reading and a checklist of tasks at the end of each chapter.

Goal-Setting Prompts: Set yourself up for success by identifying your unique goals for writing a book, then use these goals as a yardstick as you work your way through the self-publishing process.

Interactive Tools: Download free PDFs and interactive worksheets created to guide you on each step of the journey, ensuring the process is front-loaded and streamlined. These include copyright updates, creative briefs for designers, and blurb testimonial trackers.

Expert Insights: Read real-life examples and recommendations from industry experts and fellow authors.

And much more. *The Self-Publishing Roadmap* is not just a guide; it's your passport to a successful publishing journey.

JENNA ROSE ROBBINS is a best-selling author, editor, and ghostwriter. Her clients' works have hit multiple best-seller lists, including the *New York Times*, *Wall Street Journal*, and *USA Today*. A former journalist, she has worked as a writer, editor, or publisher at some of the nation's most prominent media companies and currently teaches publishing at UCLA Extension.

SARA STRATTON is a writer, editor, and publishing consultant. She has spent years helping authors navigate the complexities of self-publishing and bring their stories to life. Together, they share a passion for empowering writers to take control of their publishing journey.

Publisher: Redwood Publishing, LLC

**JENNA ROSE ROBBINS
& SARA STRATTON**

FROM THE CREATORS OF **THE BOOK-A-GO-GO PODCAST**

THE
SELF-PUBLISHING
ROADMAP

**Everything You Need to Know
About Becoming an Indie Author**

PAPERBACK COVER

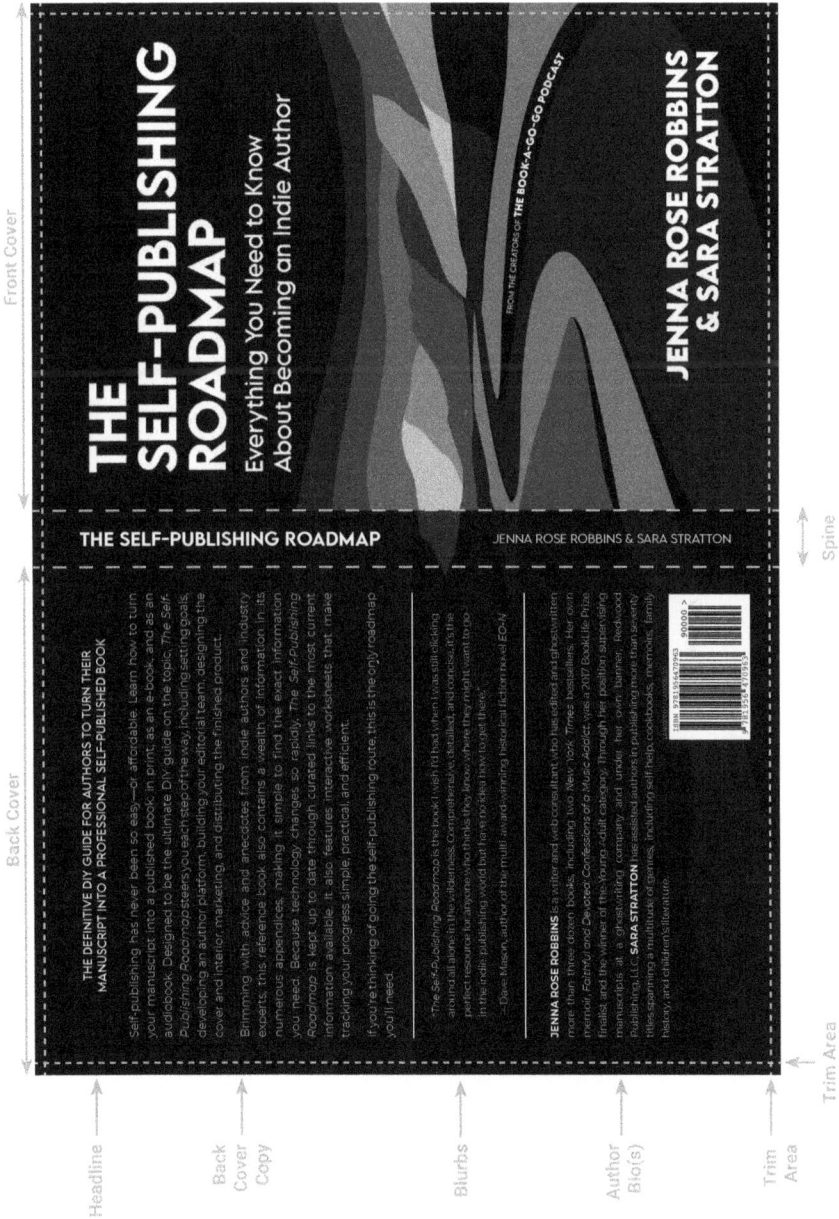

Back Cover | Front Cover | Spine

THE SELF-PUBLISHING ROADMAP

Everything You Need to Know About Becoming an Indie Author

FROM THE CREATORS OF **THE BOOK-A-GO-GO PODCAST**

JENNA ROSE ROBBINS & SARA STRATTON

THE SELF-PUBLISHING ROADMAP · JENNA ROSE ROBBINS & SARA STRATTON

THE DEFINITIVE DIY GUIDE FOR AUTHORS TO TURN THEIR MANUSCRIPT INTO A PROFESSIONAL SELF-PUBLISHED BOOK

Self-publishing has never been so easy—or affordable. Learn how to turn your manuscript into a published book: in print, as an e-book, and as an audiobook. Designed to be the ultimate DIY guide on the topic, *The Self-Publishing Roadmap* steers you each step of the way, including setting goals, developing an author platform, building your editorial team, designing the cover and interior, marketing, and distributing the finished product.

Brimming with advice and anecdotes from indie authors and industry experts, this reference book also contains a wealth of information in its numerous appendices, making it simple to find the exact information you need. Because technology changes so rapidly, *The Self-Publishing Roadmap* is kept up to date through curated links to the most current information available. It also features interactive worksheets that make tracking your progress simple, practical and efficient.

If you're thinking of going the self-publishing route, this is the only roadmap you'll need.

"*The Self-Publishing Roadmap* is the book I wish I'd had when I was still clicking around all alone in the wilderness. Comprehensive, detailed, and concise, it is the perfect resource for anyone who thinks they know where they might want to go in the indie-publishing world but have no idea how to get there."

— Bess Mason, author of the multi-award-winning historical fiction novel *EON*

JENNA ROSE ROBBINS is a writer and web consultant who has edited and ghostwritten more than three dozen books, including two *New York Times* bestsellers. Her own memoir, *Faithful and Devoted: Confessions of a Music Addict*, was a 2017 Book Life Prize finalist and the winner of the Writing-Craft category. Through her position supervising manuscripts at a ghostwriting company and under her own banner, Redwood Publishing, LLC, **SARA STRATTON** has assisted authors in publishing more than seventy titles spanning a multitude of genres, including self-help, cookbooks, memoirs, family history, and children's literature.

ISBN 9781956470963
90000 >

Headline · Back Cover Copy · Blurbs · Author Bio(s) · Trim Area

Creative Brief

Some authors know exactly what they want for their book's cover, while others need a little help figuring it out. If you fall in the latter category, the following exercises could help point you in the right direction. It's also not uncommon for an author to be dead set on a concept only to be unhappy with the mockup, so these exercises can help crystallize your vision if you're in the former category. It's important to remain flexible and open-minded so that, even if you end up choosing your original vision, you can rest assured that you're happy with your design.

Over her many years of working with authors on their book covers, Michelle Manley of Graphique Design Co. has compiled the following exercises to help you prepare for the introductory call with your designer. Having this information will also aid the designer in providing a more accurate estimate of design costs from the beginning so there are no surprises later. After you have completed these steps, fill out the creative brief that follows and provide that to your designer before your call. (Note that the creative brief template can be used for other design requests, such as logos, illustrations, ads, etc.)

1. **Establish your book's genre.** Design trends vary by genre, so it's important you know for sure which one your book belongs in.
2. **Visit your genre's section at a local bookstore.** If you know someone in your target audience, take them with you to get their perspective. Review the books in your genre's section, noting the size, colors, imagery, fonts, and styles most often used, as well as which you like and which you don't. Take note of the following:
   - Are the books in your genre most often hardcovers, paperbacks, or something else?

- What size feels most comfortable to hold and flip through?
- Do the interiors contain a lot of pictures?
- Are there any special bindings?
- What color and thickness is the paper?
- Which covers stood out to you and why?

3. **Explore the rest of the store.** Make sure to look at the books by some of your favorite authors, even if they're outside your genre. Note any designs that catch your attention. Are these techniques being used in your genre? If not, can you see them working? Even if you're unsure, it's worth mentioning an idea to your designer if it interests you, as they might be able to suggest similar techniques or workarounds.

4. **View books in your genre online.** Visit Amazon, Barnes & Noble, Bookshop.org, and other book sites—and repeat step 2. Pay particular attention to whether you can read the title in the cover's thumbnail. If potential readers cannot read your title, they may skip over it.

5. **Do keyword research.** Make a list of keywords relating to your book's subject matter. (See page 40 for a brief overview of keywords.) Then visit Google Images (images.google.com) and perform a search, one keyword at a time. Note what imagery comes up—this may inspire a look you never imagined, or you might see results unrelated to your book, which could lead you to rethink your keywords. Repeat the search process with your keywords, only this time, search stock photo sites, such as:

- **Alamy:** alamy.com
- **Dreamstime:** dreamstime.com
- **iStock:** istockphoto.com
- **Shutterstock:** shutterstock.com

Use your notes from all of the above exercises to complete the following creative brief, developed by cover designer Lluvia Arras (lluviaarras.com), which you can then provide to your designer. Visit bookagogo.com/worksheets to download a blank version of this creative brief.

Project Name							
Date Submitted							
Production Timeline	Round 1:		Round 2:		Final Delivery:		Live Date:	
Requestor							
Key Project Stakeholders							
Deliverable(s) (Include specs, e.g., Digital: social media or ad—RGB, 72 DPI, JPEGs Print: Ad, OOH, Book—CMYK, 300 DPI, PDFs)							
Background/Objective							
Outcome/End Goal							
Measurements of Success							
Key Insights							
Featured Products							
Consumer Profile (Target Audience)							

APPENDIX M

Sample Interior Design Pages With Interior Choices

Here are some examples of various interior design elements, with our book serving as a model. Consider what you want your book to look like based on your genre. For example, fiction and romance typically feature a simple design, while a memoir may incorporate images throughout. Visit bookagogo. com/infographics to view a larger version of this infographic.

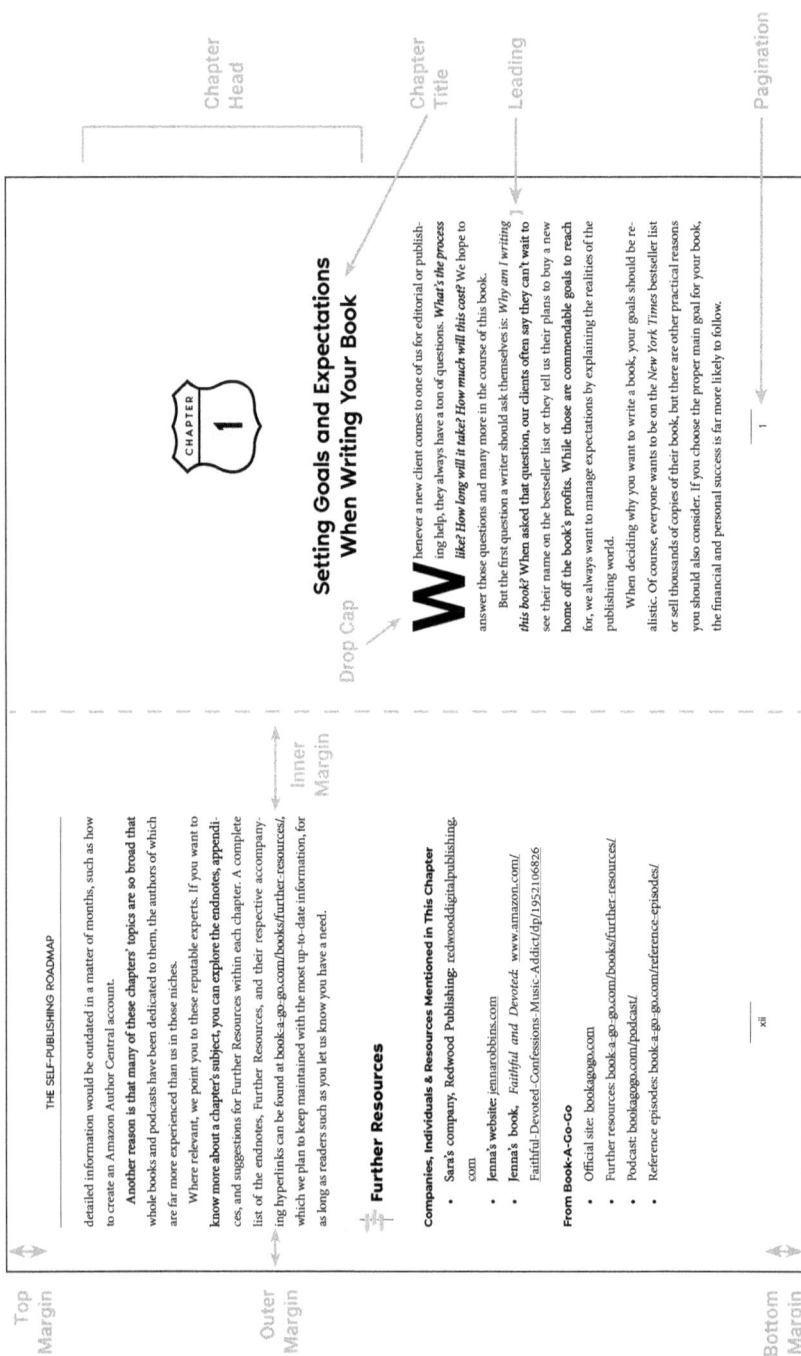

detailed information would be outdated in a matter of months, such as how to create an Amazon Author Central account.

Another reason is that many of these chapters' topics are so broad that whole books and podcasts have been dedicated to them, the authors of which are far more experienced than us in those niches.

Where relevant, we point you to these reputable experts. If you want to know more about a chapter's subject, you can explore the endnotes, appendices, and suggestions for Further Resources within each chapter. A complete list of the endnotes, Further Resources, and their respective accompanying hyperlinks can be found at book-a-go.com/books/further-resources/, which we plan to keep maintained with the most up-to-date information, for as long as readers such as you let us know you have a need.

Further Resources

Companies, Individuals & Resources Mentioned in This Chapter
- Sara's company, Redwood Publishing: redwooddigitalpublishing.com
- Jenna's website: jennarobbins.com
- Jenna's book, *Faithful and Devoted:* www.amazon.com/ Faithful-Devoted-Confessions-Music-Addict/dp/1952106826

From Book-A-Go-Go
- Official site: bookagogo.com
- Further resources: book-a-go-go.com/books/further-resources/
- Podcast: bookagogo.com/podcast/
- Reference episodes: book-a-go-go.com/reference-episodes/

xii

CHAPTER 1

Setting Goals and Expectations When Writing Your Book

Whenever a new client comes to one of us for editorial or publishing help, they always have a ton of questions. *What's the process like? How long will it take? How much will this cost?* We hope to answer these questions and many more in the course of this book.

But the first question a writer should ask themselves is: *Why am I writing this book?* When asked that question, our clients often say they can't wait to see their name on the bestseller list or they tell us their plans to buy a new home off the book's profits. While those are commendable goals to reach for, we always want to manage expectations by explaining the realities of the publishing world.

When deciding why you want to write a book, your goals should be realistic. Of course, everyone wants to be on the *New York Times* bestseller list or sell thousands of copies of their book, but there are other practical reasons you should also consider. If you choose the proper main goal for your book, the financial and personal success is far more likely to follow.

1

Chapter Head

Chapter Title

Leading

Pagination

Gutter Margin

Inner Margin

Drop Cap

Top Margin

Outer Margin

Bottom Margin

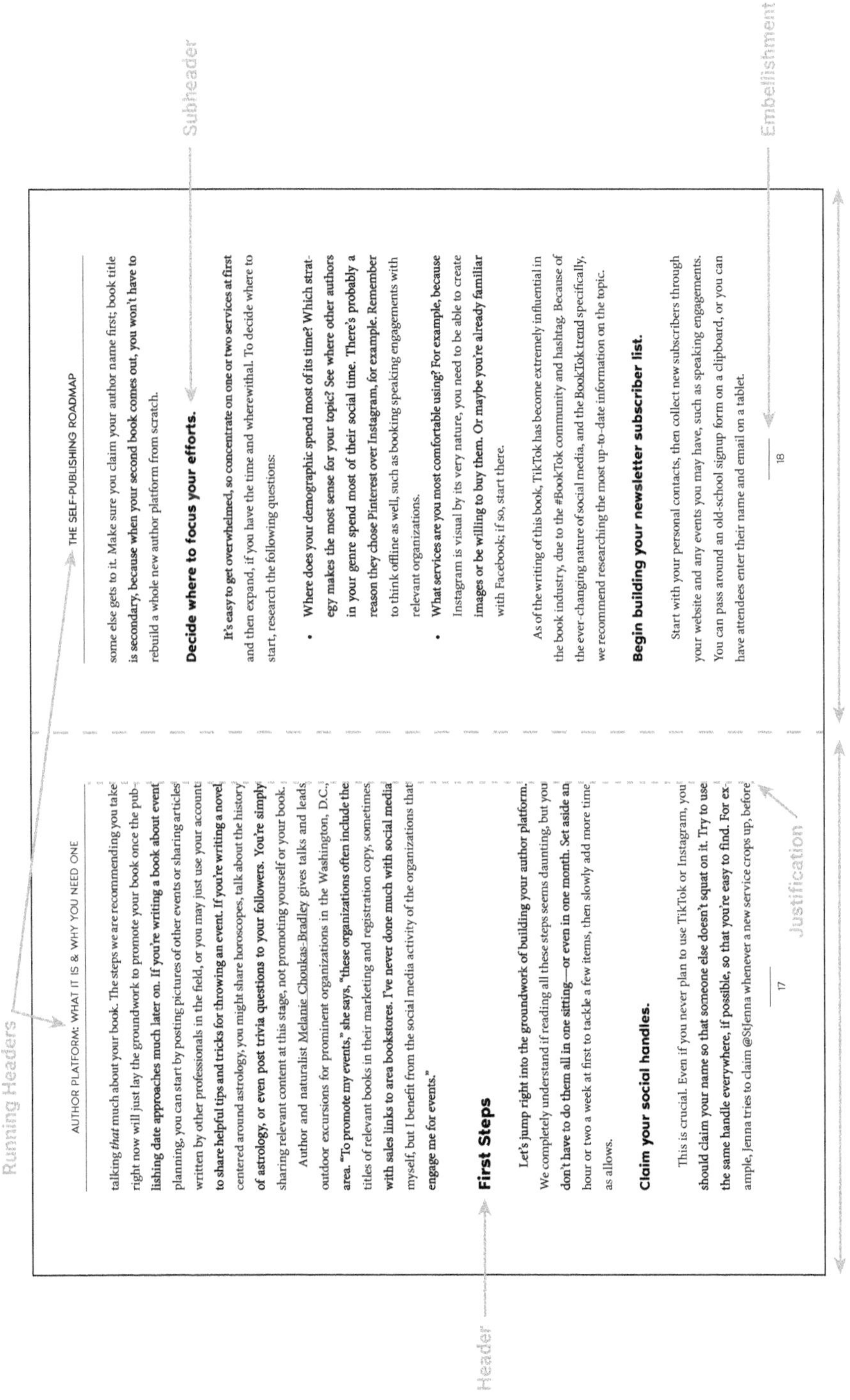

Running Headers
Header
Subheader
Justification
Embellishment
Verso
Recto

AUTHOR PLATFORM: WHAT IT IS & WHY YOU NEED ONE

talking *that* much about your book. The steps we are recommending you take right now will just lay the groundwork to promote your book once the publishing date approaches much later on. **If you're writing a book about event** planning, you can start by posting pictures of other events or sharing articles written by other professionals in the field, or you may just use your account **to share helpful tips and tricks for throwing an event. If you're writing a novel** centered around astrology, you might share horoscopes, talk about the history **of astrology, or even post trivia questions to your followers. You're simply** sharing relevant content at this stage, not promoting yourself or your book.

Author and naturalist Melanie Choukas-Bradley gives talks and leads outdoor excursions for prominent organizations in the Washington, D.C., **area. "To promote my events," she says, "these organizations often include the** titles of relevant books in their marketing and registration copy, sometimes **with sales links to area bookstores. I've never done much with social media** myself, but I benefit from the social media activity of the organizations that **engage me for events."**

First Steps

Let's jump right into the groundwork of building your author platform. We completely understand if reading all these steps seems daunting, but you **don't have to do them all in one sitting—or even in one month. Set aside an** hour or two a week at first to tackle a few items, then slowly add more time as allows.

Claim your social handles.

This is crucial. Even if you never plan to use TikTok or Instagram, you **should claim your name so that someone else doesn't squat on it. Try to use the same handle everywhere, if possible, so that you're easy to find. For ex**ample, Jenna tries to claim @StJenna whenever a new service crops up, before

17

THE SELF-PUBLISHING ROADMAP

some else gets to it. Make sure you claim your author name first; book title **is secondary, because when your second book comes out, you won't have to** rebuild a whole new author platform from scratch.

Decide where to focus your efforts.

It's easy to get overwhelmed, so concentrate on one or two services at first and then expand, if you have the time and wherewithal. To decide where to start, research the following questions:

- **Where does your demographic spend most of its time? Which strategy makes the most sense for your topic? See where other authors in your genre spend most of their social time. There's probably a reason they chose Pinterest over Instagram, for example. Remember** to think offline as well, such as booking speaking engagements with relevant organizations.
- **What services are you most comfortable using? For example, because** Instagram is visual by its very nature, you need to be able to create **images or be willing to buy them. Or maybe you're already familiar** with Facebook; if so, start there.

As of the writing of this book, TikTok has become extremely influential in the book industry, due to the #BookTok community and hashtag. Because of the ever-changing nature of social media, and the BookTok trend specifically, we recommend researching the most up-to-date information on the topic.

Begin building your newsletter subscriber list.

Start with your personal contacts, then collect new subscribers through your website and any events you may have, such as speaking engagements. You can pass around an old-school signup form on a clipboard, or you can have attendees enter their name and email on a tablet.

18

E-Book Side-by-Side Comparison

The following images illustrate how the appearance of different sections of a flowable-format e-book can differ from those of its printed counterpart, as well as how an e-reader's settings affect display. Note that, as of the printing of this book, Kindles display only in monochrome (black and white), although a color version is rumored to be in the works. However, if you are reading a book on a Kindle app on a device such as a phone or tablet, the book will display in color, if available.

If you are reading a black-and-white version of *The Self-Publishing Roadmap*, visit bookagogo.com/infographics to view the following images in color. While there are a number of e-readers and apps to choose from, the following images are from a 6.8" Kindle and an 9.7" iPad.

1. Front Cover

Both the Kindle device and app usually jump straight to the front matter when a new book is opened. Readers generally only see the cover when purchasing, in their library list, or if they manually go to the cover.

- Cropping/margins vary by format, even when using the same image file.

  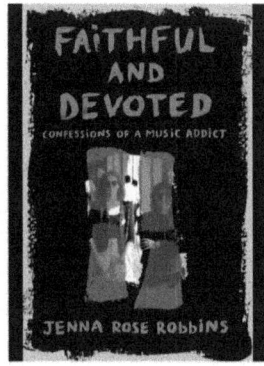

| Print | Kindle | iPad |

2. Table of Contents

Not all books contain a table of contents, but it is advisable that e-books have them, as e-readers offer readers the option to view one. On both Kindle and iPad, users access the table of contents from a dropdown menu at the top of the screen.

- Print version lists page numbers. (Note that the example book does not have a table of contents, as it does not have chapter titles.)
- For books without tables of content, Kindle shows location (the e-reader version of a page number) of the chapter, while the iPad does not. For books with tables of content, the full chapter title and location are shown on both devices.

Go To ✕

| Contents | Popular Highlights |

Beginning

Page or Location ►

Cover

► Front Matter 2

Preface 29

Prologue 65

Chapter 1 86

Chapter 2 298

Chapter 3 554

Chapter 4 664

Faithful and Devoted: Confessions of a Depeche Mode Addict
Robbins, Jenna Rose

Acknowledgements

Preface

Prologue

Chapter 1

Chapter 2

Chapter 3

Chapter 4

Chapter 5

Chapter 6

Chapter 7

Chapter 8

Chapter 9

Chapter 10

About the Author

Back Cover

Kindle   iPad

3. Chapter Head

E-book versions can use elements such as drop caps and custom imagery, although not all do. If using custom imagery, the image needs to be locked in place and the text formatted around it.

- The spacing between the imagery and chapter number, as well as around the drop cap, varies on each device.
- The amount of text displayed in digital versions depends on the e-reader settings.
- Not all fonts available for print are available for digital versions.
- Although the same file was used for both the Kindle and iPad versions below, the iPad shows a running header on the first chapter page while the Kindle does not.

 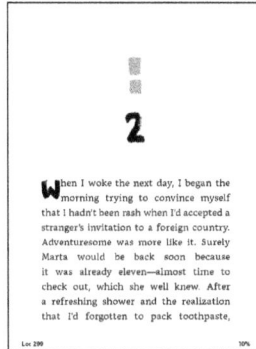 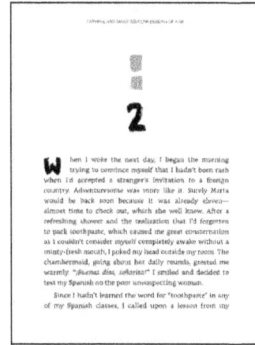

Print   Kindle   iPad

4. Interior Spread

*When held horizontally, an iPad shows a two-page spread; vertical mode displays a single page, which can often display more text than the two pages combined.

- Print version shows a two-page spread with running header and page numbers at bottom.
- E-readers display only one page at a time and typically less text overall, although the amount of text depends on the e-reader's settings.

Faithful and Devoted

knowing that it would only incite annoyance from the person who least understood my infatuation. My mother ignored my question and concentrated her efforts on dabbing the squirming raccoon, who had spit up evaporated milk on the front of her shirt.

Marta's letter of promises burned in my hand, urging me to press harder. I aimed for my mother's Achilles' heel. "It'll be a lot less expensive if I do both countries in one long trip, rather than crossing the ocean twice."

My mother shoved the bottle back in the raccoon's mouth. Finally, as the critter once again took to sucking, she sank into the chair, heaving the sigh of resignation I'd hoped for. Her back still to me, she said, "Ask your father. See what he says."

If there'd been such a thing as black pompoms, I would have been shaking them and doing cartwheels like the cheerleaders I so despised. I'd won the battle. There was no way my father would turn down an opportunity to expand my cultural and linguistic knowledge. I rushed to my candy-apple-red Firebird and sped across town to ask him. His grin nearly split his face in two and, moments later, he was calling over his colleagues to share in the celebration. "My daughter's going to Spain and France!" he announced to all who'd listen. And there were many. "She's going to practice her Spanish *and* French! She speaks two foreign languages, you know." In that respect, he was stretching the truth as much as his smile was splitting his face.

Although my father had agreed and my mother had gone along with his decision, in the weeks leading up to my departure, she prodded me with off-putting remarks. "Why Spain? You've never shown any interest in going there." My Spanish grades from the last two years must have somehow eluded her. I reminded her that in addition to having taken Spanish classes, I'd cared enough to seek

6

Chapter 1

a deep kinship, an understanding that went far beyond the typical angst teenagers share. Despite our different nationalities, we spoke the same covert language, so much so that I knew that my mother, were she ever to read our letters, would think we communicated in some sort of new-wave transatlantic slang that I'd learned from listening to CDs backwards.

My mother was used to being on the outside of my conversations. The summer before I left for college, my family hosted a French exchange student. Marion and I became fast friends, switching between our two languages depending on our mood and desired level of privacy. My mother would try to pick out a word here and there—"Cat! I know you were talking about a cat!"—but she could only manage a few French words, one of which was not Marion's name. "*Mary-on*," she would drone like some Southern hick on methadone, and I would roll my eyes. When I told her to pronounce it normally, "like an American," my mother still insisted on mangling our guest's name, infusing it with an accent that made my teenage-self cringe in embarrassment. "I'm saying it just the way you say it," she insisted.

In a roundabout way, it was because of Marion that I was in Spain. As part of the exchange program, I was to visit her the summer after her stay in the States. (Unbeknownst to both my parents, I had ticked the option of "reciprocal exchange" rather than "monetary compensation" on the host-family application.) Had I not already been planning a trip to France, I would never have considered hitting up my parents for two extra weeks in Spain.

I didn't *need* to go to Spain. I answered my mother, who was now picking a flea from the raccoon's groin. But I was already hopping the Pond, I reasoned, so why not make the most of the airfare? I didn't share my real reason for wanting to visit a second foreign country.

5

Print

left the warm spot I'd created for myself. The underside of my body that had been in contact with the wall and floor felt exceptionally cold, and I shivered as a chill passed down my spine.

I glanced through the sliding glass door that separated the hallway in front of the compartments from the area where Marta, myself, and several other seatless passengers stood about. Several men—one of whom seemed to wear a uniform of authority—were arguing. A younger man, who looked thoroughly perplexed, kept repeating over and over again, "I don't speak Spanish! I can't understand what you're saying!" I glanced at Marta.

"He understands," she whispered. "He just doesn't want to pay the fare."

We gathered our bags and crossed between the cars, where we stayed only a few moments before the younger man

Loc 559   19%

Kindle

can't understand what you're saying!" I glanced at Marta.

"He understands," she whispered. "He just doesn't want to pay the fare."

We gathered our bags and crossed between the cars, where we stayed only a few moments before the younger man entered and walked briskly past us. Marta's eyes followed him, then widened with a twitch of her eyebrow. "Not bad. He can come back if he likes."

I nodded in agreement. "Kind of a California look to him. Definitely not bad."

The fare-hopper muttered aloud to himself as he passed through. When I thought the doors had closed behind him, I turned to Marta. "Australian," I said with an air of authority. Finally, I could have the upper hand on language. "He's Australian."

"Am not!" I turned to find the subject of my conversation leaning through the doorway. For a moment I was at a loss for words. "New Zealand, actually." And with that, the traveler joined me and Marta in our luxurious accommodations on the floor. Although we never learned his name, despite listening to his stories the better part of four hours, Marta and I later came to refer to him as "Kiwi," and we cared little how derogatory the moniker might be. We soon learned that Kiwi had left his home in New Zealand three years earlier with his bike to begin his

Result 3 of 11

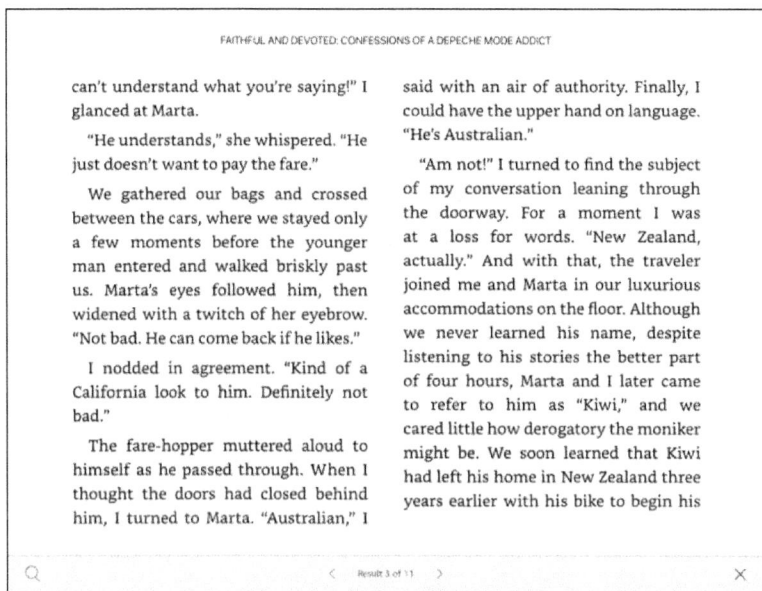

iPad (horizontal)

where Marta, myself, and several other seatless passengers stood about. Several men—one of whom seemed to wear a uniform of authority—were arguing. A younger man, who looked thoroughly perplexed, kept repeating over and over again, "I don't speak Spanish! I can't understand what you're saying!" I glanced at Marta.

"He understands," she whispered. "He just doesn't want to pay the fare."

We gathered our bags and crossed between the cars, where we stayed only a few moments before the younger man entered and walked briskly past us. Marta's eyes followed him, then widened with a twitch of her eyebrow. "Not bad. He can come back if he likes."

I nodded in agreement. "Kind of a California look to him. Definitely not bad."

The fare-hopper muttered aloud to himself as he passed through. When I thought the doors had closed behind him, I turned to Marta. "Australian," I said with an air of authority. Finally, I could have the upper hand on language. "He's Australian."

"Am not!" I turned to find the subject of my conversation leaning through the doorway. For a moment I was at a loss for words. "New Zealand, actually." And with that, the traveler joined me and Marta in our luxurious accommodations on the floor. Although we never learned

Result 3 of 11

iPad (vertical)

5. Same Page with Different Device Settings

A device's settings can alter the way a book displays. The following images show a page in print compared with the same page in Kindle and iPad, with the font at two different sizes.

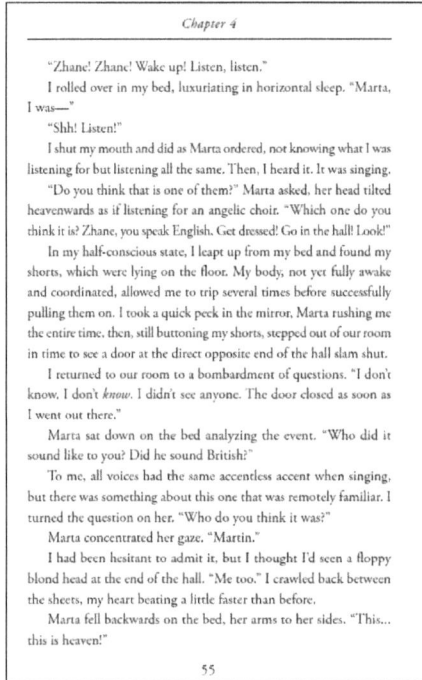

Chapter 4

"Zhane! Zhane! Wake up! Listen, listen."

I rolled over in my bed, luxuriating in horizontal sleep. "Marta, I was—"

"Shh! Listen!"

I shut my mouth and did as Marta ordered, not knowing what I was listening for but listening all the same. Then, I heard it. It was singing.

"Do you think that is one of them?" Marta asked, her head tilted heavenwards as if listening for an angelic choir. "Which one do you think it is? Zhane, you speak English. Get dressed! Go in the hall! Look!"

In my half-conscious state, I leapt up from my bed and found my shorts, which were lying on the floor. My body, not yet fully awake and coordinated, allowed me to trip several times before successfully pulling them on. I took a quick peek in the mirror, Marta rushing me the entire time, then, still buttoning my shorts, stepped out of our room in time to see a door at the direct opposite end of the hall slam shut.

I returned to our room to a bombardment of questions. "I don't know. I don't *know*. I didn't see anyone. The door closed as soon as I went out there."

Marta sat down on the bed analyzing the event. "Who did it sound like to you? Did he sound British?"

To me, all voices had the same accentless accent when singing, but there was something about this one that was remotely familiar. I turned the question on her. "Who do you think it was?"

Marta concentrated her gaze. "Martin."

I had been hesitant to admit it, but I thought I'd seen a floppy blond head at the end of the hall. "Me too." I crawled back between the sheets, my heart beating a little faster than before.

Marta fell backwards on the bed, her arms to her sides. "This... this is heaven!"

55

Print

"Zhane! Zhane! Wake up! Listen, listen."

I rolled over in my bed, luxuriating in horizontal sleep. "Marta, I was—"

"Shh! Listen!"

I shut my mouth and did as Marta ordered, not knowing what I was listening for but listening all the same. Then, I heard it. It was singing.

"Do you think that is one of them?" Marta asked, her head tilted heavenwards as if listening for an angelic choir. "Which one do you think it is? Zhane, you speak English. Get dressed! Go in the hall! Look!"

In my half-conscious state, I leapt up from my bed and found my shorts, which were lying on the floor. My body, not yet fully awake and coordinated, allowed me to trip several times before successfully pulling them on. I took a quick peek in the mirror, Marta rushing me the entire time,

Loc 743   25%

Franks, and she left the room with the same ecstatic look on her face. "I'm going to go look. Maybe they are even *on this floor*."

* * *

"Zhane! Zhane! Wake up! Listen, listen."

I rolled over in my bed, luxuriating in horizontal sleep. "Marta, I was—"

"Shh! Listen!"

I shut my mouth and did as Marta ordered, not knowing what

Loc 741   25%

Kindle

"Zhane! Zhane! Wake up! Listen, listen."

I rolled over in my bed, luxuriating in horizontal sleep. "Marta, I was—"

"Shh! Listen!"

I shut my mouth and did as Marta ordered, not knowing what I was listening for but listening all the same. Then, I heard it. It was singing.

"Do you think that is one of them?" Marta asked, her head tilted heavenwards as if listening for an angelic choir. "Which one do you think it is? Zhane, you speak English. Get dressed! Go in the hall! Look!"

In my half-conscious state, I leapt up from my bed and found my shorts, which were lying on the floor. My body, not yet fully awake and coordinated, allowed me to trip several times before successfully pulling them on. I took a quick peek in the mirror, Marta rushing me the entire time, then, still buttoning my shorts, stepped out of our room in time to see a door at the direct opposite end of the hall slam shut.

I returned to our room to a bombardment of questions. "I don't know. I don't *know*. I didn't *see* anyone. The door closed as soon as I went out there."

Marta sat down on the bed analyzing the event. "Who did it sound like to you? Did he sound British?"

Marta hadn't stopped smiling since she had laid eyes on Andy Franks, and she left the room with the same ecstatic look on her face. "I'm going to go look. Maybe they are even *on this floor*."

* * *

"Zhane! Zhane! Wake up! Listen, listen."

I rolled over in my bed, luxuriating in horizontal sleep. "Marta, I was—"

"Shh! Listen!"

I shut my mouth and did as Marta ordered, not knowing what I was listening for but listening all the same. Then, I heard it. It was singing.

"Do you think that is one of them?" Marta asked, her head tilted heavenwards as if listening for an angelic choir. "Which one do you think it is?

iPad

Printing in Signatures Diagrams

The following diagrams demonstrate how a printer can utilize a single sheet of paper to print multiple pages of a book. The text is printed on both sides, and subsequent folding, cutting, and binding with other signatures culminate in the creation of the finished book. The illustrations provided are based on a 16-page signature, with dashed lines indicating fold locations.

Front Side

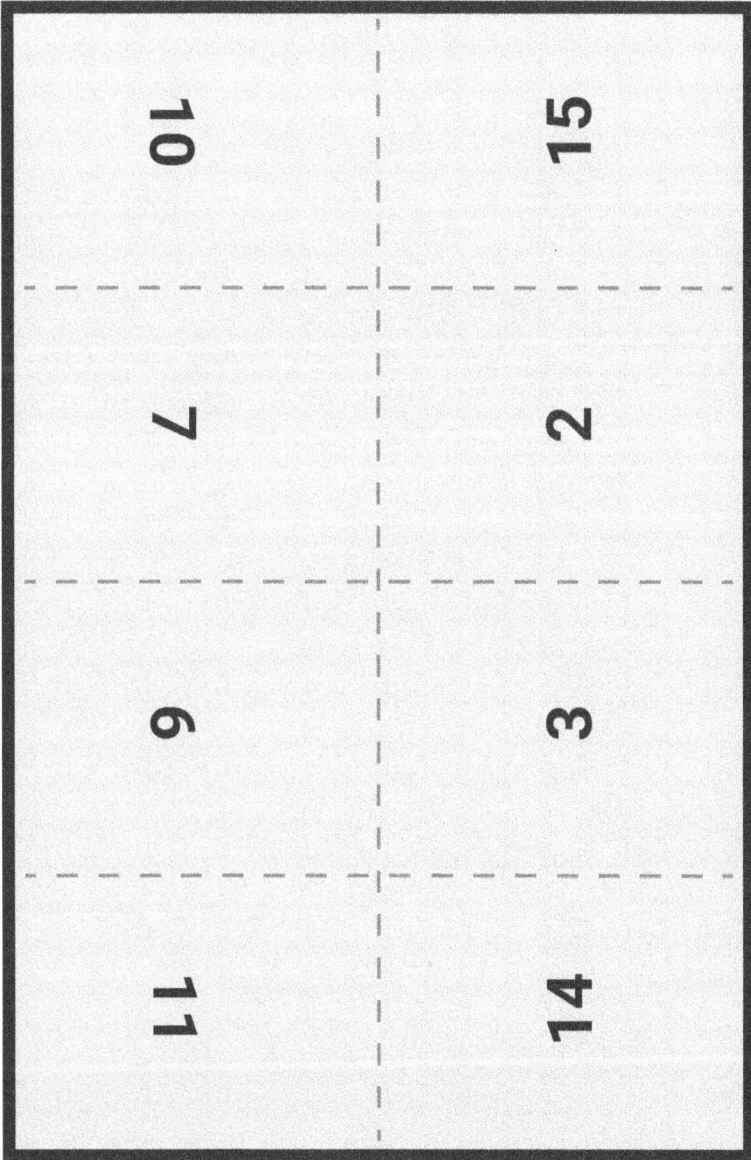

Back Side

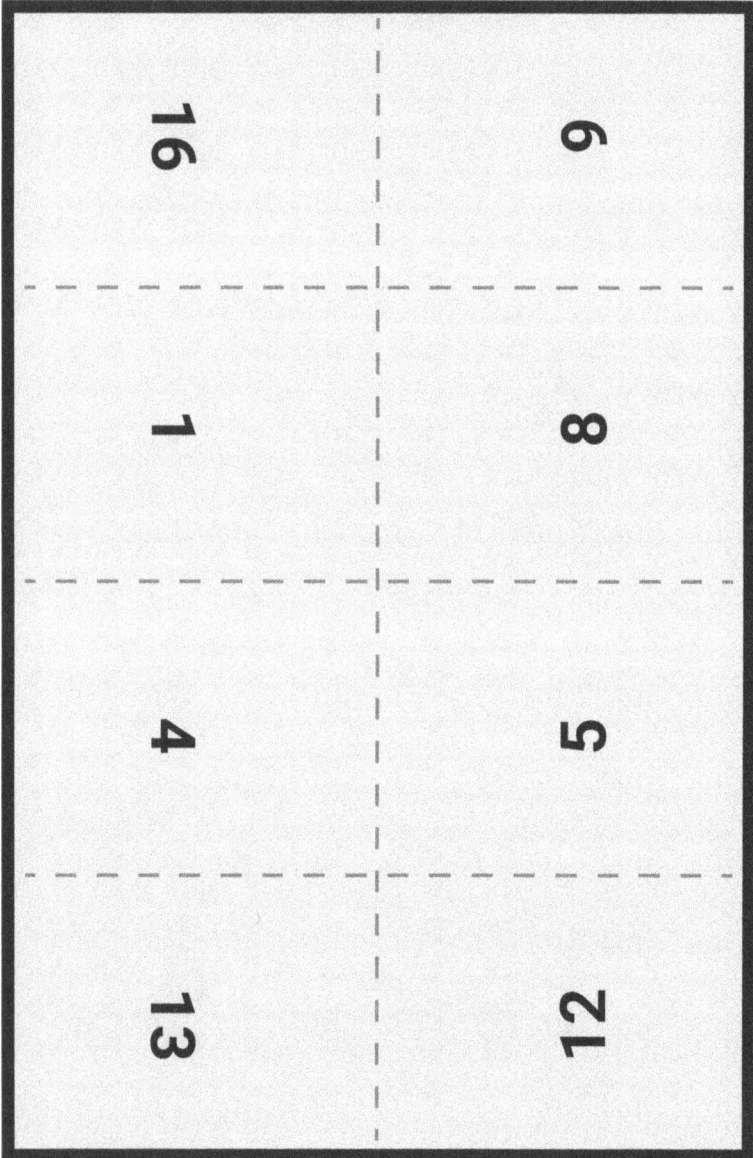

Allowable Changes
After Publication

If you wish to make changes to your book after it's been published, your options might be limited, depending on the publishing service (Amazon, IngramSpark, etc.).

Data	Can it be changed after being published?	Notes
Title	N	
Subtitle	N	
Author Name	Depends	Some allow this to be changed as long as cover/interior files are revised accordingly.
ISBN	N	
Publisher/ Imprint Name	Depends	Although some allow a change to imprint name, many do not. Some may require the imprint name registered with Bowker be changed before it can be changed in their system.
Interior File	Y	Can be changed if you update your book (e.g., to correct typos)/add more information; however, changing 20% or more of content usually requires the release of a new edition.

Page Count	Y	Can be changed; however, uploading a reformatted cover could be required depending on the number of pages added or subtracted.
Cover File	Y	
Book Size, Paper Selection & Cover Material	Depends	Some allow modification of book size and printing details (e.g., changing from color to black-and-white pages).
About the Book	Y	
About the Author	Y	

Comparison of
Print-on-Demand Companies

The following chart shows the most commonly requested features and services of some of the most popular POD companies. Note that printing costs and options for trim size are not included, as they change often and vary greatly depending on quality, type of book, and print time frame. For those companies that also offer bulk printing in addition to POD, additional options may be available. Visit bookagogo.com/infographics to view a larger version of this infographic.

		AMAZON KDP	BOOK-BABY	INGRAM-SPARK	LULU	OVER-DRIVE	RAKUTEN KOBO
DISTRIBUTION SERVICES		Print, e-book	Print, e-book	Print, e-book	Print, e-book	E-book, audiobook	E-book, audiobook
ISBN		Provide your own or use a free one provided by Amazon KDP	Provide your own or purchase through BookBaby	Provide your own or purchase through IngramSpark	Provide your own or use a free one provided by Lulu	Provide your own	Provide your own
COVER FORMATS	Hardcover	Case laminate	Case laminate, dust jacket with printed case cover	Case laminate, jacketed case laminate, dust jacket with cloth linen	Case laminate, jacketed case laminate, dust jacket with cloth linen, linen wrap with no dust jacket	N/A	N/A
	Paperback	Perfect binding	Perfect binding	Perfect binding	Perfect binding, coil binding, saddle stitch	N/A	N/A
COVER MATERIALS	Finish	Glossy or matte	Glossy or matte	Glossy or matte	Glossy or matte	N/A	N/A
	Custom Options	N/A	N/A	Gold-foil stamping available for cloth linen hardcover	Gold-foil stamping available for cloth linen hardcover	N/A	N/A
INTERIOR	Printing Color	Black-and-white or color printing	Black-and-white or color printing	Black-and-white or color printing	Black-and-white or color printing	N/A	N/A
	Paper Color	Cream or white	Natural (similar to cream), opaque (white), or gloss	Cream or white; paperback also offers groundwood	Cream or white	N/A	N/A
	Paper Weight	55 or 60 lb.	60 or 80 lb.	50 or 70 lb.	60 or 80 lb.	N/A	N/A
MINIMUM PRINT RUN		None	Varies depending on type of service (typically starts at 25 copies)	None	None	None	None
CUSTOMER SERVICE	Medium	*Email, phone	Email, phone	Email	Email, phone	Email	Email
	Dedicated Support Contact	No	Yes	No	Yes	No	No
ROYALTY STRUCTURE	Print	**100% of profit after retailer discount and print fees	Most titles generate 10%–30%	**100% of profit after retailer discount and print fees	80% of profit after print and distribution fees	***Up to 46% of the list price	N/A
	E-Book	35% or 70% of list price	45%–70%, depending on retailer	70% of retail	Varies depending on retailer	***Up to 46% of the list price	20%, 45%, or 70%
DESIGN SERVICES		DIY cover design; no interior design services	Full design services for both interior and cover	Authors must upload files to their specifications; does not assist with editing files	Full design services for both interior and cover	N/A	N/A
SETUP COST		$0	$0	Free, but may charge to upload new files	Varies by package	$0	$0

*Clients cannot call Amazon, but Amazon customer service agents can call clients at a requested time and number.

**Based on retail price set by author.

***When using Draft2Digital as your distribution service to release on OverDrive.

Metadata Worksheet

Use this document to keep all of your book's metadata in one place so that you can refer to it as needed, such as when uploading your book to different publishing sites (e.g., Amazon, IngramSpark). Items with an asterisk (*) are required information for most publishing sites, while the other items are used only by some sites. Because some of the information will vary based on book format and edition, you may want a separate worksheet for the e-book, hardcover, each country's edition, etc. You also need to have a final front cover image for each version of your book. Visit bookagogo.com/worksheets for a PDF download of this worksheet.

General

*Title: _____

*Subtitle: _____

*Publication Date: _____

Edition Name (e.g., revised edition, book club edition): _____

Edition Number: _____

Series Name: _____

Series Number: _____

Publisher/Imprint Info

*Name: _____

*Address: _____

*Phone: _____

*Email: _____

ISBNs & Serial Numbers

*Paperback: _____

*Hardcover: _____

*E-Book: _____

*LCCN: _____

*Language: _____

Author Details

*Author 1 First Name: _____

*Author 1 Last Name: _____

*Author 1 Middle Name: _____

Author 1 Country: _____

Author 1 State: _____

Author 1 City: _____

Author 1 Role (e.g., translator): _____

*Author 1 Biography (~2,000 characters):

_____

_____

_____

_____

Author 1 Prior Work (i.e., book titles):

_____

_____

Author 1 Affiliations (e.g., memberships):

_____

_____

_____

Author 2 First Name: _____

Author 2 Last Name: _____

Author 2 Middle Name: _____

Author 2 Country: _____

Author 2 State: _____

Author 2 City: _____

Author 2 Role (e.g., translator): _____

Author 2 Biography (~2,000 characters):

_____

_____

_____

_____

_____

Author 2 Prior Work (i.e., book titles):

_____

_____

Author 2 Affiliations (e.g., memberships):

_____

_____

_____

Author 3 First Name: _____

Author 3 Last Name: _____

Author 3 Middle Name: _____

Author 3 Country: _____

Author 3 State: _____

Author 3 City: _____

Author 3 Role (e.g., translator): _____

Author 3 Biography (~2,000 characters):

_____

_____

_____

_____

_____

Author 3 Prior Work (i.e., book titles):

_____

_____

Author 3 Affiliations (e.g., memberships):

_____

_____

_____

Book Description and Subject Details

*BISAC Category 1: _____

*BISAC Category 2: _____

*BISAC Category 3: _____

*Audience/Readership (options vary by service; choose one):

- ○ Juvenile (child, 0–12)
- ○ Young Adult (child, 13–18)
- ○ Elementary School/High School (textbook)
- ○ College (textbook)
- ○ Professional/Scholar (adult)
- ○ Trade/General (adult)
- ○ Other: _____

*About the Book (long description):

_____

_____

_____

_____

_____

*About the Book (short description; 200 words or fewer):

_____

_____

_____

Key Facts About the Book: [Describe anything new/fun/interesting about your book, such as: "first book by a new author," "TEDx speaker releasing first book," "every page has color illustration by author," "inspired by viral TikTok trends," etc.]

_____

_____

_____

*Keywords: _____

_____

*Quotes From Reviews/Blurbs: _____

_____

_____

_____

Print Details

*Trim Size: _____
*Book Binding:
- Paperback (also called perfect binding or softcover)
- Hardback (also called hardcover or hardbound)
  - Case Laminate (no dust jacket)
  - Dust Jacket (cloth linen)
  - Jacketed Case Laminate

*Page Count: _____
*Interior:
  - Black-and-White
  - Color

Number of Illustrations/Photos: _____
  - Black-and-White
  - Color

*Paper Selection:

- ○ White
- ○ Cream

*Cover Finish:

- ○ Gloss
- ○ Matte

Pricing

*Paperback:

    *Retail Price: _____

    *Retail Discount: _____

    *Return Option:

- ○ Yes (destroy books)
- ○ Yes (return books)
- ○ No

*Hardcover:

    *Retail Price: _____

    *Retail Discount: _____

    *Return Option:

- ○ Yes (destroy books)
- ○ Yes (return books)
- ○ No

*E-Book

    *Retail Price: _____

Contact Information

Name: _____

Phone Number: _____

Email: _____

Relation to Author: _____

Glossary

The following is a collection of publishing-related words, organizations, and companies found in this book, as well as those you might come across on your publishing journey.

80/20 Rule—a guideline to follow when creating content, such as on blogs or social media, that states that 80% of your posts should be useful to your audience (meaning the post should educate, entertain, or offer solutions), while 20% should be promotional.

ACX—*See* Audiobook Creation Exchange.

advance—an up-front payment made to an author before a book is published. The author must earn back the advance in sales before any royalties are paid. *See also* royalty.

advance reader—an individual such as a reviewer and or wholesale book buyer who is provided the book prior to its official release date in order to build early buzz, increase sales, and collect professional reviews and/or testimonials to place on the book cover or use in marketing. *Called also* advanced reader.

advance reader copy (ARC)—a pre-published version of a book sent to advance readers prior to its official release date in order to build early buzz and collect professional reviews and/or testimonials to place on the book cover or use in marketing. *Called also* advance reader copy, advanced review copy.

afterword—a section of the book, located in the front matter, usually written by somebody other than the author, often to provide an extended testimonial for the book. *See also* foreword.

AMA Manual of Style—the American Medical Association's style guide, which is used for publications such as journals or reference books in medicine, health, and other life sciences. *See also Associated Press Stylebook, Chicago Manual of Style.*

Amazon A+ Content—an Amazon marketing feature, allowing authors to customize book detail pages.

Amazon Ads—Amazon services available to their sellers to promote and advertise their products. Previously known as Amazon Marketing Services (AMS), which is how some sources still refer to it.

AMS—*See* Amazon Ads.

appendix—supplemental material such as charts and diagrams placed in the back matter so as not to disrupt the flow of content in the main matter and to make the content easy to refer to.

ARC—*See* advance reader copy.

Associated Press Stylebook, The—a grammar, style, and usage guide that sets the standard for spelling, punctuation, and formatting in journalism and news writing, such as magazines and newspapers; often referred to as *The AP Style Guide. See also AMA Manual of Style, Chicago Manual of Style.*

Audible—an Amazon company that sells audiobooks. *See also* Audiobook Creation Exchange.

Audiobook Creation Exchange (ACX)—an Amazon-owned marketplace for narrators, recording engineers, and other audiobook professionals to offer their services, and for authors, agents, and publishers to create and release audiobooks on Audible.

author copies—final printed copies of a book charged to the author at a cheaper rate than the retail price so they can be sold directly from the author's website, provided for giveaways, or used for other promotional purposes.

author's note—*See* preface.

author tour—*See* book tour.

back flap—the part of a dust jacket that wraps around the rear of the book's cover and that typically has the author's bio and photo or spillover copy from the front flap. *Called also* back panel. *See also* front flap.

back matter—material that exists as supplementary and/or reference material and which is found at the back of the book, after the main matter. *See also* front matter.

back panel—*See* back flap.

bad break—when a word is incorrectly hyphenated (broken) during the interior formatting of the manuscript. *Breaking the word publishing as publishing is a bad break.*

BAGG—a crucial element in the self-publishing process, the Book and Author Gameplan and Goal is a clearly defined objective that authors should establish at the beginning of their publishing journey. The BAGG serves as a guiding principle, helping authors track their progress and make informed decisions. It is recommended to revisit and potentially revise your BAGG as you learn more about the publishing process, ensuring it remains relevant and aligned with your evolving goals.

bastard title—*See* half-title page.

beta reader—an individual, usually nonprofessional, who provides feedback on a near-final draft of the book at a stage when the author is still open to making changes. *See also* expert reader, peer review, sensitivity reader.

bibliography—a list of the books and/or articles used as reference material when writing a book.

Big Five—the five biggest book publishers in the United States, all of which are based in New York City: Hachette Book Group, HarperCollins, Macmillan, Penguin Random House (PRH), and Simon & Schuster.

binding—the physical material used to join together the different parts of a book, such as the cover and pages. Although the most popular types of binding are case or sewn (for hardcover) and glue (paperback), spiral binding and saddle stitch (brochures) are also used.

BISAC code—a nine-character alphanumeric code that indicates to book retailers, distributors, and librarians which categories (and subcategories) an author's book belongs in.

blank—a page intentionally left empty but included in the book's final page count. *Let's add a blank at the beginning of the book so that you have a place to sign at book signings.*

bleed—a printing term used to indicate if a book's interior or cover will have content (such as images, graphics, or color) extend past where the printer will trim the book after printing.

blog—a website or section thereof consisting of informally written, regularly published posts that showcase the author's or authors' viewpoints, ideas, knowledge, or commentary. The term is a shortened version of *weblog*.

blurb—1. a short piece of copy, usually taken from a review or testimonial, that is used to promote a book, such as on the back cover or in ads. 2. to provide a testimonial of a book or an author. *Stephen King said he would blurb my book!*

board—the thick cardboard used for certain types of book printing, such as children's picture books or the material under the dust jacket of a hardcover.

body—*See* main matter.

book proposal—a document that includes an overview of the book, an author biography, competitive research on comparable titles, marketing strategies, chapter outline, table of contents, and one or two sample chapters, as well as anything else an author feels is pertinent to pique the interest of agents and publishers.

book tour—a promotional activity meant to promote an author's newly published title, in which the author plans a series of events, usually consisting of talks, readings, and interviews, to sell books and meet readers.

book trailer—a marketing video that promotes the book in the same way a movie trailer promotes a film.

Bowker—the official ISBN agency for the United States.

C1S—a term for printing that stands for *coated one side,* meaning the coating selected (matte or glossy) is applied to only one side of the paper. *We can print your paperback book cover in full color, C1S.*

call to action (CTA)—a prompt for the reader to perform a specific action, such as a button on a website that reads, "Learn more."

caption—a brief explanation or description of an image, usually placed directly beneath it. *Called also* cutline.

case binding—a bookbinding method that creates a hard cover to protect a book's pages and spine. *Called also* case wrap.

case laminate—a hardcover book in which the cover art and text are printed directly onto the case rather than onto a dust jacket.

case wrap—*See* case binding.

Cataloging in Publication (CIP) record—a bibliographic record prepared by the Library of Congress for an as yet unpublished book that is included on the book's copyright page once published so that places like libraries can process the book in their system. *Called also* CIP data.

center spread—the pair of facing pages in the center of a book that often contains special content, such as photos.

chapbook—a published book, most often of poetry, that is typically forty to sixty pages and often of lower production quality than a traditional paperback or hardcover book.

chapter head—the content that comprises the start of a chapter, such as the chapter number and title, an illustration, or a quote. Chapter heads often appear only on recto pages.

character sheet—a document used to track character facts and traits to maintain consistency throughout the manuscript.

Chicago Manual of Style, The—a grammar, style, and usage guide that sets the standard for spelling, punctuation, and formatting in books, corporate materials, and some scientific publications. *See also AMA Manual of Style, Associated Press Stylebook.*

CIP—*See* cataloging in publication record.

clean copy—a copy of an author's manuscript with all edits incorporated and notations removed. *My publicist asked for a clean copy of the manuscript to review.*

click-through rate (CTR)—a measure of the performance of a link, such as an ad or a CTA, calculated by dividing the number of clicks that an ad receives by the number of times it is shown. An ad that has two clicks and 100 impressions would have a CTR of 2%.

cloth—the material stretched around the board that a hardcover book's dust jacket is wrapped around. The cloth is typically linen and can often be printed on, embossed, or stamped with the book's title and/or author's name.

CMS—*See* content management system.

CMYK—a printing process that uses four colors—cyan, magenta, yellow, and key (black)—that is often required for all-color printing. *Called also* four-color printing. *See also* Pantone Matching System.

coated one side—*See* C1S.

co-author—any of the multiple credited authors of a manuscript.

coil binding—*See* spiral binding.

colophon—a brief statement in a book noting the type of font used in the book, the name of the printer and/or publisher, the publisher's logo, and the date of printing; typically placed on the last page of the back matter.

color printing—a printing option that allows authors to produce a book (or a portion of it) in full color rather than black-and-white.

concordance—an alphabetical list of the most important words and phrases in a text, usually in context as to how the words appear in the manuscript.

content management system (CMS)—software that allows for the creation and organization of digital content, such as for a blog.

cooperative publishing—*See* subsidy publishing.

copy—the text of a manuscript.

copyeditor—an editor who checks for issues with sentence structure, grammar, and consistency in punctuation and formatting, and who sometimes fact-checks. *See also* developmental editor, line editor, proofreader.

copyright—an intellectual property that confers the legal right of ownership to a work.

copyright infringement—the unauthorized use of a copyrighted work.

copyright notice—the section of a book's copyright page that states the copyright owner and the date of copyright.

creative brief—a document that provides information to a designer or other creative to guide them on a project.

cross-reference—a note or notation in the text that directs the reader to another section of the document.

CTA—*See* call to action.

CTR—*See* click-through rate.

cutline—*See* caption.

dedication—a statement in a book's front matter that shows the author's appreciation, affection, or respect for a person or entity.

depth—the number of lines of text on a page. Book designers manipulate depth to make text visually appealing and to avoid issues such as widows and orphans.

design proof—a copy of a manuscript created to check elements of design such as page numbering, consistency in running headers, etc.

developmental editor—an editor who evaluates, critiques, guides, and sometimes helps shape a manuscript, most often during its early stage. *Called also* substantive editor. *See also* copyeditor, line editor, proofreader.

digital assets—everything on the web that an author owns and/or controls (e.g., website, blog, social media handles, logins, etc.).

digital printing—a printing method, used for short-run book printing and print-on-demand publishing, that employs a laser or inkjet printer to print straight from a computer file. *See also* offset printing.

Digital Text Platform—*See* Kindle Direct Publishing (KDP).

distributor—a company or individual responsible for selling books to bookstores and other retailers, online and off.

domain host—a company that manages domain names. *See also* web host.

domain name—the core part of a website address, under which all the site pages reside. *Our website's domain name is bookagogo.com.*

dots per inch (DPI)—a measurement of the resolution of an image both on-screen and in print.

DPI—*See* dots per inch.

drop cap/dropcap—*See* dropped capital.

dropped capital (drop cap)—a design element used at the start of each chapter and displayed via a large first letter of the first sentence, often spanning several lines.

dust jacket—the removable paper sleeve of a book, usually a hardcover.

EAN—*See* European Article Number.

earn out—to bring in profits equal to the book advance so that the author begins to collect royalties.

e-book—a digital version of a book, usually in .epub or .mobi format.

elevator pitch—a short synopsis of a book used for sales and marketing; so named because it can be stated during an elevator ride.

embellishment—an aesthetic element that serves to elevate the visual appeal of a book's design without overshadowing the text; may be used in headers, to denote text breaks, and/or to add character to page numbers.

embossing—when text or images are raised from the flat surface of a material, such as the title on the front cover of a book.

endband—a small strip of colored material a printer uses to attach the block of text pages to the top and bottom of the spine of a hardcover book. *See also* headband, tailband.

endnote—like a footnote, an endnote flags to the reader that additional information or a citation for specific text is available and is indicated via a superscript numeral; however, the citation is placed at the end of the chapter or book rather than on the bottom of the page. *See also* footnote.

endpaper—*See* endsheet.

endsheet—a page, thicker than those throughout the rest of the book, that is glued to the inside of the front and back covers of a case-bound hardcover book. *Called also* endpaper.

epigraph—a short quote, poem, or statement placed at the beginning of a book, usually on its own page.

epilogue—a part of the manuscript often used to tie up loose ends or provide concluding thoughts.

EPK—an electronic (digital) press kit.

.epub—a computer file format for e-books that is compatible with most e-readers, smartphones, tablets, and computers. *See also* .mobi.

e-reader—a device that allows for the reading of e-books.

errors and omissions insurance—a type of insurance used to protect an author or publisher from being sued in the case of a problem with the manuscript, such as plagiarism or copyright infringement; sometimes referred to as professional liability insurance, although the two sometimes differ.

European Article Number (EAN)—a standard barcode and numbering system, similar to a UPC (Universal Product Code), used to identify unique products at point of sale and their country of origin. For books, a prefix of 978 is used so that the EAN is the same as the ISBN.

evergreen—used to describe content that is accurate and relevant regardless of the publication date. *He was born in 1984* is evergreen, while *He is twenty years old* is not.

expert reader—an individual who has a personal connection to or professional expertise in a book's subject matter and who can thus provide specialized feedback on a manuscript before publication. *See also* beta reader, peer review, sensitivity reader.

fair use—a legal doctrine that allows for limited use of copyrighted material without permission under certain circumstances.

favicon—a small symbol that represents a website on a browser tab.

flap copy—written content on the part of the dust jacket that gets folded inside of the book.

foil—1. a printing option for adding metallic material to a surface, such as a book jacket. 2. a character in a narrative who acts as a contrasting figure, often to the protagonist.

folio—1. the page number on a book page. 2. a printed sheet that is folded once to produce four pages.

foot—*See* footer.

footer—the text placed above the bottom margin of the book, usually including the page number or, when no page number appears, from the bottom of the page up to the last line of text. *Called also* foot.

footnote—ancillary information or a citation pertaining to a specific section of text, indicated by a superscript numeral and placed at the bottom of the page. *See also* endnote.

foreword—a section of a book, located in the front matter, usually written by somebody other than the author, often to provide an extended testimonial for the book. *See also* afterword.

four-color printing—*See* CMYK.

front flap—the part of a dust jacket that wraps around the front side of a book's cover and that most often contains a synopsis of the book. *Called also* front panel. *See also* back flap.

frontispiece—artwork that goes to the left of the title page. *See also* tailpiece.

front matter—the beginning sections of a book that precede the main matter and that typically consist of promotional and legal details, and sometimes longer introductory material, usually written by someone other than the author. *See also* back matter.

front panel—*See* front flap.

fulfillment—the process of delivering books to retailers, wholesalers, and individual customers.

full-title page—a page in the front matter of a book that includes the title, subtitle, author name, and, optionally, publishing company name. *See also* half-title page, title page.

galley—*See* advance reader copy.

ghostwriter—the writer, usually anonymous, of a manuscript that gets credited to someone else.

glossary—a collection of the definitions of important words and terms from a manuscript, usually included in the back matter.

glue binding—a bookbinding method, used mainly with paperback books, in which the interior pages are gathered together and glued into the spine of the cover, such that the pages and cover are bound together through the adhesive. *See also* sewn binding, saddle stitching, Smyth sewn, spiral binding.

groundwood—an inexpensive and high-opacity paper, often used for newsprint and low-cost books.

gutter—the inner margin of a book.

gutter margin—the blank space where two pages (recto and verso) meet in the inner margin of a book. *Called also* gutter.

half-title page—a page in the front matter that lists only the title of the book, typically in the same font and style as the front cover. *See also* full-title page, title page.

head—*See* header.

headband—a small strip of colored material that a printer uses to attach the block of text pages to the top of the spine of a hardcover book. *See also* endband, tailband.

header—the text placed under the top margin of each page and above the body copy, usually with the title on the recto and the author name or book chapter on the verso. *See also* running header.

hed—*See* header.

homepage—the main page of a website.

hybrid publishing—a cross between traditional and self-publishing in which the author is responsible for the up-front publishing costs while the hybrid publisher handles the tasks of design, printing, and distribution. *See also* self-publishing, subsidy publishing, traditional publishing, vanity publishing.

imprint—the trade name under which a publisher publishes a book. Many traditional publishers have several imprints, each catering to a specific demographic. An example of an imprint is Ladybird, an imprint of Penguin Random House, which publishes mass-market children's books.

index—a key to a book, found in the back matter, that identifies the pages of each occurrence of a topic.

indie publishing—1. the segment of traditional publishing handled by smaller companies (i.e., not the Big Five). 2. self-publishing. Short for *independent publishing*.

informational social influence—*See* social proof.

IngramSpark—an online self-publishing company that allows authors to print and distribute their books to the websites of all major book retailers, such as Amazon, Barnes & Noble, Books-A-Million, etc.

in print—available for sale from the publisher. With the advent of print on demand, it is now financially feasible to keep a book in print in perpetuity. *See also* out of print, out of stock.

International Standard Book Number (ISBN)—a unique numeric identifier for a book, purchased from an affiliate of the International ISBN Agency.

introduction—a section of the book, often written by the author, that presents the main matter. If the introduction is critical to the reader understanding the book's content, the section is included in the main matter. If the introduction is written by somebody else and/or presents the background story of the topic, the introduction goes in the front matter.

ISBN—*See* International Standard Book Number.

jacket—*See* dust jacket.

KDP—*See* Kindle Direct Publishing.

kerning—the spacing between individual letters and/or words. *See also* leading.

keyword—a word or phrase used to categorize online content.

Kindle—Amazon's proprietary e-reader, which uses primarily the .epub file format.

Kindle Direct Publishing (KDP)—Amazon's self-publishing service; originally called Digital Text Platform.

launch—the overarching book release strategy, which may include marketing, PR, book tours, virtual appearances, etc. Also sometimes called a release, although there are subtle differences. *See also* release date.

layout—how the content of a book is designed, including the spacing, fonts, placement of photos, chapter heads, etc.

LCCN—*See* Library of Congress Control Number.

leading—the vertical space between lines of text. *See also* kerning.

libel—defamation in a physical form, such as in text or images, that is injurious to the individual. *See also* slander.

Library of Congress Control Number (LCCN)—a number that acts as a unique identifier for the U.S. Library of Congress.

limited edition—a version of a book produced in a small quantity, usually fewer than 1,000 copies, and not printed again.

line editor—an editor who focuses on a manuscript's use of language, such as whether the writing is clear and applicable to the intended audience, and who ensures that the copy flows and makes for an enjoyable read. *See also* copyeditor, developmental editor, proofreader.

list price—*See* retail price.

main matter—all the content of a book that falls between the front and back matter. *Called also* body.

manuscript—the original, unpublished copy of a book, often just the main matter.

manuscript critique—a professional assessment of a manuscript's most important elements: plot, character development, and pacing.

margin—the space, including the header and footer, around the main text and images on a page, comprising the top margin, bottom margin, inner margin, and outer margin.

mass-market paperback (MMPB)—a mass-produced version of a book, often printed at a lower quality and in a smaller size than the hardcover or trade paperback versions.

media kit—a package of information, photos, and/or videos provided to the media for use in promoting a brand or product, such as a book. *See also* press kit.

MMPB—*See* mass-market paperback.

.mobi—a deprecated computer file format that was specific to Kindle e-readers. *See also* .epub.

mockup—a preliminary design, such as for a book cover.

model release—a contract that grants permission to use an individual's likeness in a work such as a video or photograph.

narrative arc—the progression of a story, usually consisting of a setup, confrontation, and resolution.

NDA—*See* nondisclosure agreement.

nom de plume—*See* pseudonym.

nondisclosure agreement (NDA)—a legal contract or part thereof that restricts one or more parties from sharing or disclosing particular information to parties outside the contract.

offset printing—a printing process, used by all major traditional publishers, that utilizes large ink rollers to transfer a book's image to paper in mass quantities.

one-pager—*See* one-sheet.

one-sheet—a single-page document used for promotional purposes. *Called also* one-pager.

on submission/on sub—being shopped around to publishers. *My agent has had my manuscript on sub for the last six months.*

option—1. a clause in an author's publishing agreement that gives the publishing house the right of first refusal on the author's next work. 2. the right, but not the obligation, to dramatize a book or script within a given time frame, after which the option expires and the work can be optioned by another party.

orphan—a single word on its own line at the bottom of a paragraph. *See also* widow.

out of print (OOP)—no longer available from the publisher. *See also* in print, out of stock.

out of stock (OOS)—unavailable for immediate purchase. *See also* in print, out of print.

page depth—*See* depth.

page proof—a digital or printed copy of the interior of a book after it has been designed, in order to show how it will appear when the book is printed. *See also* proof.

pagination—how the laid-out text affects the number of pages and the numbering sequence in a publication.

Pantone Matching System (PMS)—a system that allows for a wide range of printing colors and accurate color matching. *See also* CMYK.

pass—1. a cover-to-cover read of a manuscript. *The proofreader needed two passes of the galley to ensure all errors were caught.* 2. a polite way of saying a manuscript has been rejected. *The publisher passed on my second novel.*

peer review—a much more in-depth read of a manuscript, sometimes done anonymously. *See also* beta reader, expert reader, sensitivity reader.

pen name—*See* pseudonym.

perfect binding—a bookbinding method in which the cover and pages are printed, glued together on the spine, and then trimmed perfectly to give the book sharp, even edges. This is the most common printing style for paperback books.

permissions editor—a professional who specializes in tracking down and negotiating with copyright holders to obtain the proper legal documentation to use a copyrighted work.

plagiarism—fraudulently representing someone else's work as your own without permission.

plate—a metal device used in offset printing to transfer the contents of a book onto paper.

PLR—*See* private label rights.

PMS—*See* Pantone Matching System.

POD—*See* print on demand.

preface—an optional part of the front matter that contains an author's note to the reader, such as how the book came about or the inspiration behind a particular character. Although *preface* is the standard industry term for this section, some authors choose to title it "Author's Note," "A Note From the Author," or "An Invitation From the Author" to entice readers.

preorder—the process when a book is listed for sale but with a date in the future, meaning customers will be able to purchase the book but will not receive it until the future date.

press check—an on-site proofing that can sometimes be performed at local print shops and that allows an author to ensure color accuracy as well as perform a last-minute review of the project before all copies print.

press kit—a type of media kit that contains information for more immediate coverage, such as a special event or breaking news. *See also* media kit.

print on demand—a printing process in which a book is produced only if a copy is ordered. *See also* offset printing.

print run—the number of copies of a book printed at one time.

private label rights (PLR)—a work sold with the purpose of the buyer branding it as their own. PLR documents are frequently used as website freebies, despite the often low quality of the content and presentation.

prologue—an optional part of the manuscript's main body that serves as a way to advance the storyline, provide key background information, or tantalize the reader for the rest of the book. Prologues are most often used in works that follow a narrative arc, such as novels, biographies, and memoirs, and so are rarely used in nonfiction.

proof—a printed copy of a book used for quality control before the full run is published. *See also* page proof.

proofreader/design proofreader—an editorial professional who reviews a manuscript for issues such as missing words, typos, and punctuation mistakes; a design proofreader looks specifically for design-related issues, such as page numbers and consistency in formatting. *See also* developmental editor, copyeditor, proofreader.

proposal—*See* book proposal.

pseudonym—a name used by an author in place of their real one. *Called also* pen name, nom de plume.

public domain—the body of creative work to which no exclusive intellectual property rights apply, due to the rights having expired, been forfeited, been waived, or any of several other reasons.

publishing expert—an individual familiar with traditional book publishing who can help an author navigate the steps to getting published.

query letter—a formal letter sent from an author and/or agent to publishing houses to propose a book idea.

reading line—text on a book cover that is not part of the title and that is intended to explain the book's contents. One of the most common reading lines is "A Novel."

recto—the right-hand page of a book. *See also* verso.

redlining—a method of tracking changes between each version of an author's manuscript, particularly between members of the editorial team.

reissue—*See* reprint.

release date—a date or short window of dates when a book is first available for sale. *My book will be released for purchase on November 1, 2023. See also* launch.

reprint—a new publishing of a book, often one that has gone out of print, with the original content intact. *See also* revised edition.

retail price—the full price of an item, such as that printed above the barcode on the back of a book, before any discounts are taken. *Called also* list price.

return on investment (ROI)—the measure of profitability of an investment, such as the cost of publishing versus book sales.

review copy—a copy of an author's book, preferably in its most final form, provided to professional critics and reviewers.

revised edition—an edition of a book that includes major revisions, by either the author or editor, such as additional chapters, supplementary materials, or revised and updated copy. *See also* reprint.

right of first refusal (ROFR)—a contractual right to enter into a business transaction with a person or company before anyone else can.

rights reserved notice—a required element to any copyright page, typically placed underneath or beside the copyright notice, that serves to let readers know your work is protected. The most common rights reserved notice is "All rights reserved."

ROFR—*See* right of first refusal.

ROI—*See* return on investment.

royalty—the amount of net profit that an author receives for each book sold, minus any fees associated with using a publisher and/or a printer. *See also* advance.

running footer—the repeated bottom part of a book's page that displays information not included in the running header.

running header—the repeated top part of a book's page that displays identifying information such as the author name, the book title, or the chapter title. *Called also* head, header, hed.

saddle stitching—a relatively quick and cost-effective, though uncommon, bookbinding method that involves stapling full sheets of paper together in the center, then folding the cover along the line of the staple. *See also* glue binding, sewn binding, Smyth sewn, spiral binding.

search engine optimization (SEO)—the practice of creating and presenting web content in a way so that it ranks higher organically in search engine results.

self-publishing—a publishing process in which the author pays for all costs related to the publication of a book and retains all copyright ownership. *See also* hybrid publishing, subsidy publishing, traditional publishing, vanity publishing.

self-publishing expert—an individual or company who helps authors navigate the self-publishing process.

sensitivity reader—an editorial professional who reviews how characters and populations of certain backgrounds are represented. *See also* beta reader, expert reader, peer review.

SEO—*See* search engine optimization.

sewn binding—*See* Smyth sewn.

short run—the printing of a small number of books, usually less than 1,000.

signature—a group of pages that are printed on both sides and then folded, trimmed, and bound together.

slander—defamation in oral form, such as on the radio or television, that is injurious to the individual. *See also* libel.

Smyth sewn—a usually expensive bookbinding process in which the signatures of a book's page are sewn together. *Also called* Smythe sewn. *See also* glue binding, saddle stitching, spiral binding.

social proof—the psychological and social phenomenon in which people emulate others' actions in certain situations in order to feel accepted or fit in. *Called also* as informational social influence.

spine—the middle of a book's binding that joins the front and back covers and that contains the title and, usually, the author name and publisher.

spiral binding—a bookbinding method that uses a spiral wire or plastic coil to fasten all pages together to the front and back cover. *Called also* coil binding. *See also* glue binding, saddle stitching, sewn binding, Smyth sewn.

spread—two facing pages (verso and recto) viewed together when a book is open; often used in layout planning to ensure that visual and textual elements align across both pages, especially in illustrated books and design-heavy nonfiction.

stack—the appearance in copy of the same word directly above or below itself.

standard trim—the industry standard size of a hardcover or paperback book once cut and bound by a printer; for paperback, the standard trim is 5.5" x 8.5", while hardcover is 6" x 9".

style guide—1. a grammar, style, and usage manual that sets standards for spelling, punctuation, and formatting. The most common style guides are *The Chicago Manual of Style*, *The Associated Press Stylebook*, and the *AMA Manual of Style*. 2. a document that contains a style sheet and which may also contain branding information, such as Pantone colors, font faces, etc.

style sheet—a document used to keep track of any deviations from the master style guide (for books, usually *The Chicago Manual of Style*), such as spelling of character names or a preferred way to format a word (e.g., *t-shirt* vs. *T-shirt* vs. *tee shirt*). *See also AMA Manual of Style, Associated Press Stylebook.*

subheader—a secondary heading or title that provides more specific information about the content of a section within a book. It usually follows the main chapter or section title and offers additional context or details to guide the reader through the organization of the material. *Called also* subhead, subhed.

subsidy publishing—a publishing process similar to self-publishing in that the author pays for the publication of the book and the publisher distributes it under its own imprint but with the difference that the publisher, not the author, retains copyright ownership, while the author receives royalties. *Called also* cooperative publishing. *See also* hybrid publishing, self-publishing, traditional publishing, vanity publishing.

substantive editor—*See* developmental editor.

subtitle—a secondary title, most often used in nonfiction, that provides further information about the book's contents and allows for the inclusion of more keywords.

table of contents—a directory in a book's front matter that details the names and page numbers of the book's sections.

tailband—a small strip of colored material a printer uses to attach the block of text pages to the bottom of the spine of a hardcover book. *See also* endband, headband.

tailpiece—a decorative image at the bottom of a page or end of a chapter. *See also* frontispiece.

testimonial—a recommendation, often from a client or colleague but also from solicited parties, about an author's work, services, or knowledge. *See also* blurb.

thumbnail—a smaller version of an image; for books, this is typically the cover shown in search results.

title page—a page in the front matter that includes the title, subtitle, author, publisher, and edition, and is often artistically decorated. *See also* full-title page, half-title page.

trade name—*See* imprint.

trade paperback—a mass-produced version of a book, often printed at a higher quality and in a larger size than the mass-market paperback. *See* mass-market paperback.

trade publisher—a publisher that produces books of general interest to be sold through regular retail channels, such as Amazon or Barnes & Noble.

traditional publishing—the process by which a book is produced through an established company that purchases the rights to a book, handles the printing and distribution processes, and, in turn, pays royalties to the author. *See also* hybrid publishing, self-publishing, subsidy publishing, vanity publishing.

trim area—the portion of the book that could be cut and so should not contain important text or graphics.

trim size—the actual dimensions of a book's page once it has been cut to be bound.

typesetting—the manual process of arranging type on a page to make it ready for print. Although the term is now considered antiquated, some book designers still use it to refer to the process of designing the word-based portion of a book's layout.

UI—*See* user interface.

Uniform Resource Locator (URL)—the address of a webpage, e.g., bookagogo.com/contact.

URL—*See* Uniform Resource Locator.

user experience (UX)—how a user interacts with a product or service.

user interface (UI)—the means by which a user interacts with a computer, such as through a touch screen, mouse, or other device, as well as how that interaction looks and behaves.

UX—*See* user experience.

vanity publisher—a company paid to publish an author's work, often with few, if any, services that provide quality control. The term was traditionally used interchangeably with *self-publishing* until the latter gained more credibility. Today, it is still sometimes used interchangeably with subsidy publishing, although an author usually retains the rights with a vanity publisher. *See also* hybrid publishing, self-publishing, subsidy publishing, traditional publishing.

verso—the left-hand page of a book. *See also* recto.

virtual book tour—a virtual version of a traditional book tour, involving an author booking appearances with bloggers, podcasts, and webinars to promote their title.

web host—a company that houses all of the files for a website. *See also* domain host, domain name.

widow—a single line of text that appears at the top of a column. *See also* orphan.

work for hire—a work created explicitly so that a third party, not the creator, is the owner.

working title—the temporary title for a book until a final one has been chosen.

Endnotes

For the complete collection of all the links mentioned in the endnotes, visit bookagogo.com/books/endnotes.

Introduction

1. "The Truth About Audible 'Passive Income' Scams." Lean Media, June 29, 2022. Video, https://www.youtube.com/watch?v=zqSOK8nquQg

1. Setting Goals and Expectations When Writing Your Book

2. Alter, Alexandra and Elizabeth A. Harris. "A New Way to Choose Your Next Book." *The New York Times*, June 8, 2022. https://www.nytimes.com/2022/06/07/books/new-book-apps-tertulia.html

3. Newman, Terry L. "Amazon Is Un-Publishing COVID-19-Themed Poetry Without Explanation." Medium, April 20, 2020. https://medium.com/@terrylnewman/amazon-is-un-publishing-covid-19-themed-poetry-without-explanation-5ae5b9899f9c

2. Author Platform: What It Is & Why You Need One

4. Friedman, Jane. "A Definition of Author Platform." JaneFriedman.com, September 24, 2023. https://www.janefriedman.com/author-platform-definition

5. Wenstrom, E. J. "Author Platform: How to Build Your Online Audience and Stay Sane." *Writer's Digest*, February 28, 2019. https://www.writersdigest.com/getting-published/author-platform-how-to-build-your-online-audience-and-stay-sane

3. Author Website: Why You Need One & What It Should Include

6. Burke, John. "The Complete Guide to Creating an Author Website." IngramSpark, February 17, 2021. https://www.ingramspark.com/blog/what-should-i-put-on-my-author-website

7. Brewer, Robert Lee. "Should Writers Have a Website?" *Writer's Digest*, December 10, 2019. https://www.writersdigest.com/publishing-insights/should-writers-have-a-website

8. "Usage Statistics of Content Management Systems." W3Techs. Accessed October 5, 2023. https://w3techs.com/technologies/overview/content_management

4. Why Blogging Is Important for Authors

9. Dickerson, Kelly. "Some of the Trickiest Science in 'The Martian' Came from the Book's Biggest Fans." *Business Insider*, October 8, 2015. https://www.businessinsider.com/andy-weir-the-martian-science-crowdsourcing-2015-10

10. Milliot, Jim. "Number of Self-Published Titles Jumped 40% in 2018." *Publishers Weekly*, October 15, 2019. https://www.publishersweekly.com/pw/by-topic/industry-news/publisher-news/article/81473-number-of-self-published-titles-jumped-40-in-2018.html

11. Kolmar, Chris. "23 Gripping Book Industry Statistics [2023]: How Many Books Were Published in 2022." *Zippia*, June 27, 2023. https://www.zippia.com/advice/us-book-industry-statistics

12. "Q&A: Best Practices for Author Websites and Blogs." The Authors Guild. Accessed October 10, 2022. https://www.authorsline.org/whats-new/seminars-member-events/business-webinars-writers/qa-best-practices-author-websites-blogs

13. Grimes, Shaunta. "If You're a Fiction Writer, You Absolutely Should Be Blogging." *Medium*, October 13, 2019. https://medium.com/the-1000-day-mfa/if-youre-a-fiction-writer-you-absolutely-should-be-blogging-6ef9e2bb439

5. Writing Collaborators: Ghostwriters vs. Co-Authors vs. Writing Coaches vs. Flying Solo

14. Heller, Karen. "James Patterson Mostly Doesn't Write His Books. And His New Readers Mostly Don't Read—Yet." *The Washington Post*, June 6, 2016. https://www.washingtonpost.com/lifestyle/style/james-patterson-doesnt-write-his-books-and-his-newest-readers-dont-read/2016/06/06/88e7d3c0-28c2-11e6-ae4a-3cdd5fe74204_story.html

15. Bernoff, Josh. "Ghostwriting Trends: A Report from the Gathering of the Ghosts in New York City." Jane Friedman, January 25, 2024. https://janefriedman.com/ghostwriting-trends-a-report-from-the-gathering-of-the-ghosts-in-new-york-city

16. Ibid

6. Choosing the Members of Your Editorial Team

17. Atwood, Blake. "How Many Words in a Novel? (Guide to 18 Genres)." The Write Life, September 22, 2023. https://thewritelife.com/how-many-words-in-a-novel

18. Tolkien, J. R. R. *The Fellowship of the Ring*, HarperCollins, 1994.

19. "What Is a Beta Reader? How to Find and Work With an Author's Best Friend." Reedsy, September 7, 2022. https://blog.reedsy.com/beta-readers

20. Rowlands, Rachel, Zsofia Macho, Lisa Poisso, and Mike Fishbein. "Sensitivity Reading: What You Need to Know, and Why It Matters." BookMachine, January 15, 2019. https://bookmachine.org/2019/01/15/sensitivity-reading-what-you-need-to-know-and-why-it-matters

7. Choosing a Title for Your Book

21. Hobart, Hobie. "8 Mistakes That Will Absolutely Kill Your Book." Self-Published Author. July 30, 2013. https://pre.selfpublishedauthor.com/content/8-mistakes-will-absolutely-kill-your-book

22. Klems, Brian A. "Can You Copyright a Title?" *Writer's Digest*, October 13, 2009. https://www.writersdigest.com/copyrights/can-you-copyright-a-title

8. Legal Review, Fact-Checking & Compliance of Your Book

23. Grady, Constance. "Book Publishing's Fact-Checking Failure, as Illustrated by the Sally Kohn Controversy." Vox, April 20, 2018. https://www.vox.com/culture/2018/4/20/17246784/book-publishing-fact-checking-sally-kohn-aminatou-sow-controversy

24. Royston, Jack. "Prince Harry's Attack on the Royal Family Has Backfired Spectacularly." *Newsweek*, January 22, 2023. https://www.newsweek.com/prince-harry-attack-royal-family-backfired-spectacularly-book-spare-poll-1775062

25. Atwal, Sanj. "Prince Harry's Spare Becomes Fastest-Selling Non-Fiction Book Ever." *Guinness World Records*, January 13, 2023. https://www.guinnessworldrecords.com/news/2023/1/prince-harrys-spare-becomes-fastest-selling-non-fiction-book-ever-732915

26. Eisenberg, Emma Copley. "Fact-Checking Is the Core of Nonfiction Writing. Why Do So Many Publishers Refuse to Do It?" *Esquire*, August 26, 2020. https://www.esquire.com/entertainment/books/a33577796/nonfiction-book-fact-checking-should-be-an-industry-standard

27. Wogahn, David. "Does Your Book Need a Legal Review? A Simple 5-Item Checklist." A Word with You Press, August 1, 2017. https://awordwithyoupress.com/book-legal-review-checklist

28. Rich, Motoko. "Rowling to Testify in Trial Over Potter Lexicon." *The New York Times*, April 14, 2008. https://www.nytimes.com/2008/04/14/books/14potter.html

29. Hawkins, Derek. "Olivia De Havilland's Lawsuit Against 'Feud' Creators Gets Tossed: She 'Does Not Own History.'" *The Washington Post*, March 27, 2018. https://www.washingtonpost.com/news/morning-mix/wp/2018/03/27/olivia-de-havillands-lawsuit-against-feud-creators-gets-tossed-she-does-not-own-history

30. Wikipedia. "Poor Man's Copyright." Last modified July 14, 2023. https://en.wikipedia.org/wiki/Poor_man%27s_copyright

31. "What Are Statutory Damages and Why Do They Matter?" Copyright Alliance. Accessed October 4, 2023. https://copyrightalliance.org/faqs/statutory-damages-why-do-they-matter

32. Copyright Review Board. "Paradise (AI) Draft Review Board Letter." United States Copyright Office, February 14, 2022. https://www.copyright.gov/rulings-filings/review-board/docs/a-recent-entrance-to-paradise.pdf

10. How to Get Testimonials for Your Book

33. Urban, Diana. "How to Get Blurbs for Your Book & Use Them in Your Marketing." BookBub Partners Blog, August 25, 2015. https://insights.bookbub.com/how-to-get-blurbs-for-your-book-use-them-in-your-marketing

14. Producing Your Audiobook

34. Kozlowski, Michael. "Audiobook Trends and Statistics for 2020." Good e-Reader, June 20, 2020. https://goodereader.com/blog/audiobooks/audiobook-trends-and-statistics-for-2020

35. "Global Audiobooks Market Size, Share & Growth Report, 2030." Grand View Research. Accessed October 5, 2023. https://www.grandviewresearch.com/industry-analysis/audiobooks-market

36. "Global Audiobook Revenues Set to Eclipse $4.8bn in 2021." Omdia, July 6, 2021. https://omdia.tech.informa.com/pr/2021-jul/global-audiobook-revenues-set-to-eclipse-4bn-in-2021

37. Sweney, Mark. "Pandemic Drives Ebook and Audiobook Sales by U.K. Publishers to All-Time High." *The Guardian*, November 14, 2020. https://www.theguardian.com/books/2020/nov/14/

pandemic-drives-ebook-and-audiobook-sales-by-uk-publishers-to-all-time-high-covid

38. Anderson, Porter. "A First: APA Research Sees 50 Percent of Americans Listening to an Audiobook." *Publishing Perspectives*, April 29, 2019. https://publishingperspectives.com/2019/04/apa-research-sees-50-percent-of-americans-listening-to-an-audiobook-2019-survey

39. Haselton, Todd. "How to Borrow Free Audiobooks From Your Local Library on Your Phone." *CNBC*, July 25, 2018. https://www.cnbc.com/2018/07/25/how-to-borrow-audiobooks-from-library-on-phone-using-libby-app.html

40. Renton, Catherine and Barbara Booth. "How to Listen to Audiobooks and Where to Get Them: Beginner's Guide." *NBC News*, September 20, 2022. https://www.nbcnews.com/select/shopping/audiobooks-guide-how-listen-audiobook-ncna1134076

41. Doctorow, Cory. "We Need to Talk About Audible." *Publishers Weekly*, September 18, 2020. https://www.publishersweekly.com/pw/by-topic/industry-news/libraries/article/84384-we-need-to-talk-about-audible.html

42. "How Long Does It Usually Take Someone to Produce 1 Finished Hour of an Audiobook?" ACX. Accessed May 5, 2023. https://help.acx.com/s/article/how-long-does-it-usually-take-someone-to-produce-1-finished-hour-of-an-audiobook

43. Wax, Alyse. "What is PFH? Everything to Know About Per-Finished-Hour Rates." Backstage. Accessed September 29, 2025. https://www.backstage.com/magazine/article/pfh-audiobook-rates-explained-76681

15. Printing & Distributing Your Self-Published Book

44. Langmaid, Virginia and Brandon Tensley. "He thought he ordered a book by a black financial adviser. the Nazi symbols inside shocked him." CNN, September 25, 2022. https://www.cnn.com/2022/09/25/us/book-black-author-nazi-symbols-reaj/index.html

17. Author Service Accounts

45. "What Is Amazon A+ Content and Why Should Authors Care?." NY Book Editors. https://nybookeditors.com/2023/01/what-is-amazon-a-content-and-why-should-authors-care

18. You're Published! What Next?

46. Haines, Derek. "There Are Now Well Over 12 Million Amazon Kindle Ebooks." Just Publishing Advice For Writers and Authors, March 10, 2023. https://justpublishingadvice.com/there-are-now-over-5-million-kindle-ebooks

INDEX

About the Authors

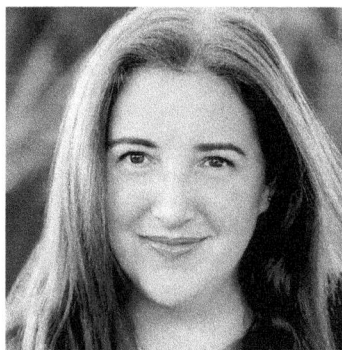

Photo: pixievision.com

Jenna Rose Robbins is a writer, ghostwriter, editor, and web consultant with extensive online and publishing experience. While the majority of her work has fallen in the entertainment and travel realms, the scope of her projects has ranged from politics and finance to sports and health.

After graduating from the University of Michigan, Jenna went on to receive her Master of Professional Writing (a specialized MFA) from the University of Southern California. In addition to ghostwriting two *New York Times* bestsellers, her 2017 book, *Faithful and Devoted: Confessions of a Music Addict*, was a finalist for the BookLife Prize, awarded by a division of *Publishers Weekly*.

Jenna is available as a freelance writer, editor, and consultant and is a member of the Los Angeles Editors and Writers Group (LAEWG, laeditorsandwritersgroup.com).

Contact: jennarobbins.com

jenna@jennarobbins.com

Sara Stratton, founder of Redwood Publishing, LLC, is a recognized expert in the self-publishing industry. In 2012, she created, developed, and implemented the self-publishing division of one of the most prominent ghostwriting firms in the United States. After running that department for four years, and producing more than ninety titles with them, she fell in love with all things self-publishing and made it her goal to give every author the ability to not just tell their story but also get it out into the world.

Since founding Redwood Publishing, Sara has helped publish more than seventy titles, from self-help to business books, cookbooks to fitness guides, personal memoirs to family histories and the occasional children's book. Redwood's goal is to create a book that can compete against others in the same category in the traditional publishing space, from content to the final printed product.

Contact: sara@redwooddigitalpublishing.com
redwooddigitalpublishing.com

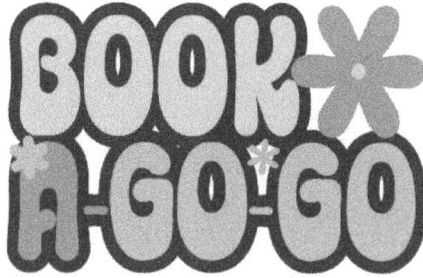

For the latest publishing news and interviews with authors and industry experts, download the Book-A-Go-Go podcast and sign up for our newsletter:

- **Podcast info:** bookagogo.com/podcast
- **Newsletter signup:** bookagogo.com/newsletter
- **Facebook:** facebook.com/bookagogo

To book Jenna and/or Sara for speaking engagements or to inquire about buying this book in bulk, please contact them at info@bookagogo.com. Both Jenna and Sara are also available for writing and publishing consulting.

If you enjoyed reading this book, please leave a review wherever you purchased it.

www.ingramcontent.com/pod-product-compliance
Lightning Source LLC
Chambersburg PA
CBHW052108030426
42335CB00025B/2886